Bicycling
The Cy

BICYCLING ANTIETAM NATIONAL BATTLEFIELD

The Cyclist's Civil War Travel Guide

Sue Thibodeau

The one and only book
that you need to bicycle Antietam!

Bicycling Antietam National Battlefield:
The Cyclist's Civil War Travel Guide

Published by Civil War Cycling
Digital (PDF) companion maps are sold separately by
www.civilwarcycling.com and www.suethibodeau.com
(E-mail) inquiries@civilwarcycling.com
154 Cobblestone Court Drive #110
Victor, New York 14564

Consult your doctor before any form of exercise, including bicycling. The bicycling directions provided in this book and all companion maps are for planning purposes only. Actual conditions (road, traffic, weather, or other events) may require you to adjust your route or actions, especially as required to obey all laws, signs, alerts, and notices. If there are mistakes in this book, or if the park road network or policies have changed since this writing, it remains your responsibility always to act in ways that are safe, healthy, and legal. The author and publisher disclaim any and all liability. Please visit www.nps.gov/anti and www.nps.gov/choh for official and up-to-date information about park roads, amenities, and policies.

ISBN 978-1-7326038-1-3 (pbk)

20201026-L6-3.6i
First Printing

About the Author

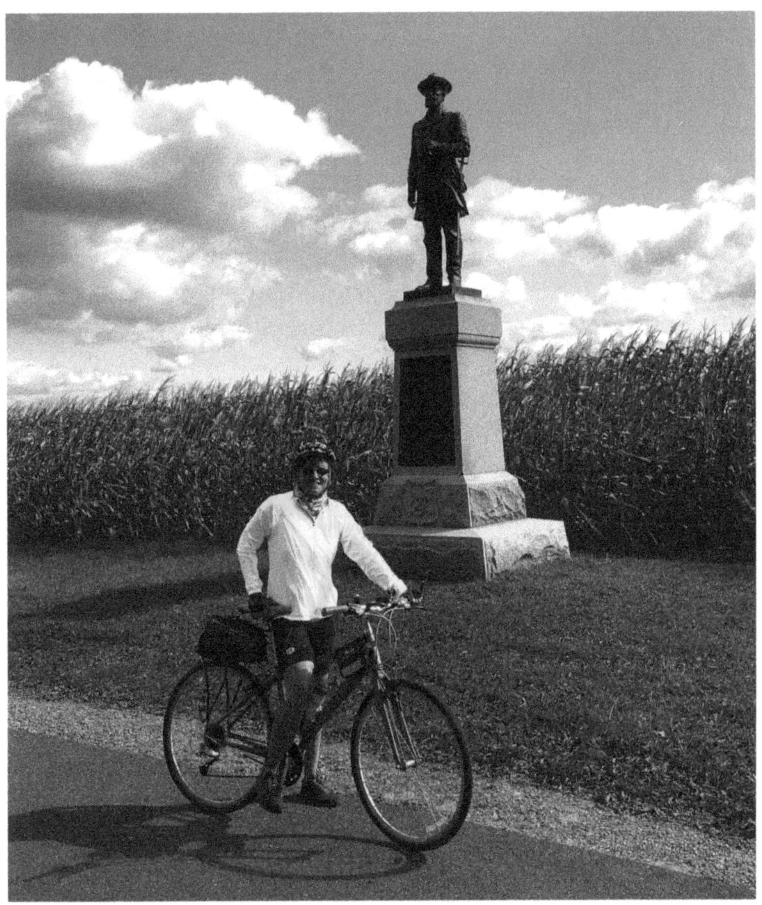

Antietam National Battlefield (Sharpsburg, Maryland)

Sue Thibodeau is a bicycling enthusiast, computer scientist, and former teacher. A native Marylander now living near Rochester, New York, Sue frequently visits Antietam National Battlefield and rides along the Chesapeake & Ohio Canal to Harpers Ferry. She is also the author of the guidebook, *Bicycling Gettysburg National Military Park*, and publishes digital touring maps through Civil War Cycling.

Battlefield touring on a bicycle?

Once you start riding through Antietam National Battlefield (in Sharpsburg, Maryland), you won't want to stop unless it's to catch your breath. The scenery is breathtaking, and the rolling landscape offers several short but challenging climbs.

Not wanting to stop is a bittersweet feeling. After all, we ride our bikes partly for the thrill of exploring freely new places and landscapes. But bicyclists also want to learn American history while touring a national military park. And that means that you will want to stop frequently: to find and study monuments; read wayside exhibits; and mentally connect the story of the battle to battlefield geography.

This guidebook is designed to help "bicycling historians" overcome the exciting tension between riding and learning. The book's 43 color maps will direct you through the battlefield, and also provide a geographic context for understanding the Battle of Antietam. Bicycle cue sheets suggest historically significant places to stop, and point you to additional photos and reading material in Part IV. For a smooth riding experience, this book does not identify all of Antietam's 96 monuments, but instead, preselects monuments by theme: state monuments; Maryland infantry and artillery monuments; and mortuary cannons. The book includes 100 color photos that will help you to find monuments, bridges, barns, and important landmarks like Dunker Church; and to understand battlefield geography as it relates to battle events.

You will learn the most if you read this book before your bicycle tour. Thus prepared, this book's touring directions offer opportunities to "stop and learn," while also supporting your freedom to modify your tour in whatever way that you see fit.

Please visit civilwarcycling.com to purchase (optional) digital companion maps for bicycling Antietam National Battlefield and also for C&O Canal Towpath access points near Sharpsburg, Maryland.

Dedication

This book is dedicated to my parents, August (Bud) and Jean Corazza, longtime Maryland residents who loved and served their country in countless ways. Our family home was located about thirty-five miles from Antietam Creek and thirteen miles from the Monocacy Aqueduct at the Chesapeake & Ohio Canal. We toured many Civil War sites within driving distance of our home, including the lesser known Sugarloaf Mountain near our family's church in Barnesville, where Union and Confederate signalmen took turns reconnoitering the movement of armies. When Mom and Dad suddenly passed away from cancer in 2019, our family was crushed, and my work on this guidebook—something of a family interest—came to a screeching halt for nearly one year. But soon enough, their voices tapped like a drum in my head to finish the job. I dedicate this guidebook in their memory.

CONTENTS

MAPS

TABLES

Take a Ride Back in Time

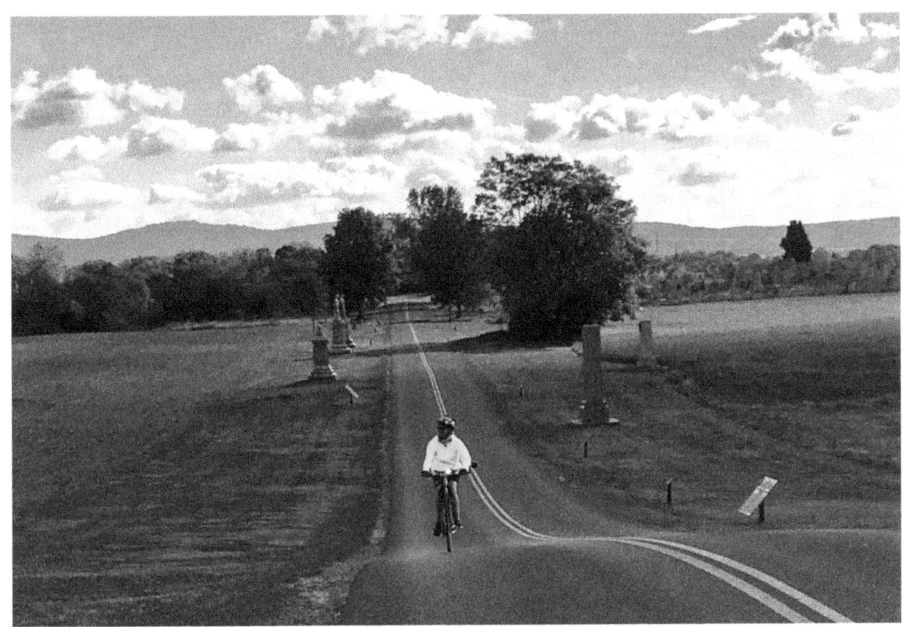

Riding West on Cornfield Avenue

Bicycling Antietam National Battlefield

For its rolling hills and pristine rural Maryland landscape, Antietam National Battlefield (ANB) is an ideal destination for bicyclists who want a visceral lesson in U.S. Civil War history—an outdoor learning adventure on two wheels. The battlefield park covers more than 2,700 acres[1] and retains much of its nineteenth-century appearance when two armies clashed here on September 17, 1862. It was the deadliest one-day battle in American military history. Here, Union Gen. George B. McClellan's 87,000 soldiers in the Army of the Potomac fought to expel the invasion of Confederate Gen. Robert E. Lee's 45,000-man Army of Northern Virginia.[2]

An estimated 22,717 federal and confederate soldiers sustained mortal wounds or were counted as missing or captured in this climactic battle of Lee's Maryland Campaign.[3] They fought on farmland surrounded by ripe corn, clover, plowed fields, and woodlots. They died in farm lanes, beside wood fences, on a bridge that spanned a creek, in farm houses turned field hospitals, and near a church built by German immigrants. Although perhaps unimaginable in September, 1862, the significance of the Battle of Antietam would extend far beyond its horrific death toll and the near total annihilation of a Maryland town. For it was this battle that motivated President Abraham Lincoln to issue the Preliminary Emancipation Proclamation to free all enslaved people residing in "states in rebellion."[4]

Located in the small western Maryland town of Sharpsburg and on the west side of Antietam Creek, the battlefield park offers bicyclists an unparalleled opportunity to connect physically with the stories of Civil War soldiers and farmers. This book provides bicyclists with a framework for understanding the battle while riding Sharpsburg's hills and valleys. At its core, the book promotes "learning on the move," where historical details are broadened to themes through the use of high-level maps. But also, this book supports learning during a touring stop, especially at battlefield monuments that advance a theme by adding historical detail.

Sharpsburg witnessed a tremendous amount of suffering and death: 3,654 dead; 17,292 wounded; and 1,771 missing or captured on both sides.[5] After the battle, William Roulette claimed that on his farm soldiers buried more than 700 Confederate men who fought at the "Sunken Road."[6] This farm lane marked part of the northeast border of Henry and Elizabeth Piper's 231-acre farm, which included a large apple orchard. The Piper house became Confederate Maj. Gen. James Longstreet's headquarters, the center of the Confederate battle line. Sharpsburg is also where Joseph and Mary Ann Poffenberger, like many local families, lost everything—dozens of animals (cattle, pigs, and sheep); tons of straw and hay; and several hundred bushels of grains, fruits, and vegetables. The Union army emptied the Poffenberger house, barns, cellars, and storehouses, and they dismantled the farm's fences for firewood.

In part, this guidebook will take you on a ride through the Poffenberger farm, near the North Woods, where Union Maj. Gen. Joseph Hooker established his 1st Corps headquarters the night before the Battle of Antietam. The next morning, Hooker's federal troops marched south from the Poffenberger farm to attack Confederate Gen. Thomas J. "Stonewall" Jackson's division. This assault through D.R. Miller's cornfield evolved quickly into a brutal back-and-forth artillery and small arms exchange.[7] On a hot and humid September day, a ride around The Cornfield will remind you of the challenges that Civil War soldiers faced. You may see ripe corn that blocks your view, feel the beating sun on your back, and maybe wipe away the grimy itch of perspiration behind your knees.

The hilly loop around the North Woods, through the East Woods, and on to the south end of The Cornfield will offer a breezy and enjoyable ride. But when you stop to visit a battlefield monument in this area, the sun and gnats can distract and pester even a nature lover. The air sometimes hangs heavy with southern humidity that draws beads of salty sweat. On two wheels, you can exercise your freedom to explore a beautiful and tranquil countryside that was once the site of unspeakable carnage.

Rather than describe all the physical sensations that I experience on the battlefield, I leave it to you to create your own bicycling memories. But having described a loop around The Cornfield, I would be remiss not to mention the famous Burnside Bridge across Antietam Creek in the south end of the battlefield. Union Maj. Gen. Ambrose E. Burnside's 9th Corps—a group of more than 13,000 men who were held on the east side of the creek by less than 500 Georgians under the command of Confederate Gen. Robert Toombs—fought for more than three hours to cross the bridge. The incredibly steep climb up to the Burnside Bridge parking area poses a significant challenge even for fit athletes. (Of course, you can walk your bicycle, and many people do just that). The climb is an unforgettable reminder of how difficult it must have been for armies to move over this hilly area.

Why I Wrote This Book

Planning a bicycle tour of Antietam National Battlefield is easier than for Gettysburg National Military Park (my first guidebook). First, with only a few minor modifications, and unlike Gettysburg, a bicyclist can complete a comprehensive loop through Antietam battlefield using the free paper map published by the National Park Service (NPS). Second, the park is easily half the size of Gettysburg and the road network not nearly as complicated. Third, the rural character of the town of Sharpsburg helps simplify the decisions that you will make on where to find food, water, or restrooms. Sharpsburg is a small town and much of the battlefield is active farmland. In part, that means that heavily trafficked public roads are not difficult to avoid.[8]

Even so, anyone who takes the time to travel to western Maryland for a bicycling adventure—especially a trip motivated by the excitement of learning U.S. Civil War history—will want the freedom to explore Antietam without wasting time wondering what to look for, in what order, and why. And perhaps most importantly, a guidebook that includes photographs, historical summaries, and conceptual military maps (without burdensome details that confuse the first-time battlefield visitor) is much more helpful than a paper map. I wrote this book because "bicycling historians" need two things: (1) bicycling directions and (2) historical images and summaries that one can commit to memory on a self-paced battlefield ride.

This guidebook and its companion digital maps—available for separate purchase from civilwarcycling.com—make it easy for bicyclists to learn about the Battle of Antietam in an active, experiential way. It also provides directions for bicyclists who want to tour the battlefield as an *excursion* from the Chesapeake & Ohio Canal Towpath, which runs along the Potomac River.

Getting Oriented

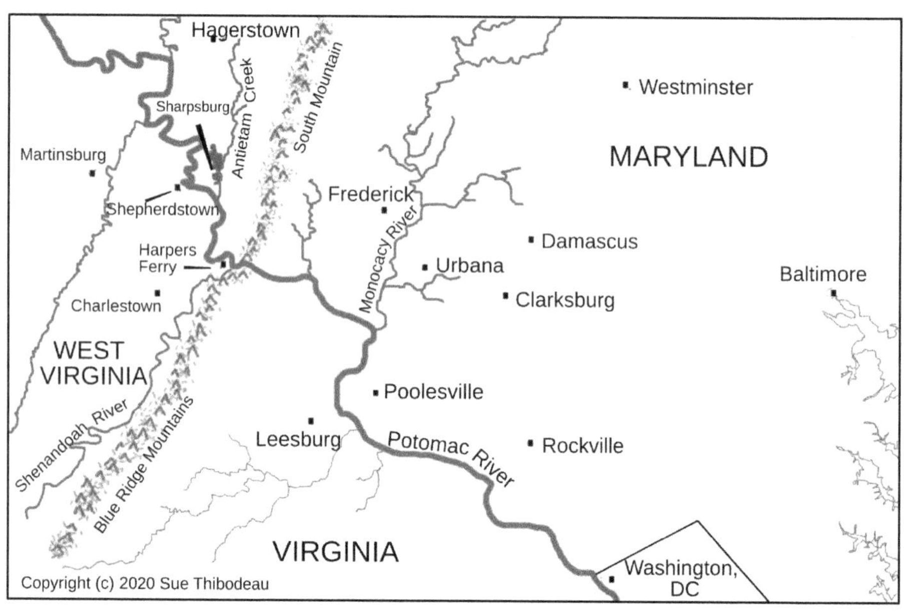

Map 1. Western Maryland (September, 1862)

My interest in bicycling the C&O Canal Towpath began after multiple visits to Antietam National Battlefield. Although I remember hiking parts of the canal when I was a kid growing up in Maryland, only as an adult did I think about the historical connections between the battlefield and the canal. I wondered how to combine two bicycling tours into one. The obvious first step was to learn a little geography.[9]

The previous map shows that Sharpsburg is located between the Potomac River and Antietam Creek. The river is the natural border between Virginia and Maryland. Antietam Creek flows south from Pennsylvania and into the Potomac River at an aqueduct south of Sharpsburg. South Mountain—the northern extension of the Blue Ridge Mountains—is about eight miles east of Antietam Creek.[10] The Blue Ridge Mountains of Virginia pass on the east side of Harpers Ferry, where the Shenandoah and Potomac Rivers meet.

The 1862 Maryland Campaign included the military conflict at Harpers Ferry and the Battles of South Mountain, Antietam, and Shepherdstown. It was Confederate Gen. Robert E. Lee's first invasion into the North.[11] Between September 4–7, Maj. Gens. Thomas J. Jackson and James Longstreet crossed the Potomac River near Leesburg at White's and Cheek's Fords.[12] Then the army marched to Frederick, Boonsboro, and Hagerstown.[13]

Maryland Side of the Confederate Crossing from Leesburg

On September 14, Union Gen. George B. McClellan secured Turner's, Fox's, and Crampton's Gaps at the Battle of South Mountain.[14] Gen. Lee's army moved toward the ridges of Sharpsburg.

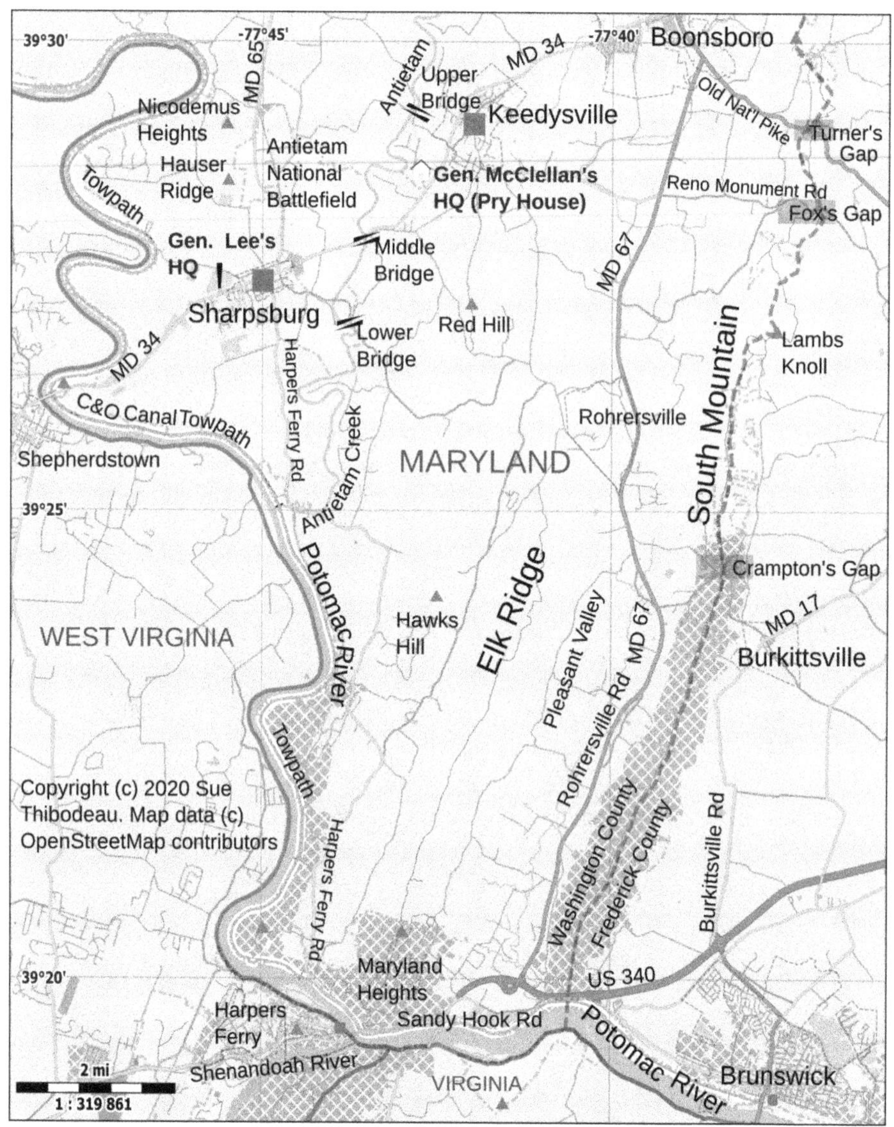

Map 2. Where is Sharpsburg, Maryland?

Having lost 2,685 men in the gaps of South Mountain, and while needing to find a strong defensive position to reassemble his army, Gen. Lee was concerned about having his back to the Potomac

River.[15] Gen. McClellan's Army of the Potomac was preparing to strike west over Antietam Creek, and Boteler's Ford was Lee's only nearby crossing point, located one mile south of Shepherdstown, (West) Virginia. Lee needed Jackson to capture the federal garrison at Harpers Ferry (on September 15) and to rejoin his army along the ridges of Sharpsburg to shore up a strong defensive battle line.[16]

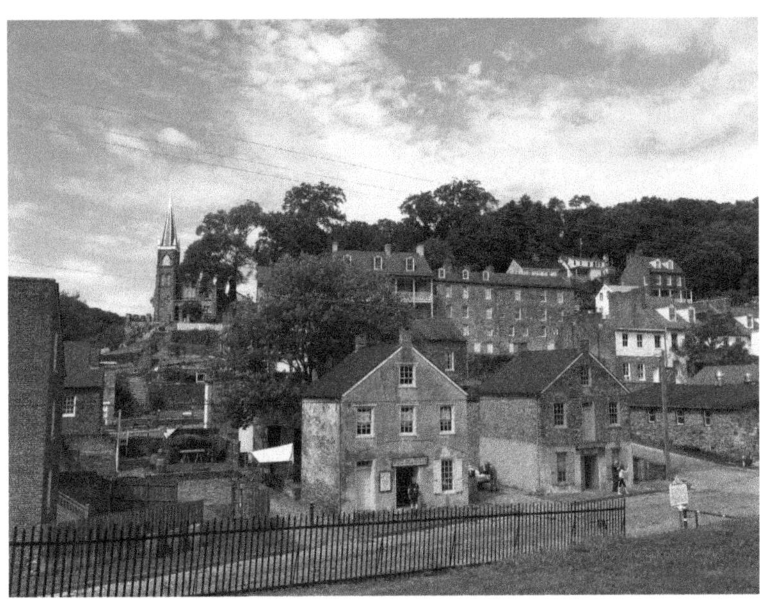

Downtown Harpers Ferry

In preparation for another battle, Gen. Lee established his headquarters in northwest Sharpsburg. Gen. McClellan did the same on a hill near Keedysville at the home of Philip and Elizabeth Pry.[17]

Pry House Near the Upper Bridge on the Antietam's East Bank

Pry Barn and Field Hospital

After some skirmishing on the west side of Antietam Creek on the evening of September 16, the Battle of Antietam started early the next morning. The battle raged for twelve hours, and ended after Confederate Maj. Gen. A.P. Hill's division arrived from Harpers Ferry to save Gen. Lee's right flank. The Confederate army retreated back to Virginia beginning on September 18, but not without one more military engagement on September 19, at the Battle of Shepherdstown. This battle is also known as the Battle of Boteler's Ford. (The ford is also called Packhorse Ford, and is identified as such on many C&O Canal maps).

Historical Approach

This guidebook is for bicycling tourists who want to learn more about the Battle of Antietam during a visit to Antietam National Battlefield. Although I designed the book specifically for bicyclists, any interested reader can benefit from what I hope will be an accessible and easy to understand description of the battle and battlefield. Since my aims are modest, I offer this description of what this book is *not*:

Although classic and recent Civil War scholarship informs my historical summaries, I do not identify or comment upon conflicting opinions or controversies that tend to spark debate among historians. For example, scholars still debate whether Gen. McClellan was slow to attack the Confederate army; whether the battle actually started on September 16; whether Gen. Burnside should have crossed Antietam Creek rather than trying to cross the lower bridge; whether Gen. Lee's offensive was bold and masterful, or blundering yet fortunate; whether the battle was a Union victory, loss, or "draw;" or whether President Lincoln's policies on slavery or martial law should be criticized. These and other strategic and tactical questions are out of scope for this type of work.

The military maps in this book are designed to help bicyclists memorize very high-level tactical movements. The battle maps are deliberately impressionistic and troop markings are not to scale. Although blue (Union) and red (Confederate) troop markings usually represent infantry divisions, this is not always the case. Please consult this book's bibliography if you prefer a military atlas.

Counts of soldiers engaged and killed ignite debates that this book intends to avoid. I accept as "close enough" all figures published by the National Park Service or the American Battlefield Trust. More broadly, I try to keep to what are commonly considered to be " facts," and I avoid "what if" questions, like "What if Gen. Israel Richardson had not been killed at The Sunken Road?" or "What if McClellan had attacked Lee's army right after the engagement at South Mountain?"

In summary, this book does not try to break new scholarly ground or make any kind of political point. I do not address the causes of the U.S. Civil War or comment on the very complicated politics of (dis)union and (anti)slavery within Maryland. Instead, this guidebook invites its reader to experience Antietam by immersing oneself in the landscape, reading wayside exhibits and monument inscriptions, and learning history in a self-directed and physically active way. I also hope that it will inspire the reader to engage in further study and reflection on the many topics associated with this landmark battle.

Riding South on Mumma Lane toward the Piper Farm

For further reading, please see this book's bibliography on p. 178. Also, the glossary on p. 173 provides a basic introduction to U.S. Civil War military terminology and concepts. Advanced students and history buffs are encouraged to read this book's endnotes for details.

For up-to-date information on park closures and alerts, you are strongly encouraged to visit these NPS websites:

ANB: www.nps.gov/anti/planyourvisit/conditions.htm

C&O: www.nps.gov/choh/planyourvisit/conditions.htm

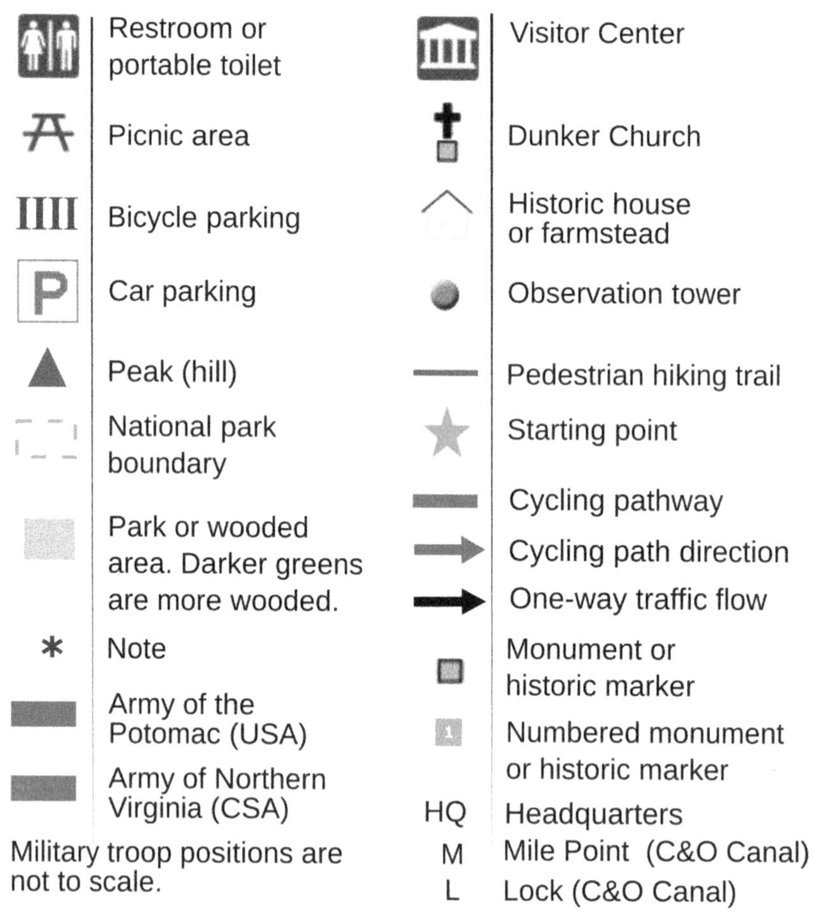
Map Key
Restroom or portable toilet
Picnic area
Bicycle parking
Car parking
Peak (hill)
National park boundary
Park or wooded area. Darker greens are more wooded.
Note
Army of the Potomac (USA)
Army of Northern Virginia (CSA)
Visitor Center
Dunker Church
Historic house or farmstead
Observation tower
Pedestrian hiking trail
Starting point
Cycling pathway
Cycling path direction
One-way traffic flow
Monument or historic marker
Numbered monument or historic marker
HQ Headquarters
M Mile Point (C&O Canal)
L Lock (C&O Canal)
Military troop positions are not to scale.
All maps have North at the top.

Map 3. Symbols, Terms and Abbreviations

PART I: INTRODUCTION

1. Antietam on a Bicycle

And never again in the deadliest hour
Of war or of peace shall we be so beset
To accomplish the purpose our spirits have met.
And what would they do if war came again?
The scarlet cross floats where all was blank then.
They would bind on their "brassards" and march to the fray,
And the man liveth not who could say to them nay;
They would stand with you now, as they stood with you then,
The nurses, consolers, and saviours of men.

Clarissa "Clara" Harlowe Barton (1821–1912) wrote and recited this verse in honor of women who—"uninvited, unaided, unsanctioned oftimes"—pressed themselves into service as nurses and logistics experts during the United States Civil War.[18] Barton's words are part of her larger poem from 1892, where she describes the heroism of women who rejected societal norms in order to nurse, console, and advocate for wounded soldiers.

Determined to serve on the battlefield, in 1862 Clara Barton left her job at the U.S. Patent Office in Washington, DC, to find the federal army. She arrived in Sharpsburg, Maryland on September 17, 1862, sometime after Union Maj. Gen. Joseph Hooker's 1st Corps marched south to fight Confederate Maj. Gen. Thomas "Stonewall" Jackson's infantry lying in wait in The Cornfield. After about four hours of attacks and counter-attacks involving both artillery and infantry, nearly 8,000 men from both armies were killed or wounded in a thirty-acre field of once tall, ripe Maryland corn. After the Battle of Antietam, Hooker commented that the corn was cut to the ground "as closely as could have been done with a knife."[19] Confederate Col. Stephen D. Lee called it "artillery hell."[20]

The inscription on the Clara Barton Monument celebrates her "act of love and mercy" on the Antietam battlefield and her 1881 founding of the American Red Cross to provide global disaster relief. The monument inscription reminds us that the Battle of Antietam is more than a story of carnage and death. It is also a story about healing, consolation, love and mercy—one in which "service" is broadly defined to include life-giving sacrifice. These concepts resonate with bicyclists whose touring goals include a deepened understanding of all types of service rendered on the fields around Antietam Creek.

While touring Antietam National Battlefield on a bicycle, and with each turn of the wheel, one is reminded of the human cost associated with the freedoms that we enjoy on the road. Protected by the mountains to the east and ridgelines throughout the battlefield, a bicyclist knows instinctively that every curve, hill, and change in light or shade is important. We know that the land over which so many people suffered and died, and under which countless and nameless men are buried, offers an opportunity to refresh our spirit and retrain our commitment to act with "love and mercy," like Clara Barton.[21]

Clara Barton Monument on Poffenberger Farm

Dedicated on September 9, 1962, the Clara Barton Monument stands on Mansfield Avenue, south of the Joseph Poffenberger farm buildings. More recently, historians conjecture that at Antietam Barton worked as a nurse east of her monument (and beyond park boundaries), at the Samuel Poffenberger farm. Using this guidebook, you will visit the Clara Barton Monument early in your tour, when you begin riding the northern half of the battlefield.[22]

The Roads at Antietam National Battlefield

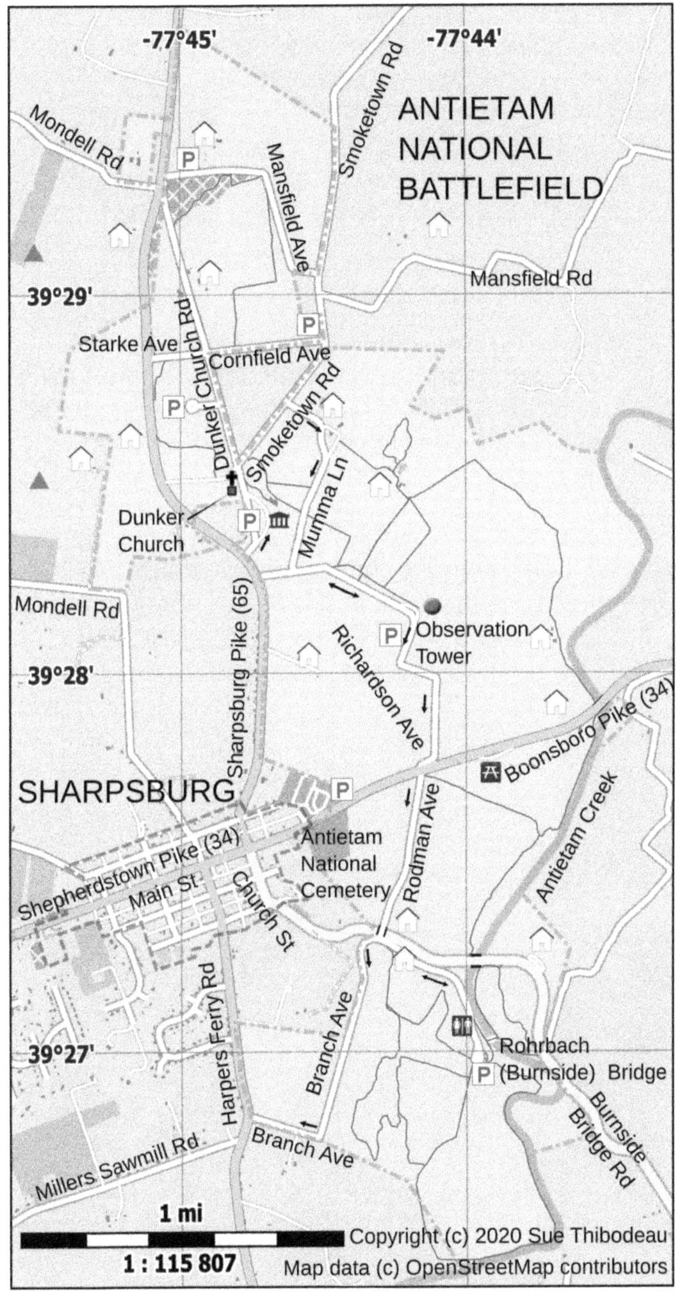

Map 4. Antietam Park Roads

Maryland Route 34 (Boonsboro Pike) cuts through downtown Sharpsburg and connects Shepherdstown, West Virginia to Boonsboro, Maryland.[23] It divides the northern and southern halves of Antietam National Battlefield. A mostly shoulder-less and sometimes bumpy public road, the bicycle routes in this guidebook avoid Route 34, except to cross it. Since the gates to Antietam National Cemetery are on Route 34 (where there are no bicycle racks), bicyclists should plan to visit the national cemetery by car. Also, as of this writing, there are portable toilets installed in the parking lot across from the national cemetery.

Maryland Route 65 (Sharpsburg Pike) is a major commercial road that runs south from Hagerstown, Maryland to downtown Sharpsburg.[24] The segment through Antietam National Battlefield has mostly double-wide shoulders. Your bicycle tour will include a 0.8-mile ride on Maryland Route 65 that passes a popular convenience store and grill near the northeast part of town.

Most of your ride through Antietam National Battlefield follows smoothly paved park avenues that, although double yellow-lined, are not heavily trafficked, especially in the early morning. Although many segments are lined with trees, they are clipped back and do not offer much if any shade while riding. This book's tour begins here:

Dunker Church Road—Looking North

For a complete battlefield tour that honors one-way traffic signs, the NPS auto tour is a reasonable option for bicyclists. However, and not surprisingly, the NPS map does not describe the bicycling terrain nor mention where extra caution may be needed. For example, early in your tour there are 0.2-mile segments that suddenly require down-shifting and then up-shifting at a peak to enjoy a fast ride downhill. These photos understate the effort required to ride up the hills:

Mansfield Avenue—Looking East to Poffenberger Farm

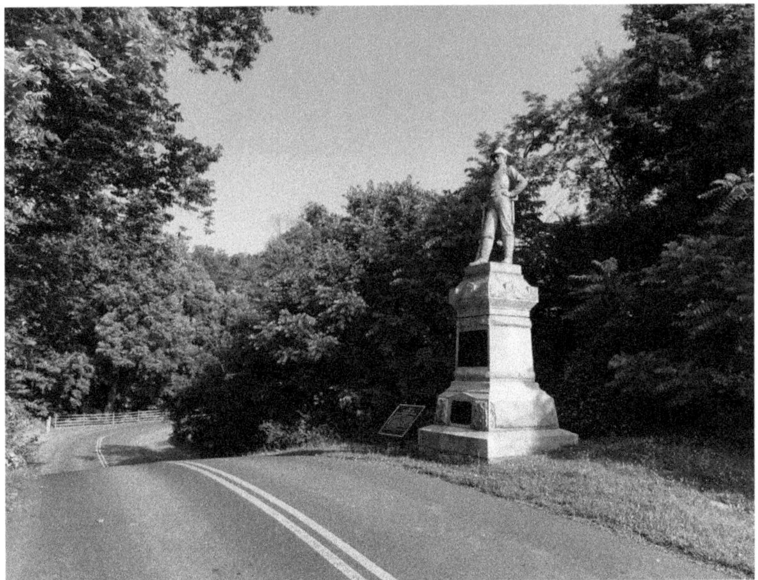

Looking Back on Mansfield Avenue near Smoketown Road[25]

Did you know ... ?

The following park avenues are named for people.

North Carolina native Confederate Brig. Gen. Lawrence O'Bryan Branch (1829–62) suffered a gunshot to his head, near a mortuary cannon that marks the site of his death on **Branch Avenue**. He led a brigade in A.P. Hill's Division, Thomas J. Jackson's Command.

Connecticut native Union Maj. Gen. Joseph K.F. Mansfield (1803–62) suffered a fatal bullet wound to his chest near a mortuary cannon that marks the site of his death on **Mansfield Avenue**. He commanded the 12th Corps (under army commander, George B. McClellan).

Mumma Lane is named for the Mumma family, owners of a large farm cut by the lane. The Union army camped on the Mumma farm for many weeks after the Battle of Antietam.

Vermont native Union Maj. Gen. Israel B. Richardson (1815–62) was mortally wounded at The Sunken Road, near a mortuary cannon that marks the site on **Richardson Avenue**. He commanded the 1st Division, 2nd Corps (under Edwin V. Sumner).

Rhode Island native Union Maj. Gen. Isaac P. Rodman (1822–1862) was mortally wounded near a mortuary cannon that marks the site on **Rodman Avenue**. He commanded the 3rd Division, 9th Corps (under Ambrose E. Burnside).

Virginia native Confederate Brig. Gen. William Starke (1814–62) suffered three bullet wounds near a mortuary cannon that marks the field on which he fought on **Starke Avenue**. He commanded a brigade in Thomas J. Jackson's Division.

Of the six generals killed or mortally wounded at the Battle of Antietam—three Union, three Confederate—all have mortuary memorials (see Chapter 11), but only one does not have a park road named for him (Confederate Brig. Gen. George B. Anderson). Six Union and six Confederate generals were wounded during the battle. One general from each side died at the Battle of South Mountain.

Overall, the 1.7-mile stretch from the Observation Tower to Burnside Bridge is the hilliest (160 feet up, 70 feet down) and most scenic part of your tour. But without question, Antietam's steepest grade hill is the 0.5-mile climb up to the Burnside Bridge parking lot.

Richardson Avenue—Looking South

Road to Burnside Bridge—Looking Southeast

For obvious safety reasons, before committing to a battlefield bicycle tour, the first-time visitor will want to anticipate what the roads are like. The above photos convey that Antietam National Battlefield has smoothly paved, 25 mph roads that wind through fields and woodlots, and carry the bicyclist over a mix of flat and very hilly terrain. If you cannot make a hill, walking your bicycle is as safe as riding. And walking affords you extra time to enjoy Antietam's monuments or to share reflections with your riding partner.

After gaining a general sense of the park road network, the next logical question is, *What will I see as I ride the battlefield?* You will want to know enough about Antietam's natural and physical landmarks so that you do not pass them by unnoticed, but also so that you can use them to stay oriented on the battlefield. The next sections provide an overview of three bicycle routes (pp. 30–35), followed by a detailed introduction to Antietam's key landmarks (p. 36–49).

Antietam Bicycle Routes

Table 1 lists one bicycle route through Antietam National Battlefield and two battlefield excursions from the Chesapeake & Ohio Canal Towpath (depending on whether you are riding south or north along the canal). Notably, the directions for exiting the towpath while riding south are not the reverse of a ride north. This is because the location of canal access points relative to battlefield roads dictates a different route when the goal is to minimize backtracking; avoid lengthy rides on public roads; and anticipate that some rural roads near the canal are incredibly steep.

#	Route Name	Miles	Est. Hours	Page
1	Half Day Loop	9.2	3–4	89
2	C&O Canal Southbound Access (includes battlefield tour)	9.5 or 11.9	4	109
3	C&O Canal Northbound Access (includes battlefield tour)	12.8 or 12.7	4	123

Table 1. Bicycle Routes Through or Connecting to ANB

In this guidebook, route distances are accurate to the nearest tenth of a mile, which is enough to find your way through the battlefield. More detail than that would be a distraction, especially since most bicyclists will dismount to explore some of the ninety-six monuments along the route,[26] which follows closely the NPS auto tour. However, unlike the NPS tour, Civil War Cycling's maps are designed to help bicyclists to complete a loop and to avoid public roads, when possible (e.g., by avoiding Boonsboro Pike).

With minimal stops, most recreational bicyclists can complete a battlefield tour in 1–2 hours. But for a leisurely, educational tour, 3–4 hours might be a more realistic plan. Of course, as a bicyclist on a self-directed learning adventure, you are free to ride in whatever style or pace that you want. This guidebook will provide the tools to plan a tour that matches your own riding and learning style.

Bicycling Antietam National Battlefield is not nearly as complicated—in terms of planning for distance, time, and safety—as bicycling Gettysburg National Military Park.[27] For that reason, this guidebook offers only one touring option, and it is one that you could easily customize. For example, you could modify Route 1 by parking your car near the Observation Tower on Richardson Avenue, where you would then unload your bicycles and use the maps in this book to ride a circuit through the northern half of the battlefield. For a longer ride, you might first eat lunch out of coolers stored in your car, and then ride a circuit through the southern half of the battlefield.

On the other hand, deciding where to exit and return to the C&O Canal Towpath is somewhat tricky. That is because so much depends on each bicyclist's road and safety skills; fitness for steep hills; tolerance for winding roads with low visibility; and willingness perhaps to trade riding distance for riding comfort.

How to Use This Guidebook and Maps

You will learn the most about the Battle of Antietam if you carry this guidebook while bicycling the park. Civil War Cycling's Antietam touring maps cover the battlefield in a way that supports a high-level chronological narrative. The maps are designed to be useful reference material for battlefield newcomers. Before your ride, study each page, one map or image at a time, and then while riding, turn to the pages with bicycling directions.

Most bicyclists will also want to photocopy some maps for personal (non-commercial) use. Having easy access to extra maps that can withstand a little drizzle is a great convenience for bicyclists.

You will not regret stuffing paper maps into plastic sleeves or baggies, and then tucking them into your jersey pocket or bag, or clipping them to your handlebars. Another option is to read directions from your PDF-enabled mobile device during a stop.[28] These digital maps are available for online purchase from Civil War Cycling at www.civilwarcycling.com. (The digital maps are *companions* to this paperback guidebook; the book itself is not available in digital format).

Route 1—Antietam Half Day Loop (9.2 miles)

Route 1

Route 1 is a 9.2-mile loop through Antietam National Battlefield, and by necessity it includes a ride through town to complete the circuit. Most people can complete the route in a leisurely 3–4 hours. The route is broken down into four detailed segment maps with bicycle cues (directions). See Chapter 6 for detailed touring maps, bicycle cues, historical summaries, photos, and tips. Note that since Routes 2 and 3 focus on C&O Canal "access points" to Antietam National Battlefield (and not the battlefield itself), they refer back to Route 1 for a complete tour.

Parked on the Walkway to the Maryland State Monument

Route 2—C&O Canal Southbound Access

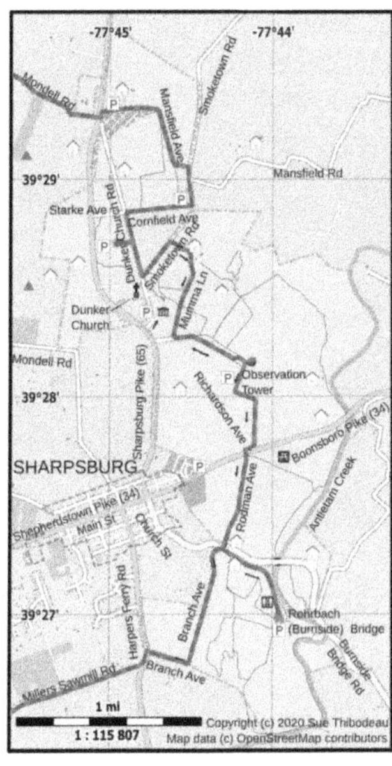

Route 2 (Option 1) Thumbnail

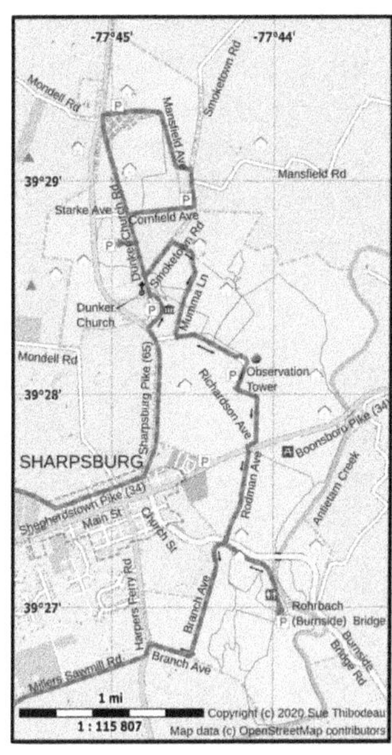

Route 2 (Option 2) Thumbnail

The C&O Canal runs in a north-south direction on the west side of the battlefield. For the southbound C&O Canal bicyclist considering an excursion through ANB, this section briefly summarizes Route 2. For help deciding exactly where to exit and return to the towpath, and for detailed touring maps and bicycle cues, see Chapter 7.

Route 2 is a pair of touring options for getting on and off the C&O Canal Towpath near Sharpsburg. The route is designed specifically for the bicyclist who is riding south on the towpath. The thumbnail images (above) show that the battlefield route for each option is similar, but the starting and ending points differ.

Option 1 [Ride at your own risk] is the shortest route to the battlefield, but it is also a long, 200-foot-climb on narrow, rural roads with poor visibility and many turns. You would exit the towpath at Taylors Landing (M80.9), tour ANB, and then return to the towpath via Millers Sawmill Road, for a total distance of 9.5 miles. The following map shows that Millers Sawmill Road will take you to about M71.[29]

Option 2 [Preferred] is to exit at Snyders Landing (M76.6) and follow a similar path through ANB, and then return to the towpath via Millers Sawmill Road, for a total distance of 11.9 miles. Although you might not guess it from looking at the two thumbnail images, most bicyclists will prefer Option 2, even though it is 2.4 miles longer. The ride from Snyders Landing to ANB is on mostly straight public roads, including downtown Sharpsburg. There are a few modest hills (190-foot gain, 30-foot loss).

Map 5. The C&O Canal Towpath and Antietam National Battlefield

Route 3—C&O Canal Northbound Access

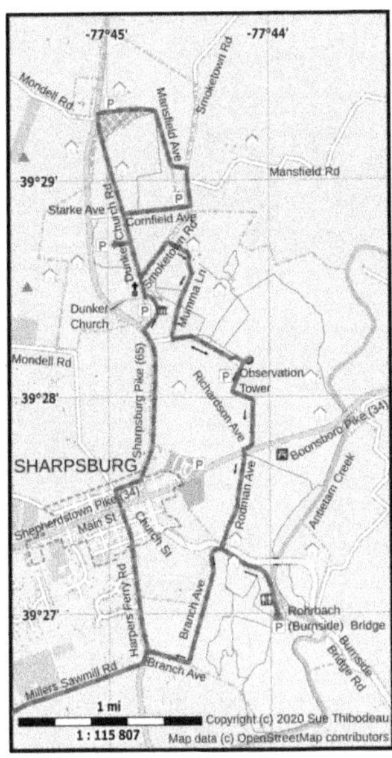

Route 3 (Option 1) Thumbnail

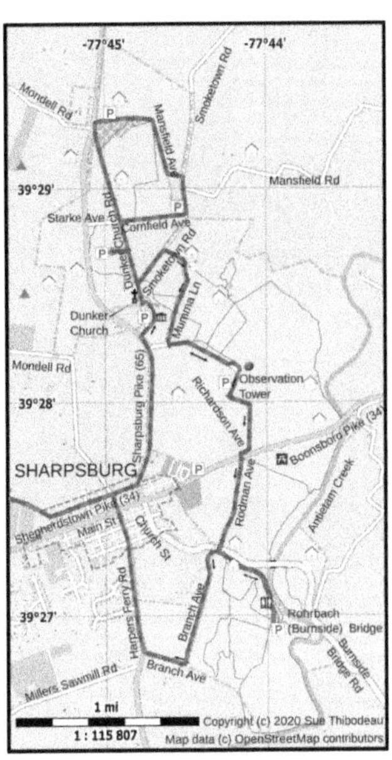

Route 3 (Option 2) Thumbnail

For the northbound C&O Canal bicyclist who wants to add a ride through the battlefield, Route 3 identifies different towpath exit and return points than for a ride south. This is largely due to this guidebook's preference for minimizing time on public roads in favor of a more complete (and looped) ride through the battlefield. If you compare the thumbnail images for Route 3's touring options with those of Route 2, you will notice that the battlefield rides are similar, but that they differ in your exposure to downtown traffic. For more details, including touring maps and bicycle cues, see Chapter 8.

Option 1 is to exit the canal towpath at M71 (to Millers Sawmill Road), tour the battlefield, and then return again to M71, for a total distance of 12.8 miles. The ride to ANB is an overall 200-foot gain and 40-foot loss. (Avoiding most of Harpers Ferry Road is a huge benefit).

Option 2 is to exit and return to the towpath at M76.6 (Snyders Landing), following a similar path through ANB, for a total distance of 12.7 miles. The ride to ANB is a 190-foot gain and 30-foot loss. The roads are mostly straight with good visibility but no shoulders.

Landmarks at Antietam National Battlefield

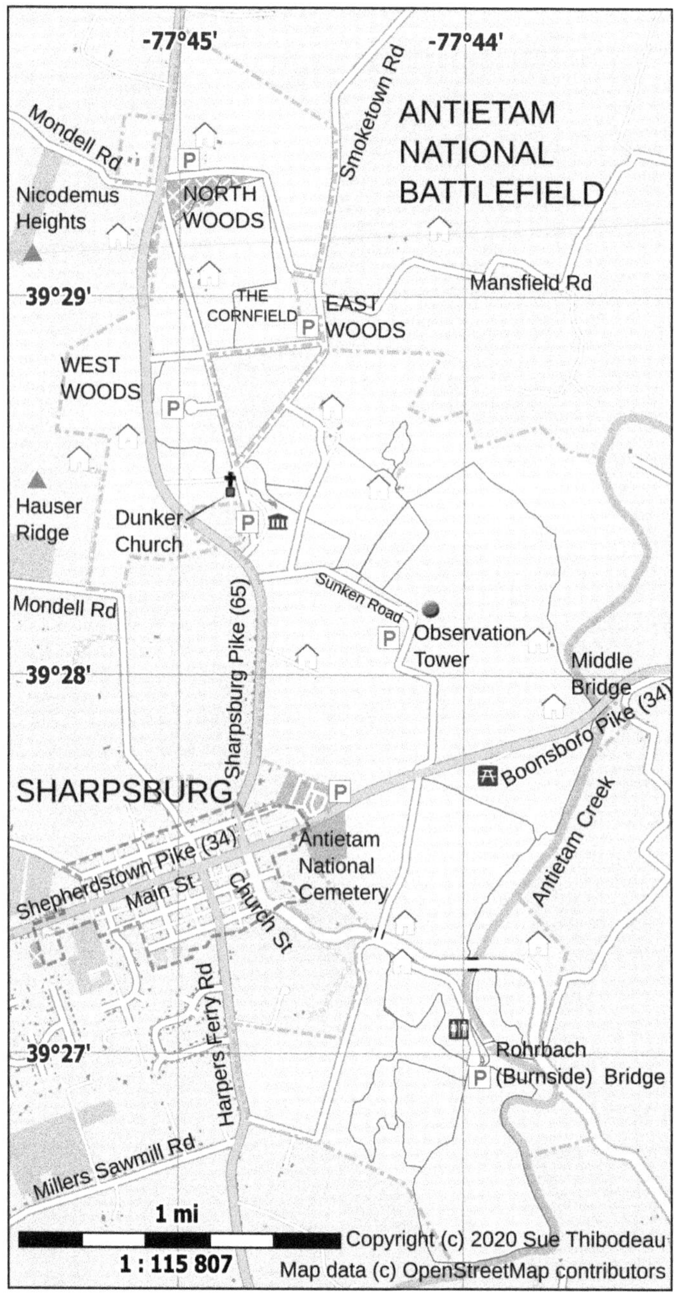

Map 6. Key Landmarks at Antietam National Battlefield

This section offers a sampling of photos and brief introductory descriptions of several significant physical and natural landmarks at Antietam National Battlefield. They are presented roughly in order of our battlefield tour, which is also generally chronological according to battlefield events of September 17, 1862. The presentation is by no means comprehensive. The intent is to provide a set of visual "data points" to help you anticipate what you will see and where you will ride. If you can recall these images while bicycling the park, it will be much easier to (re)construct and understand the battlefield story. Just as important, learning while riding will feel more fluid and enjoyable.

Map 6 identifies some notable geographic areas. Take a moment to find the Visitor Center, marked with a brown "museum" icon. Across the road is Dunker Church, a reconstructed version of the 1852 church in which members of Sharpsburg's German Baptist Brethren gathered for prayer.[30] If you trace a path north from the church, and follow in a clockwise direction, you will see West Woods, North Woods, East Woods, and the famous D.R. Miller cornfield. (The woodlots were named after the battle by U.S. army engineers). Again from the Visitor Center, look southeast to notice the location of The Sunken Road, also called "Bloody Lane." And then almost due south from the Observation Tower, identify the location of the Rohrbach ("Burnside") Bridge across Antietam Creek. (The purple lines mark hiking trails that are off-limits to bicycles).

The house-shaped icons in the map above identify nineteenth century farms. Map 8 on p. 46 identifies the names of these farms.

Antietam National Battlefield Park Visitor Center

5831 Dunker Church Road
Sharpsburg, Maryland

Antietam National Battlefield
Visitor Center (2019)

Antietam National Battlefield was established on August 30, 1890. In 1933 its management was transferred from the U.S. War Department to the National Park Service, at which time the park covered sixty-five acres, including eleven acres in Antietam National Cemetery. Antietam National Battlefield currently includes more than 3,200 acres, and more than one-third of that is active farmland. There are about 8 miles of park avenues and 14.9 miles of hiking trails.[31]

Union Col. Ezra Carman, who fought at the Battle of Antietam, was one of the principal architects of the national park. He corresponded and met with hundreds of Union and Confederate veterans to mark battle lines and commemorate significant battle events.[32] This work informed the content and placement of cast iron tablets that the War Department installed in the late 1890s. Most of the ninety-six battlefield monuments were erected between 1890 and 1910, although some were dedicated in the 1960s. The Visitor Center opened (with a bomb shelter) in 1962 and is scheduled for major renovations in 2020–2021.

One of the first things that you notice when you arrive at the Visitor Center is that the building sits on a ridge on the east side of Dunker Church Road, which roughly parallels Sharpsburg Pike (Maryland 65). This ridge was Confederate Gen. Robert E. Lee's choice for establishing a defensive battle line in preparation for the battle that would ensue after Union Gen. George B. McClellan's army marched westward from the gaps of South Mountain.

Sharpsburg Area Ridges and South Mountain

The following photo captures the view looking southeast from Dunker Church Road (see map, p. 25). Dunker church is at your back and Elk Ridge is in the distance, obscuring South Mountain until you follow the ridgeline north (not visible in the photo). In the mid-front, you can see the ridge on which Confederate Col. Stephen D. Lee's artillery battalion, part of Maj. Gen. Thomas "Stonewall" Jackson's division, posted their guns. In the early morning hours of September 17, the guns faced north and aimed at what is now known as The Cornfield, about one mile away. It is from that direction that Union 1st and 12th Corps soldiers, under the command of Maj. Gen. Joseph Hooker and Maj. Gen. Joseph K.F. Mansfield, respectively, would attack. In the next map (p. 40), infantry from the Army of the Potomac (Union) is represented as blue bars and the Army of Northern Virginia (Confederate) as red bars—and for simplicity, not to scale.

New York Monument and Battlefield Visitor Center

Because of Sharpsburg's hilly terrain that spanned beyond Antietam Creek to South Mountain, artillery played a critical role in the Battle of Antietam. For a map of western Maryland that shows Sharpsburg's location relative to South Mountain, see p. 14. A trained eye will be able to see Turner's Gap and Fox's Gap while standing on the east side of the Visitor Center, but Crampton's Gap is obscured by Elk Ridge. Together, both armies posted more than 500 cannons, both smoothbore and rifled, on the Antietam battlefield, and those guns fired about 50,000 rounds.[33]

The Confederate cannons at the Visitor Center mark an artillery position that was behind Gen. Jackson's infantry on the morning of September 17. The faded bar in Map 7 indicates the infantry's advance from Dunker Church (shown here) to The Cornfield.

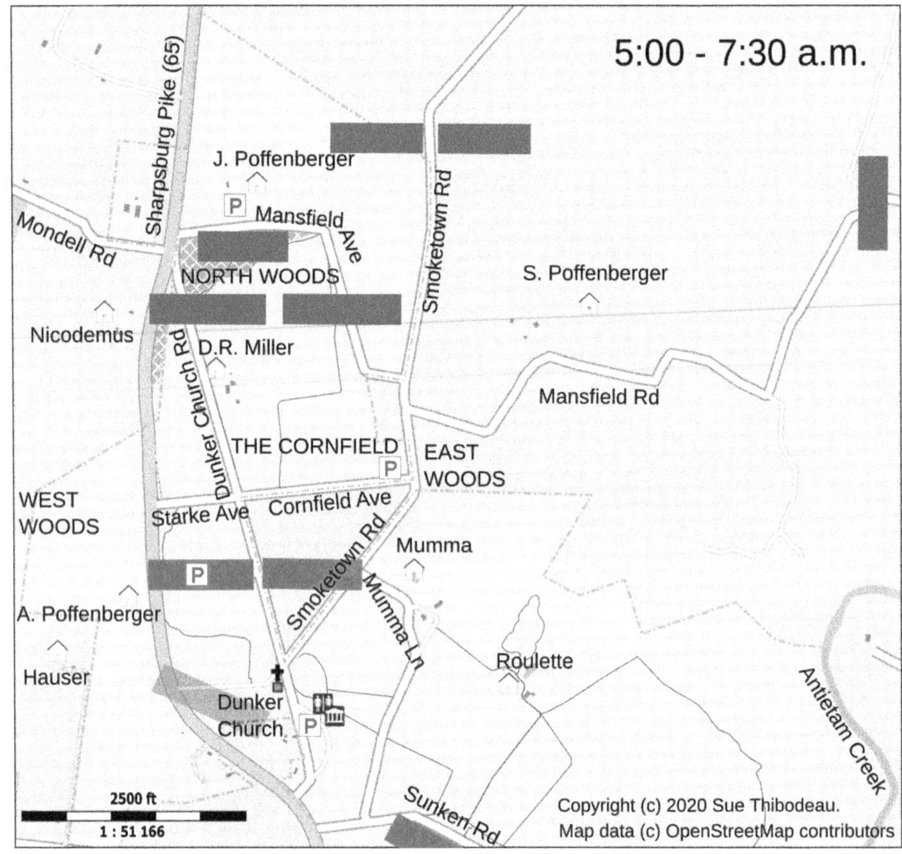

Map 7. Faceoff at The Cornfield[34]

Dunker Church

Confederate infantry advanced from around Dunker Church to prepare for a fight in D.R. Miller's cornfield. They passed through part of the Mumma farm, whose owner, Samuel Mumma, donated the land on which his pacifist neighbors built this 1852 church building. But during the Battle of Antietam, Dunker Church was not a place of worship but a shelter for wounded soldiers, a place of truce for the exchange of living and dead men, and possibly also an embalming station. Repaired and rededicated in 1864, the church was destroyed by a storm in 1921. In the 1930s, the site was a gas station and a store.

In time for the 100th anniversary of the battle, Dunker Church was rebuilt from its original foundation and rededicated in September,

1962. The cast iron tablet shown in the next photo, which shows Dunker Church in the background, says:

> "Let us here today, in the spirit of the brethren who built it more than a century ago, rededicate this building to the advancement of peace among nations .... to the brotherhood of all mankind." from address delivered by J. Millard Tawes, Governor of Maryland, September 2, 1862. Reconstruction of the historic DUNKARD CHURCH was made possible in 1961 by a special appropriation of funds by the State of Maryland.

Looking Southwest to Dunker Church from Near Smoketown Rd.

Inside Dunker Church

The placement of the tablet between Dunker Church and the Maryland State Monument (pictured below) is symbolic. In the 1960s the "brother versus brother" interpretation of the Battle of Antietam was a powerful national lens through which to make sense of the U.S. Civil War. The Maryland State Monument honors all Maryland infantry and artillery units that fought in Sharpsburg, Maryland—both Union and Confederate. The "brother versus brother" theme extended to other battlefields, even decades later, with the most notable example being the "Brothers Again" sculpture on the Maryland State Monument at Gettysburg, which was dedicated in 1994.[35]

Maryland State Monument

On May 30, 1900, President William B. McKinley spoke at the dedication of the Maryland State Monument. Nearly thirty-eight years earlier, and during the battle, Sgt. McKinley had served as a nineteen-year-old commissary sergeant in the 23rd Ohio Infantry. Former

Confederate Maj. Gen. James Longstreet and resident of Gainesville, Georgia, joined the presidential party for the monument's dedication.

The dedication's speakers struck a common theme, which was national reunion under one flag. And with respect to the State of Maryland, the sentiment extended to Maryland's "sons" who fought on both sides at the Battle of Antietam. One inscription summarized the purpose of the monument, as follows: "Erected by the State of Maryland, to her sons, who on this field offered their lives in maintenance of their principles."

The Maryland State Monument is the only Antietam memorial that honors both Union and Confederate military units, a reality that is expressed by four bas-relief battlefield scenes:

1. Wolcott's First Maryland Battery (p. 151)
2. Charge of Second Maryland on Burnside Bridge (p. 154)
3. Fifth Maryland Closing upon Roulettes Barn and House (p. 156)
4. Brockenbrough's Maryland Battery, Repelling a Charge (p. 157)

Maryland State Monument

On each end of the granite-encased bas-relief sculptures stands a column, for a total of eight columns. The monument's octagonal structure physically expresses the participation of Maryland's eight military units that fought at the Battle of Antietam.

USA (Army of the Potomac):

1. **1st Maryland Light Artillery (Wolcott's) Battery A**, Capt. John W. Wolcott, 1st Division Artillery (Upton), 1st Division (Slocum), 6th Corps (Franklin). Fired toward Dunker Church from the Mumma farm.

2. **1st Maryland Light Artillery (Snow's) Battery B**, 1st Lt. Theodore J. Vanneman, 2nd Division Artillery (Ayres), 2nd Division (Smith), 6th Corps (Franklin). Fought in the East Woods.

3. **Purnell Legion Infantry**, Lt. Col. Benjamin L. Simpson. 3rd Brigade (Goodrich), 2nd Division (Greene), 12th Corps (Mansfield). Fought in the West Woods.

4. **2nd Maryland Infantry**, Lt. Col. J. Eugene Duryea, 1st Brigade (Nagle), 2nd Division (Sturgis), 9th Corps (Burnside). Fought at Burnside Bridge.

5. **3rd Maryland Infantry**, Lt. Col. Joseph M. Sudsburg,[36] 2nd Brigade (Stainrook), 2nd Division (Greene), 12th Corps (Mansfield). Fought in the West Woods.

6. **5th Maryland Infantry**, Maj. Leopold Blumenberg, 3rd Brigade (Weber), 3rd Division (French), 2nd Corps (Sumner). Fought at The Sunken Road.

CSA (Army of Northern Virginia):

7. **Baltimore Light Artillery (Brockenbrough's) Battery**, Capt. John B. Brockenbrough, Shumaker's Artillery, J.R. Jones commanding Jackson's Division, under Jackson's Command. Fought in the West Woods.

8. **1st Maryland Artillery (Dement's) Battery**, Capt. William F. Dement, Courtney's Artillery, Ewell's Division (Lawton), Jackson's Command. Marched from Harpers Ferry to near Harpers Ferry Road, west of Antietam Creek.

On the battlefield, each of the eight Maryland military units has similar looking monuments that mark the general location of their service at the Battle of Antietam. A Union and Confederate example is provided below. For more details, see p. 143 and Chapters 9–10.

USA Purnell Legion Infantry (Behind Dunker Church)

CSA Brockenbrough's Baltimore Battery (West Woods)

While at Antietam on September 17, 1937, President Franklin D. Roosevelt spoke about the meaning of the battle from the perspective of a man who was born nearly two decades after the U.S. Civil War ended. Although President Roosevelt expressed the longstanding theme of being one people and one nation, he also mentioned what he called the "evil ways" of reconstruction. He declared:

> I believe also, that the past four years mark the first occasion... that we are not only acting but also thinking in national terms. Deeply we appreciate that the distress or difficulty of any one part of the Union adversely affects each and every other part. We stand ready in all parts of the land to lend a helping hand to those Americans who need it most.
>
> In the presence of the spirits of those who fell on this field—Union soldiers and Confederate soldiers—we can believe that they rejoice with us in the unity of understanding which is so increasingly ours today. They urge us on in all we do to foster that unity in the spirit of tolerance, of willingness to help our neighbor, and of faith in the destiny of the United States.[37]

Did you know ... ?

The following U.S. presidents visited Antietam.

16th President Abraham Lincoln (1809–65) visited the battlefield, Maj. Gen. McClellan, and the soldiers camped in the Sharpsburg area on October 2–4, 1862.[38]

17th President Andrew Johnson (1809–75) delivered the dedication speech for Antietam National Cemetery on the battle's fifth anniversary in 1867.

18th President Ulysses S. Grant (1822–85) visited Antietam National Battlefield on October 15, 1869.[39]

25th President William B. McKinley (1843–1901), a veteran of the Battle of Antietam, delivered a speech at the dedication of the Maryland State Monument on May 30, 1900.

26th President Theodore Roosevelt (1858–1919) visited Antietam National Battlefield on September 17, 1903, to dedicate the New Jersey State Monument.

32nd President Franklin Delano Roosevelt (1882–1945) delivered an address on the battle's seventy-fifth anniversary in 1937. The celebration included a reenactment at the Burnside Bridge.

35th President John F. Kennedy (1917–63) and First Lady Jackie Kennedy toured Antietam National Battlefield on April 8, 1963, seven months before he was assassinated in Dallas, Texas. The Kennedys made a point of learning about the role of the Irish Brigade in the fighting at The Sunken Road.

39th President Jimmy Carter (1924–) and First Lady Rosalynn Carter toured Antietam National Battlefield with author Shelby Foote on July 6, 1978. The Carters were particularly interested in the fighting at Burnside Bridge and the role of Georgian soldiers who fought there.

Sharpsburg Family Farms

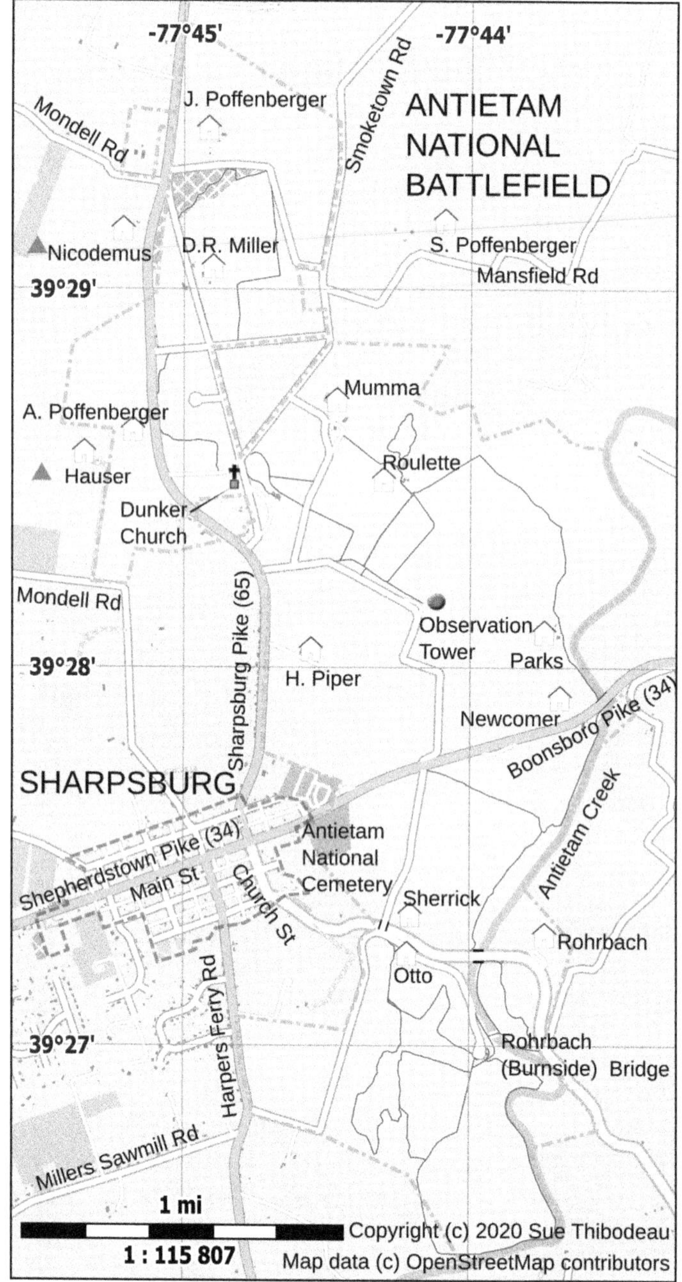

Map 8. Antietam Farms

Map 8 identifies the locations of several notable Sharpsburg family farms. On the night of September 16, Hooker's corps camped at Joseph and Mary Ann Poffenberger's farm. Then at dawn, they marched through the North Woods and onto D.R. Miller's farm while nearly forty Confederate cannons on Nicodemus Heights shelled the infantry divisions of Brig. Gens. Doubleday, Ricketts, and Meade.[40] Nicodemus Heights is located on the western part of the Nicodemus family farm[41] and north of another important artillery position on Hauser Ridge, named for the Jacob Hauser family.

Later in the morning, fighting rolled onto farmsteads owned by Samuel and Barbara Mumma, William and Margaret Roulette, and Henry and Elizabeth Piper.[42] Confederate Brig. Gen. Roswell S. Ripley, a New Yorker and U.S. Military Academy graduate, ordered his North Carolina and Georgia regiments to burn the Mumma farm buildings. At the Roulette farm, Confederate artillery hit the family apiary (bee yard) near Union infantry marching toward a dirt farm lane known as The Sunken Road; the 132nd Pennsylvania suffered stings from one direction and shells and bullets from the other.[43] On the south side of The Sunken Road, the Piper farm suffered extensive damage during attacks and counter-attacks through this "Bloody Lane," and although the fighting here claimed about 3,000 Union and 2,500 Confederate casualties, the Confederate center line held.[44]

The Sunken Road ("Bloody Lane")—Looking Southeast

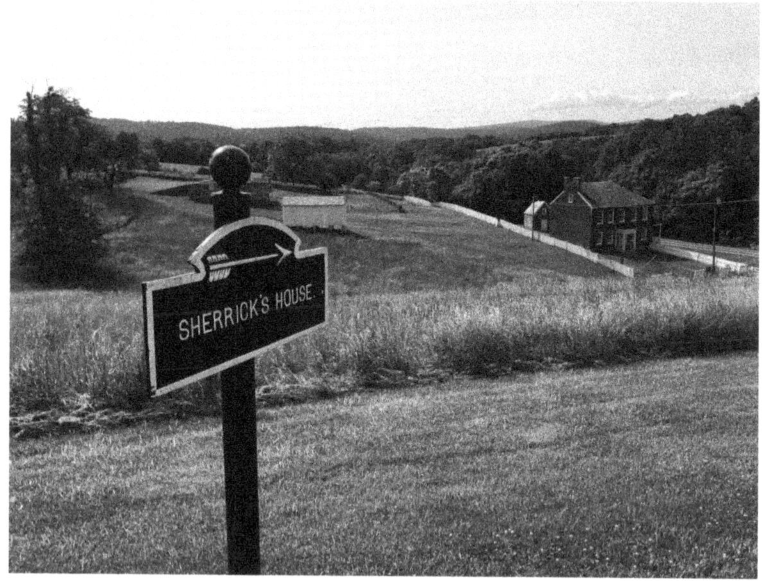

Sherrick Farmstead (About 1,000 Yards from Rohrbach Bridge)

In the late afternoon, the battle shifted to farmland south of Boonsboro Pike—property owned by Joseph and Sarah Sherrick, John and Kate Otto, and Henry and Martha Rohrbach. The Sherrick family lived on the west bank of Antietam Creek, where Joseph hid $3,000 worth of gold in a stone wall; although his orchards and crops were looted or destroyed at the Battle of Antietam, his gold remained safe from theft.[45]

Early that morning, before a brigade of half-starved Georgian soldiers would anchor the Confederate right wing on an overlook above Antietam Creek, some Georgians breeched the Otto kitchen and asked for bread, bacon, and milk. Then, for several hours later that day, the brigade kept four infantry divisions (an entire army corps) penned up on the east side of the creek, near the Rohrbach Bridge. The bridge connected the Rohrbach properties. Built circa 1836–37, it was also known as the Lower Bridge, and later, the "Burnside Bridge," named for the Union corps commander who fought here.

Rohrbach Bridge and Antietam Creek

The next photo was taken from the west bank of Antietam Creek. The tree on the far bank, near the end of Rohrbach Bridge, is a "witness tree," which means that the tree was old enough to "witness" the Battle of Antietam. Union Maj. Gen. Ambrose E. Burnside's 9th Corps tried three times to take the bridge, but they took heavy fire from a few hundred Georgians who were dug into an overlook on the west bank. Confederate Gens. Robert A. Toombs and Henry L. Benning held this commanding position for more than three hours.

A brigade of men from Ohio and Connecticut first tried to cross the bridge, but they were forced back. A brigade from Maryland and New Hampshire made the second charge, but failed. Finally, Brig. Gen. Edward Ferrero's 51st New York and 51st Pennsylvania regiments took the bridge and Burnside's 9th Corps crossed to the west bank to join the final attack of the day.

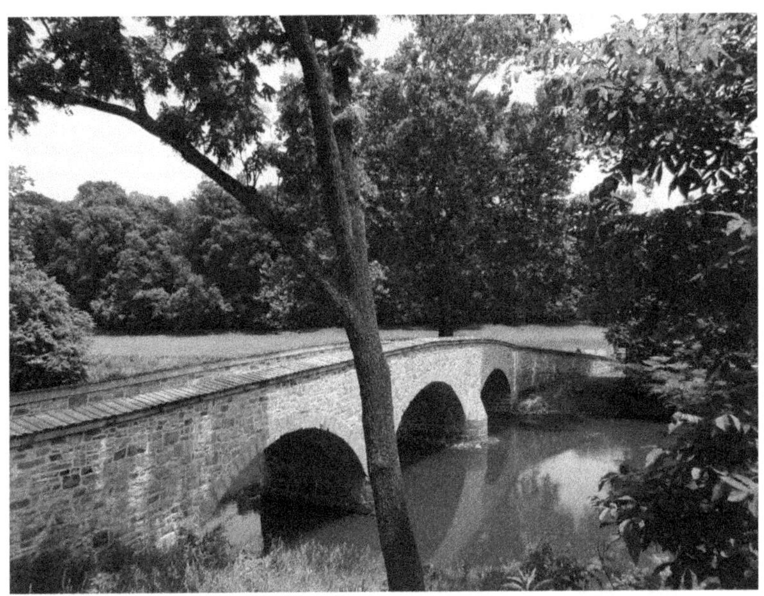

Rohrbach (Burnside) Bridge Over Antietam Creek

The fight moved westward where the two armies squared off in the hilly fields southeast of Sharpsburg from 3:00-5:30 p.m. When the Union left flank collapsed, the battle was over. You will learn more about "The Final Attack" and the battle's results on your bicycle tour.

Hopefully, this chapter has provided you enough context—in terms of significant landmarks and how they connect to the battle narrative—to keep you oriented on your ride through Antietam National Battlefield.

Antietam National Cemetery

Capt. Robert Gould Shaw—who less than one year later famously commanded the 54th Massachusetts and died in a failed assault on Fort Wagner in South Carolina—described the battlefield scene the night of September 17 in this way: "At last, night came on ... all was quiet. The crickets chirped, and the frogs croaked, just as if nothing unusual had happened all day long, and presently the stars came out bright, and we lay down among the dead, and slept soundly until daylight. There were twenty dead bodies within a rod of me."[46]

When the Battle of Antietam ended, about 4,000 dead bodies covered a once picturesque landscape. Within days, Civil War photographer Alexander Gardner and his team arrived to document the scene. For months afterwards, the small town of Sharpsburg served the nation as a massive field hospital, burial ground, and home to Gen. McClellan's Army of the Potomac.[47]

It was not until March 23, 1865, that Maryland purchased eleven acres as a burial site for soldiers. Prior to that, some men were buried in trenches, others taken home for burial, and still others transported to local cemeteries. Reburials would take years. In 1867, a Maryland newspaper reported that "five or six hundred" coffins had arrived in Clarysville (MD) to prepare bodies for reburial in Sharpsburg.[48]

Antietam National Cemetery

Federal graves radiate around the Private Soldier Monument, which was dedicated on September 17, 1880. "Not for themselves, but for their country," is the only inscription.[49] Maryland graves are on the back left side.

Private Soldier Monument

On September 17, 1867, Antietam National Cemetery was dedicated as a national burial site for federal soldiers, starting with about 4,700 Union soldiers killed or mortally wounded in Maryland during the Civil War. This included the Battles of Antietam, South Mountain, and Monocacy. President Andrew Johnson was in attendance for the ceremony.

Maryland Graves at Antietam National Cemetery

Area Confederate Cemeteries

The Cemetery Commission originally planned to bury both Union and Confederate soldiers at Antietam National Cemetery. However, bitter divisions and financial problems resulted in Maryland's decision to exclude Confederates. Confederate bodies were re-interred in Elmwood Cemetery in Shepherdstown, West Virginia; Washington Confederate Cemetery in Hagerstown, Maryland; and Mount Olivet Cemetery in Frederick, Maryland.[50]

Although not a bicycling destination, you might want to consider extending your historical touring vacation to include visits to area Confederate cemeteries. You will get the most out of your trip if you come prepared with a list of gravestones to find. For example, although most Civil War graves at Elmwood Cemetery are for ordinary soldiers, a member of Jackson's staff at Antietam, Col. Henry Kyd Douglas, is buried there. Col. Isaac E. Avery missed the Battle of Antietam due to wounds suffered at the Battle of Gaines' Mill in June, but he is buried in Washington Confederate Cemetery (where only a bronze engraved map shows the position of graves). Frederick's Mount Olivet Cemetery has a mix of Union and Confederate graves.

Elmwood Cemetery

Shepherdstown,
West Virginia[51]

Washington Confederate Cemetery

(in Rose Hill Cemetery)
Hagerstown, Maryland[52]

Mt. Olivet Cemetery

Frederick, Maryland[53]

What Next?

Chapter 1, "Antietam on a Bicycle," provides an overview of the Antietam road network (including access roads from the C&O Canal Towpath); a high-level summary of three different sets of bicycle routes; and a lengthy visual presentation of several significant physical and natural landmarks at Antietam National Battlefield. The chapter's objective is to provide a solid introduction to what a bicyclist can see, feel, and learn on a 9.2-mile ride. It also sets the stage for mastering the high-level battle chronology that is outlined in Chapter 2, "The Battle of Antietam."

Chapter 2 is a concise summary of 1862 battlefield events that relies heavily on maps and photos so that it is easier to learn on two wheels. But before turning to Chapter 2, please first familiarize yourself with the next three tables. Collectively, these tables give a "who's who" introduction to the names of Union and Confederate officers who appear on park wayside exhibits and other mini histories, including this guidebook. As you read Chapter 2, you may want to refer to Tables 2–4 to confirm your understanding of the Battle of Antietam.

Table 2. State Affiliations for Each Army

STATES AT THE BATTLE OF ANTIETAM

USA / Federal / Union (19 states + 2 other*):

Connecticut	*Maryland*[54]	Ohio
*District of Columbia	Maine	Pennsylvania
Delaware	Michigan	Rhode Island
Illinois	Minnesota	*United States Regulars
Indiana	New Hampshire	Vermont
Kentucky	New Jersey	Wisconsin
Massachusetts	New York	(West) Virginia

CSA / Confederate (9 states + Maryland secessionists):

Arkansas	*Maryland*	Tennessee
Alabama	Mississippi	Virginia
Georgia	North Carolina	
Louisiana	South Carolina	

Table 3. USA Abbreviated Order of Battle

Key: ^battlefield promotion or reassignment (often due to death or injury)
(k) killed (mw) mortally wound (w) wounded (c) captured

ARMY OF THE POTOMAC, MAJ. GEN. GEORGE MCCLELLAN

1st Corps, Maj. Gen. Joseph Hooker (w) ^Meade

1st Division, Brig. Gen. Abner Doubleday
2nd Division, Brig. Gen. James B. Ricketts
3rd Division, Brig. Gen. George G. Meade ^Truman Seymour

2nd Corps, Maj. Gen. Edwin V. Sumner

1st Division, Maj. Gen. Israel B. Richardson (mw) ^Winfield S. Hancock[55]
2nd Division, Maj. Gen. John Sedgwick (w) ^Oliver O. Howard
3rd Division, Brig. Gen. William H. French

5th Corps, Maj. Gen. Fritz John Porter

1st Division, Maj. Gen. George W. Morell
2nd Division, Brig. Gen. George Sykes
3rd Division (September 18), Brig. Gen. Andrew A. Humphreys[56]
Artillery Reserve: Lt. Col. William Hays

6th Corps, Maj. Gen. William B. Franklin

1st Division, Maj. Gen. Henry W. Slocum
2nd Division, Maj. Gen. William F. Smith
(September 18) 4th Corps, 1st Division, Maj. Gen. Darious N. Couch[57]

9th Corps, Maj. Gen. Ambrose E. Burnside (Wing Commander)

^Brig. Gen. Jacob D. Cox
1st Division, Brig. Gen. Orlando B. Wilcox
2nd Division, Brig. Gen. Samuel D. Sturgis
3rd Division, Brig. Gen. Isaac P. Rodman (mw) ^Edward Harland
4th (Kanawha) Division, Brig. Gen. Jacob D. Cox ^Eliakim P. Scammon

12th Corps, Maj. Gen. Joseph K.F. Mansfield (mw) ^Williams

1st Division, Brig. Gen. Alpheus Williams ^Samuel W. Crawford (w)
2nd Division, Brig. Gen. George S. Greene

Cavalry Division, Brig. Gen. Alfred Pleasonton

Table 4. CSA Abbreviated Order of Battle

Key: ^battlefield promotion or reassignment (often due to death or injury)
(k) killed (mw) mortally wound (w) wounded (c) captured
"Hood (Wofford)" means that Hood's Brigade was led by Wofford. Brigade numbers are for readability; they are arbitrary.

ARMY OF NORTHERN VIRGINIA, GEN. ROBERT E. LEE[58]

Maj. Gen. James Longstreet's Command (Right Wing)

Maj. Gen. Lafayette McLaws' Division

Brigades: 1-Kershaw; 2-Cobb; 3-Semmes; 4-Barksdale.

Maj. Gen. R.H. Anderson's Division[59] (w) ^Pryor

Brigades: 1-Wilcox (Cumming); 2-Mahone (Parham); 3-Featherston (Posey); 4-Armistead (w); 5-Pryor ^Hatley; 6-Wright (w).

Brig. Gen. D.R. Jones' Division[60]

Brigades: 1-Toombs (Benning); 2-Drayton; 3-Pickett (Hunton, Garnett); 4-Kemper; 5-Jenkins (Walker); 6-G.T. Anderson.

Brig. Gen. John Walker's Division

Brigades: 1-Walker (Manning); 2-Ransom.

Brig. Gen. John B. Hood's Division

Brigades: 1-Hood (Wofford); 2-Law; 3-Evans.

Maj. Gen. Thomas J. Jackson's Command (Left Wing)

Ewell's Division, Brig. Gen. Alexander R. Lawton (w) ^Early

Brigades: 1-Lawton (Douglass (k)); 2-Early ^Smith (w); 3-Trimble (Walker (w)); 4-Hays.

Maj. Gen. A.P. Hill's Division[61]

Brigades: 1-Branch (k); 2-Gregg (w); 3-Field (Brockenbrough); 4-Archer; 5-Pender; 6-Thomas.

Jackson's Division, Brig. Gen. J.R. Jones (w) ^Starke (k) ^Grigsby

Brigades: 1-Winder (Grigsby); 2-Taliaferro (Warren);

3-Jones (Penn (w) ^Page (w) ^Withers);

4-Starke (k) ^Williams (w) ^Stafford (w) ^Pendleton.

Maj. Gen. D.H. Hill's Division[62]

Brigades: 1-Ripley (w); 2-Rodes (w); 3-Garland (McRae (w)); 4-G.B. Anderson (mw); 5-Colquitt.

Brig. Gen. William N. Pendleton's Artillery Reserve

Maj. Gen. J.E.B. Stuart's Cavalry Division

Brigades: 1-Hampton, 2-Fitzhugh Lee, 3-Robertson (Munford).

2. The Battle of Antietam

When I took that color in my hand, I gave up all hope of life.
~ Maj. Rufus Dawes, 6th Wisconsin Infantry, Iron Brigade[63]

A Concise Overview of Battlefield Events

In the first week of September, 1862, the Confederate Army of Northern Virginia, under the command of Gen. Robert E. Lee, crossed the Potomac River into western Maryland. This first invasion of northern soil resulted in the Battle of South Mountain (September 14), Gen. Lee's capture of Harper's Ferry (September 15), and the Battle of Antietam (September 17) in Sharpsburg, Maryland.

The Battle of Antietam was a twelve-hour fight that evolved in three phases. The armies first clashed in the north section of today's battlefield park (North Woods, The Cornfield, and West and East Woods). Next, the battle expanded southeast to the Mumma and Roulette farms and The Sunken Road (Bloody Lane). Finally, in the late afternoon, brutal and desperate fighting raged southeast of town, from Rohrbach (Burnside) Bridge to Harpers Ferry Road.

A Visual Summary of the Battle Phases

This book's bibliography identifies many excellent references that describe, analyze, and interpret the Battle of Antietam from a military perspective. It is not our purpose to repeat those narratives in any significant detail. Instead, this chapter offers four maps that provide a general sense of the location of the Union and Confederate armies in each of three phases—described in terms of battlefield geography, and moving from north to south. For learning history on-the-go, the maps answer the most basic question, "Where were the armies?"

John Hoptak's work inspired what maps to draw, specifically with respect to battle timeframes.[64] However, unlike Hoptak's maps, the military maps in this guidebook are *impressionistic* at the army division (not brigade) level; the names of divisions and their commanders are omitted; and the geographic area is limited to the park. For more details, you are encouraged to read the park's many wayside exhibits as you find them on your ride. This chapter's maps are designed for ease of learning on two wheels; consult them each time you stop.[65] Map 6 (p. 36) and Map 8 (p. 46) will help, too.

Finally, for a nineteenth century geographic perspective, excerpts from S.G. Elliott's 1864 "Map of the Battlefield of Antietam" are provided. Blocks of hatch-marks in Elliott's map identify—not troop positions or crops—but thousands of temporary graves.[66] (Antietam National Cemetery was dedicated five years after the battle).

The Northern Portion of the Battlefield

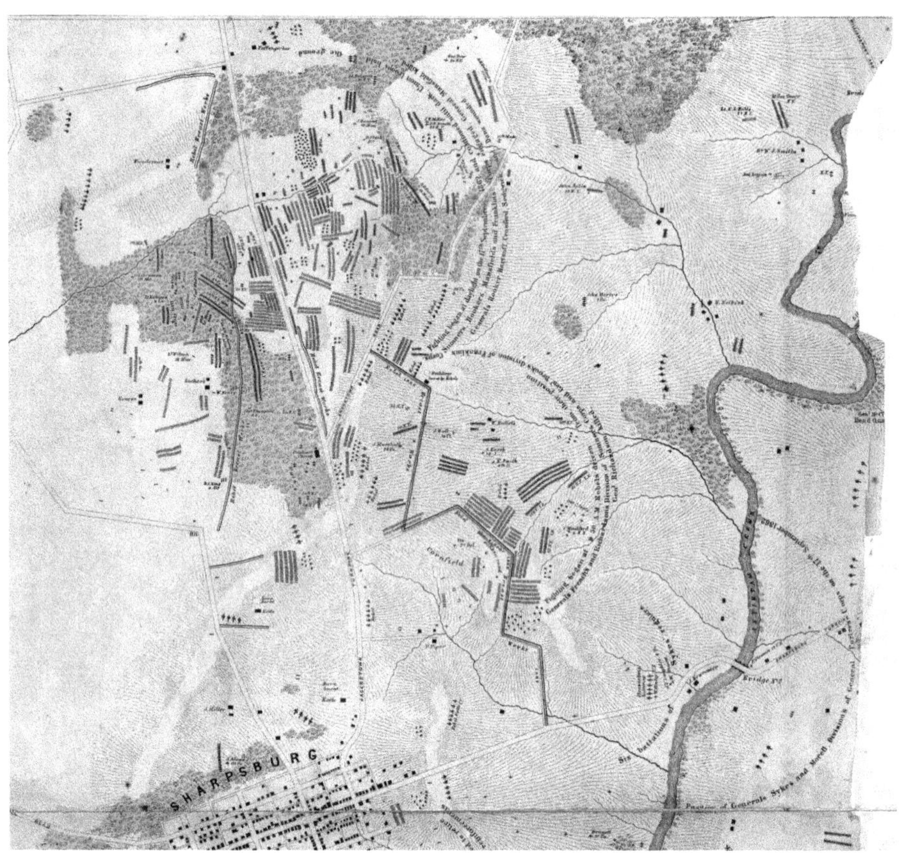

Map 9. Northern Portion of the Battlefield (S.G. Elliott, 1864)

Excerpt from The New York Public Library. White balance by author.

In the above map, the (green) West Woods, North Woods, and East Woods surround an area that included The Cornfield and Dunker Church. Antietam Creek is on the far right (east). Sharpsburg is south.

A Cartographer's Description (S.G. Elliott, 1864)

Simon G. Elliott produced detailed maps of the Antietam and Gettysburg battlefields.[67] His Antietam survey included this text:

> The ground on which Lee's army was drawn up was a crescent-shaped ridge, facing the creek, toward which it presented a gentle slope. On the farther side it was a table land, with woody coverts. It could be approached only from the creek, with the assailants exposed to a long range of fire.
>
> Antietam Creek, dividing the armies, was fordable only at points distant from each other, and the bridges were commanded by Lee's batteries. The Unionists were drawn up east side [of] the creek, behind low unwooded [sic] ridges, which, though unfavorable for infantry movements, afforded some cover for artillery. Here was posted most of the artillery, supported by reserves under Generals Sykes and Porter.
>
> General Burnside's corps was stationed on the left, forming the southern wing of the army. General Hooker, on the extreme right, began the battle late in the afternoon of the 16th, by fording the stream and gaining some advantage over the enemy's left. The battle began again with the dawn of the 17th. The field of conflict during most of the day was an open plain on the crest of the hill, a corn-field beyond, and masses of woods projecting into the plain like promontories into the sea.
>
> From 5 a.m. till 2 p.m. the battle raged with the utmost intensity. The field, which had been four times lost and won, finally, when both sides were nearly exhausted, remained in possession of the Union army. ...
>
> Such was the terrific slaughter, that divisions were reduced to brigades, and brigades to regiments. Several regiments, among which were the 34th New York and 15th Massachusetts, were nearly annihilated. Such were some of the results on the northern portion of the battle-field.
>
> ~S.G. Elliott, "Map of the Battlefield of Antietam," 1864.

Union View through The Cornfield to Cornfield Avenue

D.R. Miller's cornfield was the field that Elliott identified as "four times lost and won." The October photo (above) shows a post-harvest view of the field's southwest corner. The three monuments in the photo stand on Cornfield Avenue (left to right): 104th New York, 11th Mississippi, and Georgia State. South Mountain is in the distance.

The Cornfield is behind the 104th New York Monument in the next photo. While looking at the east face of the 11th Mississippi Monument, you can see West Woods in the distance.

104th NY Monument (South Face)

11th MS Monument (East Face)

Phase 1—In the North, The Cornfield and Woodlots

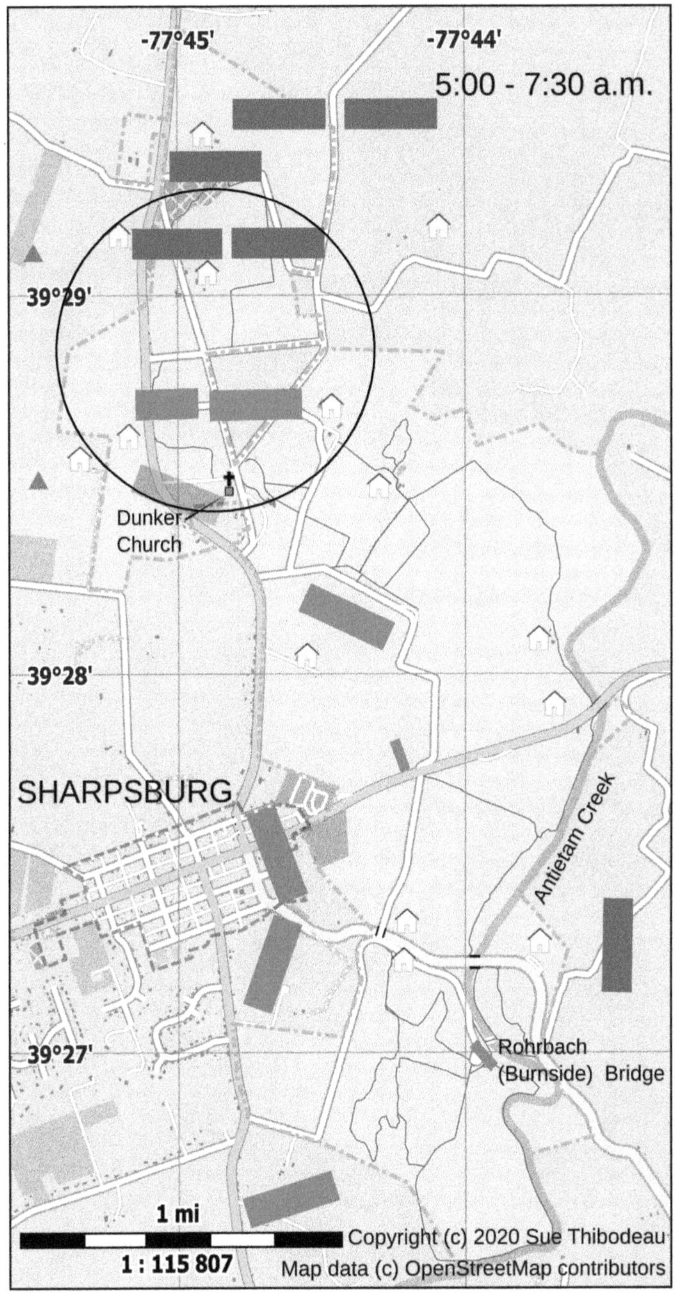

Map 10. The Battle Begins

34th NY Monument (1902)

The 34th New York and 15th Massachusetts infantry regiments (both mentioned by S.G. Elliott) fought in the West Woods and behind Dunker Church. The trefoil symbol etched on the two monuments represents the 2nd Corps, Army of the Potomac.

The 34th New York broke camp in Keedysville (see Map 2 on p. 16) to cross Antietam Creek. Upon entering the East Woods, the regiment "became heavily engaged with the Confederate forces in its front," and pressed toward the church, when "in a very brief time 43 men had been killed and 74 wounded."[68]

15th MA Monument (September 17, 1900)

"Here ... 606 men of all ranks ... within twenty minutes 330 had fallen, 75 killed and 255 wounded, 43 dying of wounds"

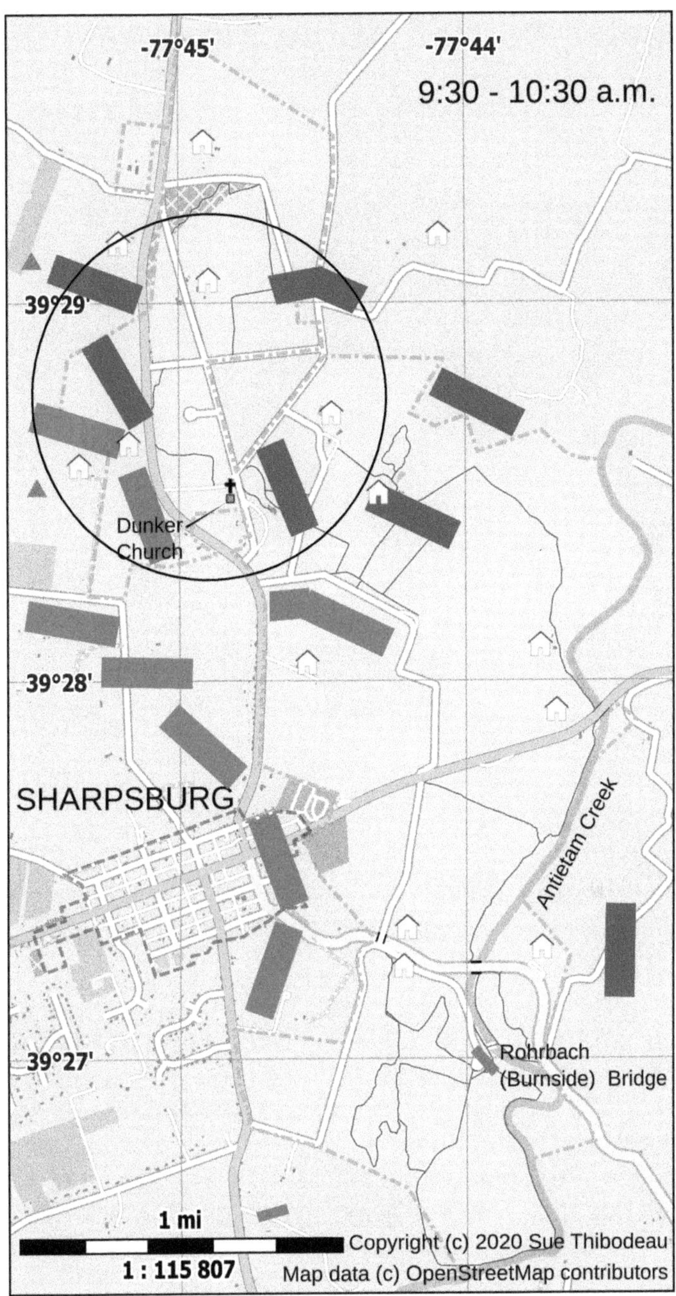

Map 11. Fighting in the East and West Woods

The fight in the battlefield's northern half produced staggering casualties—nearly 8,000 in a 700-yard radius of The Cornfield.[69]

The Center Portion of the Battlefield

Tip: Line up Elliott's map with this book's military maps by finding the "Sharpsburg" label.

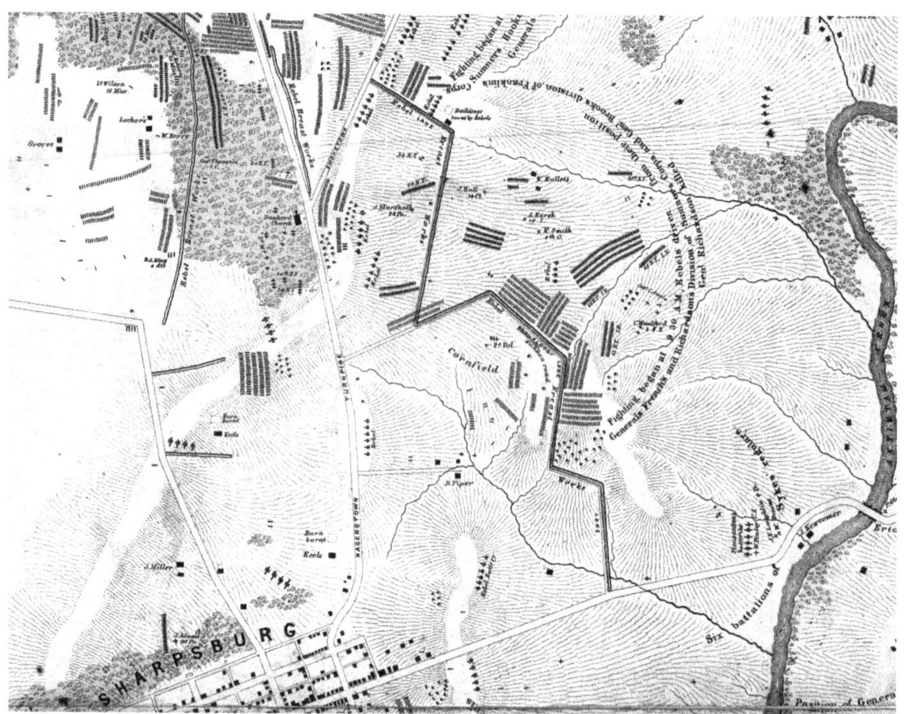

Map 12. Center Portion of the Battlefield (S.G. Elliott, 1864)

Excerpt from The New York Public Library. White balance by author.

The angled road near the center of Map 12 cuts through the Mumma, Roulette, and Piper farms. The central section is the famous Sunken Road through which Sharpsburg farmers drove their wagons. Note that Elliott's map shows a large number of temporary graves, most of which are Confederate. This is the second-most dense area of battlefield deaths, the first being the result of attacks and counter-attacks in The Cornfield and the West Woods earlier in the morning.

Map 13 shows the approximate battle line positions in what would be called "The Bloody Lane." On the Union side, there were regiments from Connecticut, Delaware, Indiana, Maryland, Massachusetts, New Hampshire, New York, Ohio, Pennsylvania, and West Virginia. On the

Confederate side, there were regiments from Alabama, Florida, Georgia, Mississippi, and North Carolina.

The Sunken Road, Looking East to the 132nd PA Monument

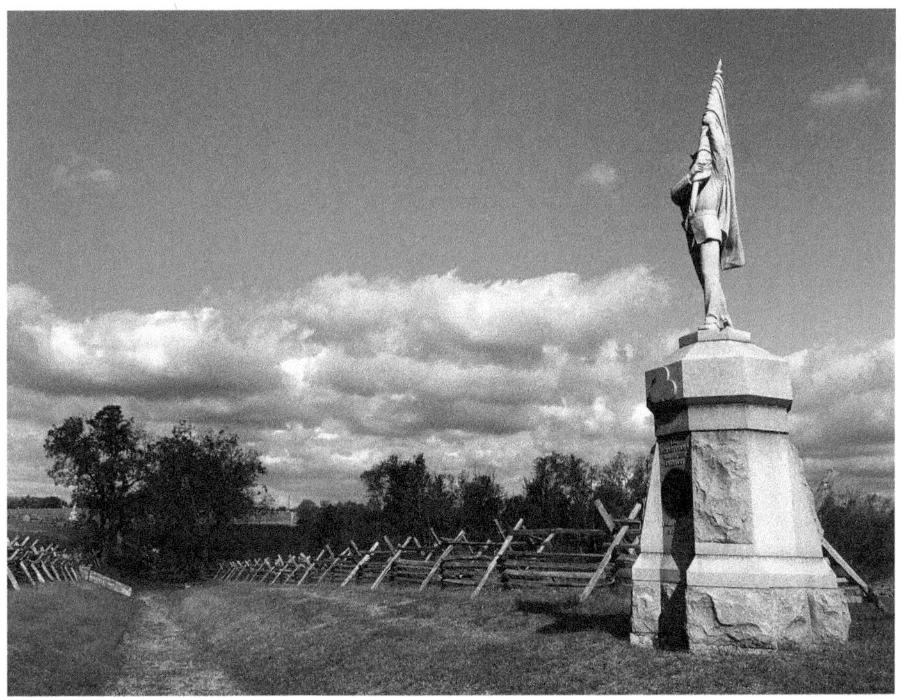

The Sunken Road, Looking West from the 132nd PA Monument

Phase 2—In the Center, Along The Sunken Road

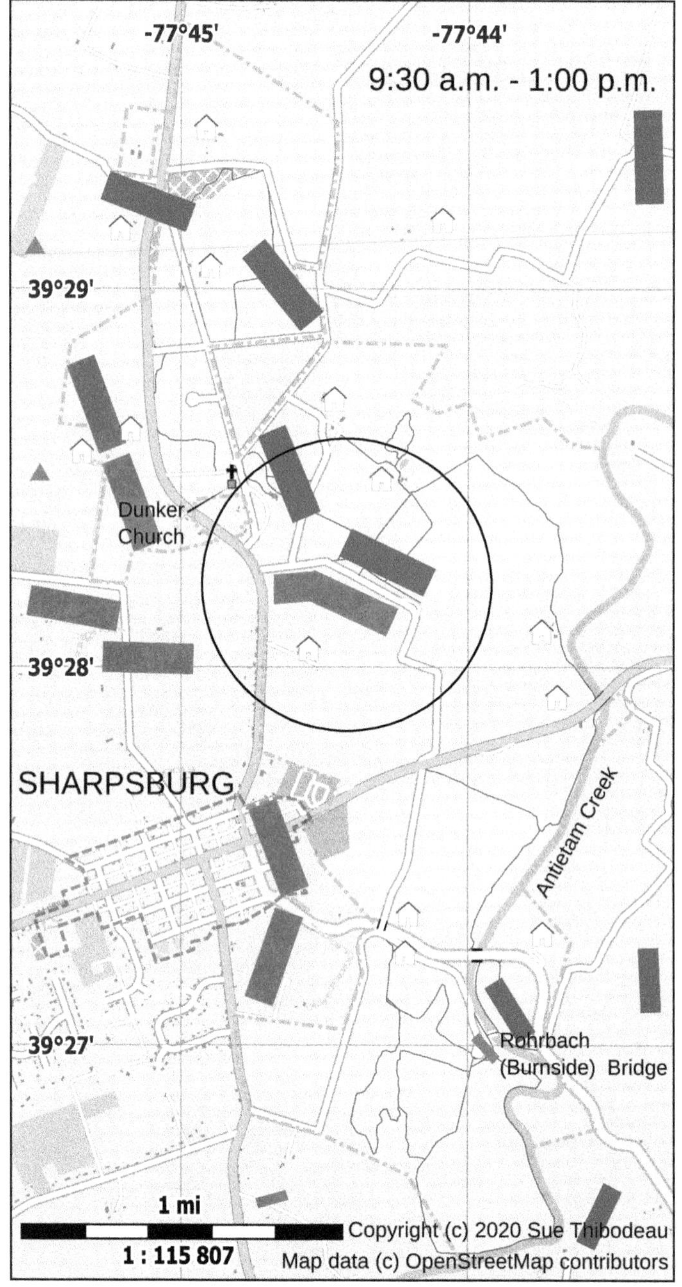

Map 13. Fighting at The Sunken Road

The Southern Portion of the Battlefield

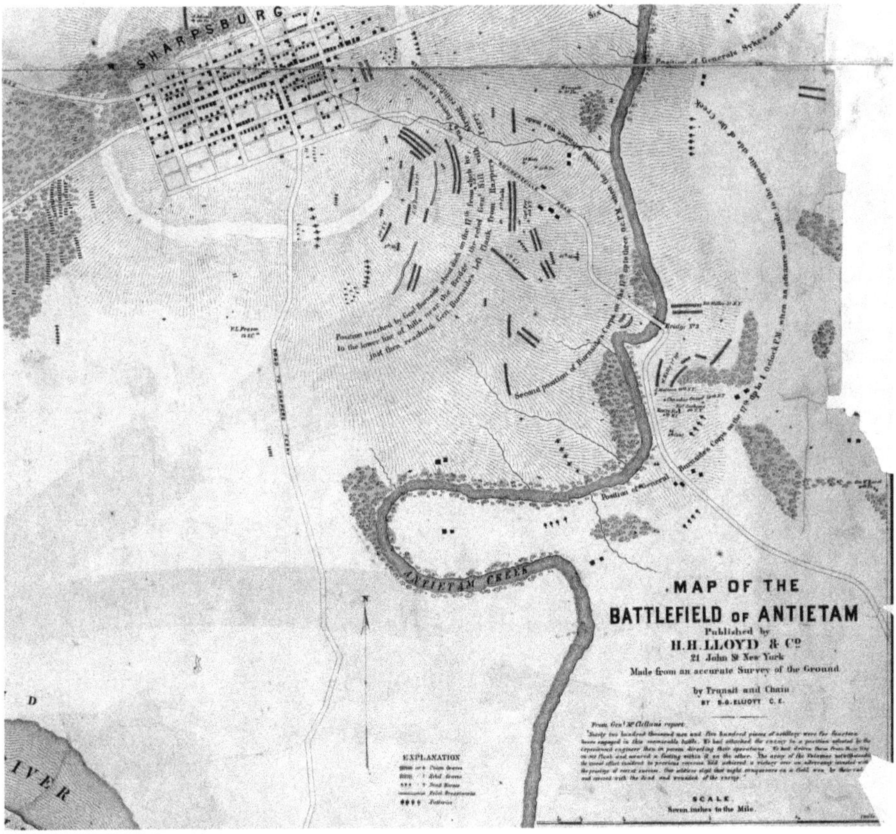

Map 14. Southern Portion of the Battlefield (S.G. Elliott, 1864)

Excerpt from The New York Public Library. White balance by author.

Pegram's Virginia Battery Gun

In Map 14, the Rohrbach (Burnside) Bridge across Antietam Creek is downstream, at the end of the first easterly bend. The nearby dark, thin blocks are temporary Union graves. In the photo, a Confederate gun points toward Antietam Creek (behind the tree line and not visible). The third and final phase of the Battle of Antietam (3:00–5:30 p.m.) was fought in these fields.

A Cartographer's Description (S.G. Elliott, 1864)

At the south the conflict was not less sanguinary. At 10 a.m. General Burnside made an attempt to cross the stone bridge upon the enemy's extreme right. This spot was commanded by the concentric fire of several of Lee's batteries, where were posted on hills that rose like an amphitheatre upon the opposite side of the creek. Three brigades made the creek run with their blood before the third carried the bridge. ...

Burnside, by the greatest gallantry, reached the brow of the hill; but, the enemy rallying, he was forced back.

~S.G. Elliott, "Map of the Battlefield of Antietam," 1864.

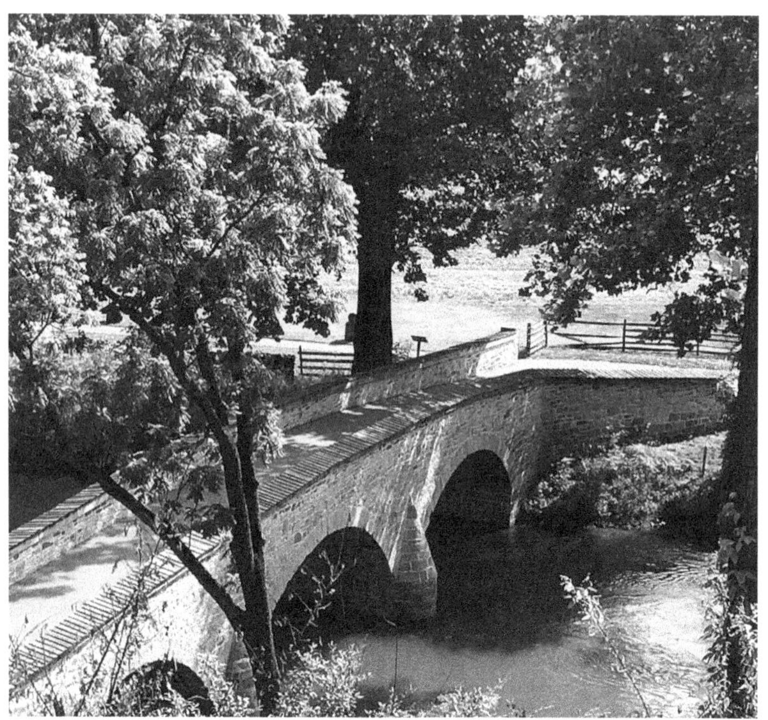

Burnside Bridge as Seen from the West Bank

Phase 3—In the South, The Rohrbach Bridge

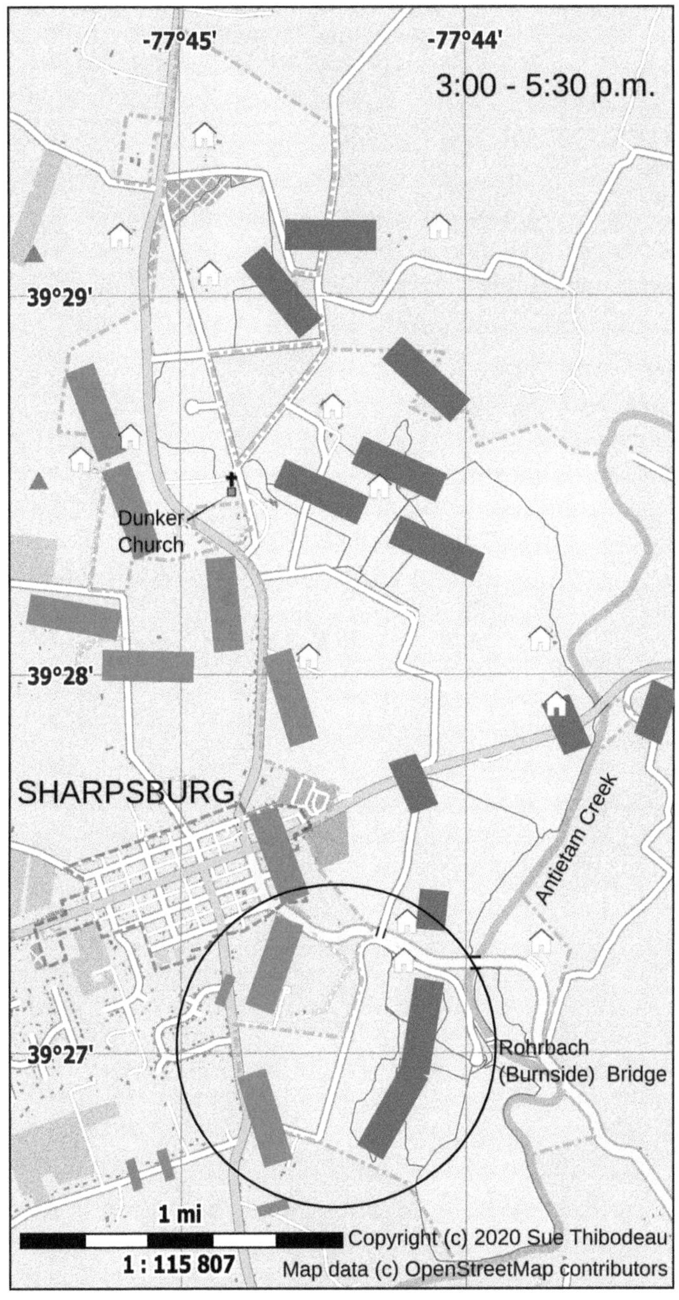

Map 15. Burnside Bridge and The Final Attack

Battle Results

	Union	Confederate	Total
Dead:	2,108	1,556	3,654
Wounded:	9,540	7,752	17,292
Missing/Captured:	753	1,018	1,771
Total:	12,401	10,316	22,717

Table 5. Antietam Casualties

Source: American Battlefield Trust, https://www.battlefields.org/learn/civil-war/battles/antietam.

Unable to win the battle in Sharpsburg, Gen. Robert E. Lee withdrew his army from Maryland and crossed the Potomac River into Virginia at Boteler's Ford on September 18 and 19. Boteler's Ford is about one mile south of Shepherdstown (now West Virginia).

The Battle of Shepherdstown began in the late morning of September 19, 1862, when Union Maj. Gen. Alfred Pleasonton, with artillery posted in Maryland, shelled Lee's Confederates. On September 20, two brigades from Union Maj. Gen. Fitz John Porter's 5th Corps crossed the river to attack A.P. Hill's Confederate division. But Maj. Gen. Thomas "Stonewall" Jackson reinforced Hill, so Porter retreated. The Army of Virginia returned home.

The Battle of Shepherdstown marked the end of the Maryland Campaign, Gen. Lee's first invasion of the North. In President Lincoln's mind, it was also the end for Maj. Gen. George B. McClellan, whom Lincoln officially removed from command on November 5, 1862, but not before visiting McClellan at one of Sharpsburg's many field hospitals, the Stephen P. Grove farmstead. On October 1, the Baltimore & Ohio Railroad carried President Lincoln through Point of Rocks (Maryland) on the way to visit his army at Harpers Ferry, Maryland Heights, and finally Sharpsburg on October 3.[70]

Human Consequences

The U.S. Civil War would not end for another two and one-half years, by which time the war claimed 1,125,453 casualties (killed, wounded, missing or captured), according to the National Park Service. The count includes 204,100 soldiers killed in action, about 40 percent of whom would not be identified, and according to one recent study, 750,000 total deaths (up from the long-standing consensus of about 620,000).[71]

For many families, the pain of not being able to locate a father or son presumed to have died—but not knowing where his body may lie—was a tragic continuation of a war that did not feel as if it had ended. Soldiers listed as "missing" might still be saved and brought home; if only the families knew where they might be. Some could be on their way home from a wartime prison as part of the prisoner exchanges in the early months of 1865.

When Clara Barton's nephew, Irving Vassall, mentioned that the federal government was struggling to notify families about the disposition of soldiers returning from Confederate prisons, Barton wrote to President Lincoln. In her February, 1865, letter, she requested that Lincoln recognize her as an official government correspondent to families. President Lincoln agreed.

With haste, Clara Barton, the "Angel of the Battlefield," nursed a different type of wound—that of the human spirit crushed by not knowing the whereabouts of a loved one. Barton began replying to many dozens of letters per day, and soon quickly hired (and paid with her own funds) a small staff whose job was, as she wrote to President Lincoln: To answer "letters from the friends of our prisoners now being exchanged," and "to obtain and furnish all possible information in regard to those that have died during their confinement."[72]

By June of 1865, Barton's "Missing Soldiers Office" published its first list of missing soldiers. The "Roll of Missing Men," as she called it, started with 1,533 names and grew to contain 6,650 names in 1868. Barton's final report to the U.S. Congress claimed that the Missing Soldiers Office had "received 63,182 inquiries, written 41,855 letters, mailed 58,693 printed circulars, distributed 99,057 copies of her printed rolls, and identified 22,000 men."[73] In a letter, Clara Barton described her service in this way:

> If it has been my privilege to lighten never [sic] so little the heavy burden of grief which has been laid upon the hearts of our suffering people, or throw the feeble weight of my arm on the side of my country in her hour of trail [sic], if I have made one heart stronger, or one war less bitter, I regard it as a blessing forever beyond my power to express.[74]

PART II: PLANNING YOUR TRIP

3. Gathering Your Gear

To bicycle Antietam National Battlefield, you need gear for a half-day ride on hilly, paved roadways. But if you are riding the battlefield as part of an excursion from a longer bikepacking tour along the C&O Canal, you are already (over)-equipped for a scenic ride. The recommendations in this chapter focus exclusively on what you need to tour the battlefield; gear considerations for bicycling the canal towpath are not considered.

Your gear should make sense for Sharpsburg's unique geography and weather. Basically, you need a bicycle, safety equipment, emergency supplies, food, water, and athletic clothing. (This chapter reproduces, and adapts for Antietam, content from *Bicycling Gettysburg National Military Park*, the first volume in Civil War Cycling's travel guide series).[75]

What Kind of Bicycle?

Obviously, you need a bicycle that is in good repair and that fits your body. Your bicycle must work well on pavement and provide sufficient gearing to climb hills while sharing the road with motor vehicles.

Fortunately, you do not need to understand the difference between a road, mountain, hybrid, touring, or electric bicycle—all of which are good choices—to select a functional and comfortable bike for your battlefield ride. If your bike is relatively modern (i.e., it has several gears that you know how to shift), and if it can help you to handle steep hills (i.e., you can retain your balance riding up and gently brake while riding down), then your bicycle is perfectly fine.

Safety Equipment

Not surprisingly, daytime rides through Antietam National Battlefield require a short list of basic safety gear. First and foremost, you need a bicycle helmet that fits your head.[76] Second, a bicycle mirror is very helpful for sharing the road with motor vehicles. And finally, a front-mounted white light helps drivers to see your bicycle in shady areas or when the sky becomes overcast.

Emergency Supplies

You will also want to carry emergency tools like a portable tire pump and a bicycle lock. Here are some additional supplies that you could pack and carry on a routine basis:

Basic First Aid Kit

- Small bandages
- Antiseptic wipes
- First aid cream
- Anti-histamine
- Pain medication
- Zinc oxide cream

Tiny Tools

- Pocket knife or razor blade
- Small flashlight
- Tire patch kit, tubes
- Tire levers, pressure gauge
- Foldable toolkit
- Duct tape, zip ties

Misc

- Touring book, maps, pen
- Insect (tick) repellent
- Comb, hand sanitizer
- Sunscreen, lip balm
- Eyeglass wipes, eye drops
- Sunglasses
- Plastic bags for trash
- Neck gaiter or wet cloth
- Fluorescent ankle bands
- Extra red LED lights
- Cell phone, extra power
- Camera, extra batteries
- Wallet, keys, cash, etc.
- Extra plastic baggies

One easy way to protect your wallet and electronics from unexpected rain is to carry extra plastic baggies. For long rides on hot summer days, consider carrying a small container of zinc oxide cream to prevent chafing behind your knees. And finally, if you are riding and camping on the C&O Canal Towpath near active railroad lines, consider adding earplugs to your normal bikepacking gear.[77]

The night before you begin a ride, check that your electronics are fully charged. Have a plan for protecting your cell phone from extended, direct exposure to heat (so that your phone works in an emergency). Consider carrying a USB power core or, lacking that, preserving your cell phone's battery for emergency use only. Because cell tower signals can be intermittent, paper maps are highly recommended.

Food and Water

If you are bicycling for longer than 2-3 hours, you need a plan for replenishing your body with food, especially carbohydrates. Most bicyclists pack and carry complex carbohydrates, especially hardy fruits and vegetables, and a small amount of protein (nuts).

More important than food, however, is a way to carry water. Refillable water bottles or backpack hydration systems are good options. With the exception of the Visitor Center restrooms, you will not find water on the battlefield. As of this writing, there is a convenience store and grill located about 0.8 miles south of the Visitor Center parking lot, on Sharpsburg Pike (Maryland 65), where you can purchase water and ice.

Restrooms and Portable Toilets

The Antietam National Battlefield Visitor Center has a restroom. The NPS opens a small number of portable toilets on a seasonal basis, but they are not always placed in the same location. Usually, there are portable toilets on the perimeter of the Burnside Bridge parking lot. Occasionally, they have been placed on Richardson Avenue near Sharpsburg Pike.

Bicycle Racks

As of this writing, Antietam National Battlefield has only one bicycle rack, which you will find near the Visitor Center. If you want to enter the building for a restroom or water break, this is an easy place to lock your bicycle. More likely, though, you will be parking your car in the Visitor Center parking lot, and your car's rack will be more convenient.

Pack and Carry

Most of your emergency supplies will fit into a front-mounted bag or bicycle trunk. Since a full battlefield tour is only 9.2 miles, you could lighten your load by leaving heavy foods, tools, and possibly clothing locked in your parked car.

If you might extend your ride for whatever reason, lightweight panniers can offer a very convenient place to store food, water, and an extra shirt or windbreaker. Of course, you could also use a student-size backpack, but please anticipate that this set up can become uncomfortable on daylong rides.

Clothing

For a half-day ride at Antietam National Battlefield, it is unlikely that you will get surprised by a change of weather during your ride. However, a tip worth remembering is that Sharpsburg can get very hot in the spring, summer, and fall months, and it can be difficult to find shade when you think you need it. On the day of your ride, as you dress and pack your bicycle bags, ask yourself four questions:

1. If I get hot, what can I take off?
2. If I get cold, what can I put on?
3. If it starts to rain or snow, how will I keep dry?
4. If it starts to get cloudy or dark, how will I be seen?

The goal is to select weather-appropriate clothing that can be assembled into layers. Inexperienced bicyclists often underestimate the value of fluorescent, athletic shirts and windbreakers that are made of moisture-wicking (synthetic) fibers. Cotton can get wet and stay wet for a long time, which can be uncomfortable and irritate your skin. For the extra expense of athletic clothing, your body will stay dry and your body temperature will be better regulated. When worn in layers, air pockets are created for extra warmth and dryness.

Maps

Pack and carry this guidebook so that you can look up monument histories in Part IV as you tour the battlefield using the book's maps. For your extra (optional) convenience, you can also purchase digital PDF companion maps from www.civilwarcycling.com. For a fraction of the cost of a paperback book, you can download and print companion maps for personal use without the hassle of license keys or passwords. Also, if your cell phone or mobile device has a PDF reader, you can consult a map during a break in your ride. (The maps are *not* intended for use while pedaling your bicycle).

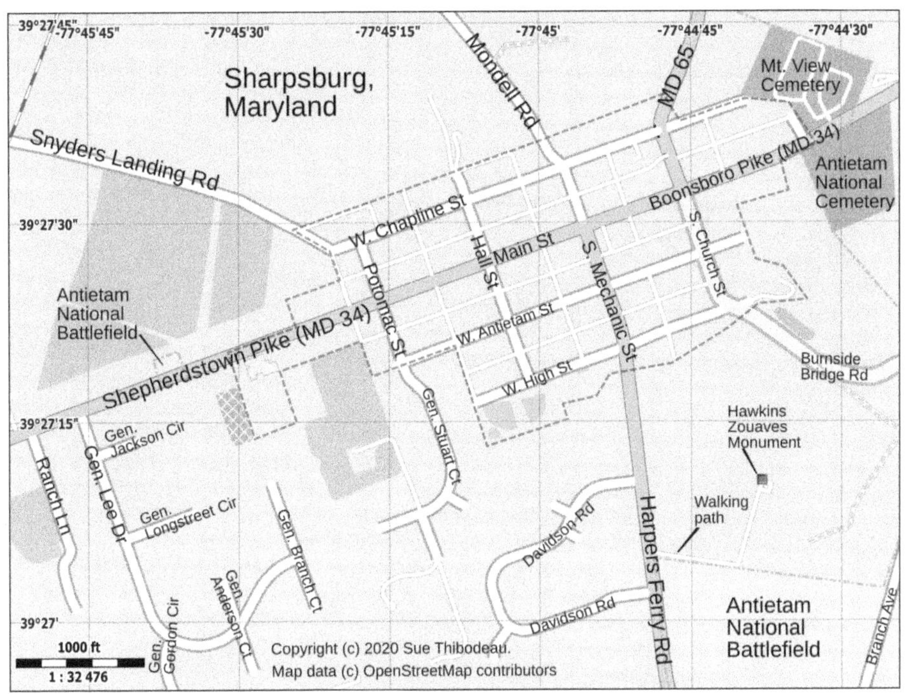

Map 16. Downtown Sharpsburg, Maryland

Walking Path Sign on Harpers Ferry Rd.

8th CT Monument

Tip: When you exit the park by turning right on Harpers Ferry Road, you will pass a sign on your right that points to a 0.3-mile walking path. Since there are no bicycle racks in this area, you can walk your bicycle on the footpath to visit three monuments: 9th New York ("Hawkins' Zouaves"), 8th Connecticut, and Brig. Gen. Isaac Rodman's mortuary cannon.

4. Transportation and Lodging

Sharpsburg, Maryland, is a rural town surrounded by farmland and mountains. Unlike Gettysburg, it has not grown into a commercial tourist center with hotels, restaurant franchises, or souvenir shops and novelty stores. As of this writing, the town population is less than 1,000 people and spans about thirty blocks, most of which are family homes. Most tourists will expand their trip planning decisions to include surrounding towns and cities, especially Shepherdstown, Hagerstown, Harpers Ferry, and perhaps as far away as Frederick.

When making arrangements to bicycle Antietam National Battlefield, bicycle rentals, transportation, storage, and lodging accommodations are important considerations. We will cover each of these topics in this short chapter.

Bicycle Renting Options

Most bicyclists who take the time to plan a tour of Antietam National Battlefield will decide not to rent. Currently, Sharpsburg does not have a bicycle shop, nor does the town have a business that offers bicycle tours. On the other hand, there are several bicycle shops in Shepherdstown, Hagerstown, Harpers Ferry, and Frederick. To pursue rental options, consult the Real Yellow Pages here, https://www.yellowpages.com/sharpsburg-md/bicycle-shops.

If you want to rent, make reservations early in the tourist season to guarantee your rental. Call or e-mail the company with your questions. Ask for pricing on twenty-four-hour bicycle rentals. Mention that you will be riding on very hilly but paved terrain. Although it is unlikely that a rented bicycle will be equipped with a mirror and a bicycle rack, a bicycle shop may be able to accommodate your request if they have sufficient notice. Finally, confirm that the rental agreement includes a helmet.

Transporting Your Bicycle

If you are driving to Sharpsburg and bringing your own bicycles, you will most likely want to mount them on your car. For safety, consult your car dealership and a local bicycle shop for advice. Make sure that the rack fits the car and the bicycles rest solidly in the rack, and then test your setup before you take your trip. Although not strictly necessary, some bicyclists use bungee cords to prevent the front wheel tires from moving. It is also a good idea to slip an inexpensive plastic cover over each bicycle's seat, since rain can damage the seat and it can take a long time for the seat to dry. If it rains, towel-dry the bicycle and be sure to apply chain lube sometime before your ride.

If you do not want to purchase a car bicycle rack, another option is to slide the bicycles into the back of a large car (with middle seats down). Use a blanket for cushioning, and bring some repair tools in case you accidentally dislodge something. Minimally, you will need to re-adjust your mirrors, which requires an Allen wrench. If your hands touch your chains, you will want a rag to wipe them.

Storing Your Bicycle

If you are staying at an inn, it is very likely that your bicycle storage options will be limited by policy. In my experience, most inns want to be accommodating, but you may be required to store your bicycle in a storage room or shed that is accessible to other patrons. Hotels are generally more predictable and will allow you to bring your bicycle to your room.

Alternatively, ask about keeping your bicycle in a storage area that is accessible only to staff. You can also lock your bicycle to the rack on your car. As a theft deterrent, remove the front wheel and the seat and store them inside your locked car. And of course, if your car is large enough, you could also lock your bicycle in your car. Many bicyclists prefer a strong bicycle lock system, like the popular but heavy Kryptonite New York Fahgettaboudit Ulock paired with a Kryptonite Kryptoflex Cable.

Lodging

If you want to experience Sharpsburg's rural charm, you might want to consider making reservations at one of the town's historic inns or guest houses; see https://www.visitmaryland.org/city/sharpsburg. Alternatively, there are many conventional and historic lodging options in nearby Shepherdstown (4 miles), Hagerstown (14 miles), Harpers Ferry (17 miles), and Frederick (22 miles).

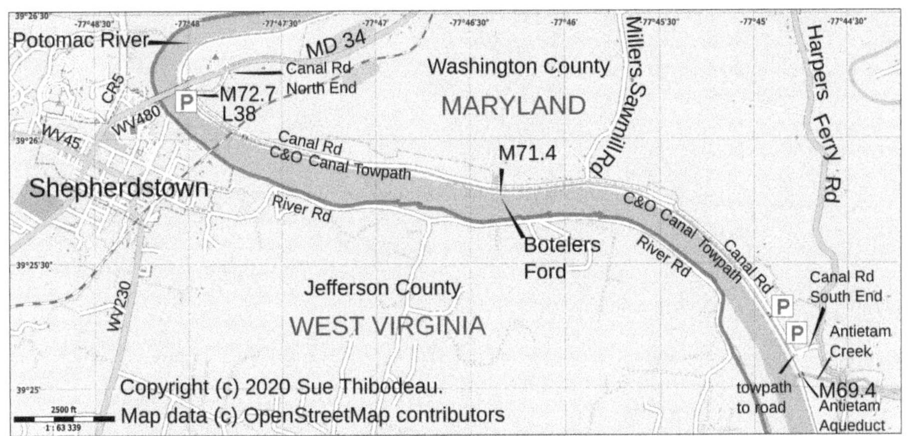

Shepherdstown (Motels and Inns) to Antietam Aqueduct (Camping)

Riding South on the C&O Canal Towpath near Harpers Ferry

Parking

Bicycle racks in or near Sharpsburg are not common, although there are many racks in Harpers Ferry. Car parking is generally not a problem, although the Visitor Center parking lot will fill up first. For a list of car parking lots and access points along the C&O Canal, see http://candocanal.org/access.html (C&O Canal Association website).

PART III: ENJOY YOUR RIDE!

5. How to Read Bicycle Cues

Segment Maps

A segment map is a detailed map of *part* of a bicycle route. When segment maps are sequenced one after the other, they describe a complete bicycle route. Route 1 for bicycling Antietam National Battlefield consists of four Segments, A—D.

Bicycle Cue Sheets

Each segment map has bicycling directions, called "cues." Distances are expressed in miles. These abbreviations are used:

L	Turn Left	**R**	Turn Right
QL	Quick Left	**QR**	Quick Right
BL	Bear Left	**BR**	Bear Right
PoL	Pass on Left	**PoR**	Pass on Right
CS	Continue Straight	**X**	Cross
U	U-Turn		
N	North	**E**	East
S	South	**W**	West

Table 6. Bicycle Cue Key

<u>**Tip 1:**</u> If you don't want to read bicycle cues, please skip over them. For most people, the maps in this book are sufficient to complete a loop through Antietam National Battlefield. The cues provide additional detail for people who like to know precise mileage details.

<u>**Tip 2:**</u> The cue sheets in this guidebook identify *optional* stopping points to visit monuments. It is highly unlikely that you will want to stop at all of them, mostly due to time restrictions. If you read this book before your trip, you can set a comfortable riding cadence that is based on your own unique touring needs and interests.

<u>**Tip 3:**</u> Park road signs are often not located or visible at a point at which a bicyclist needs to make a turning decision. The maps and cue sheets in this book should bridge that gap for you. For a key to map symbols and other abbreviations, see p. 20.

6. Route 1–Half Day Loop, 9.2 miles

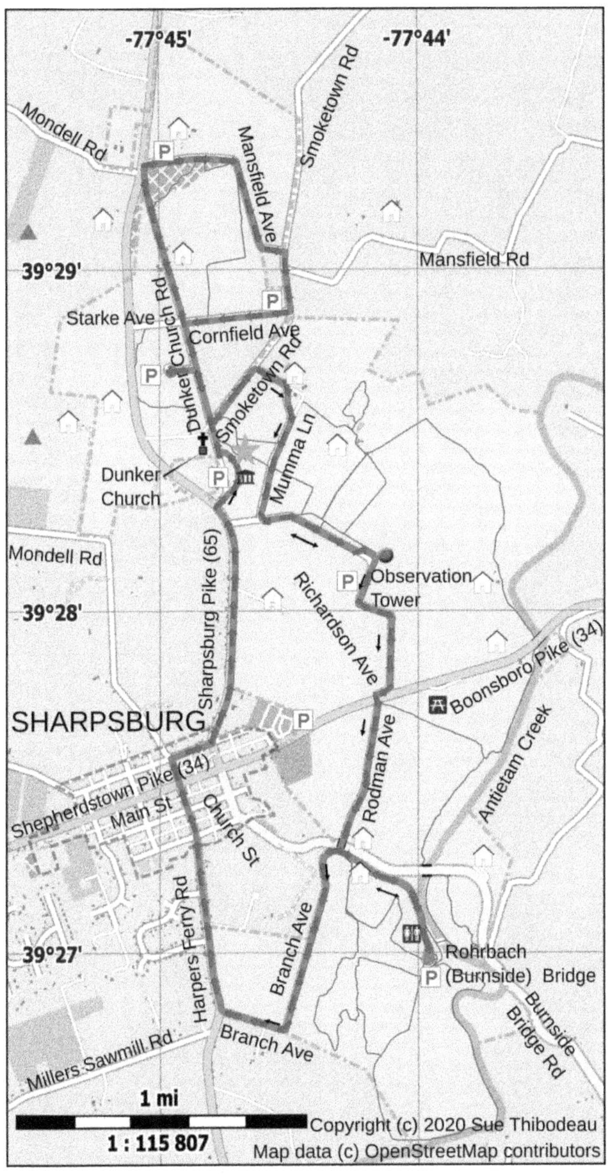

Map 17. Rt. 1 Battlefield Tour (Half Day Loop)

See p. 20 for a key to map symbols and abbreviations.

Before Your Ride

Route 1 consists of four Segments, A–D, that collectively cover the entire battlefield. The Segment maps and bicycles cues in Chapter 6 will take you on a 9.2-mile loop that begins and ends at the Visitor Center. For brevity—and knowing that bicyclists will prefer to spend more time riding the battlefield than reading at stops—historical information provided in this chapter is purposefully incomplete and certainly brief. To get the greatest educational experience from your battlefield tour, you are encouraged to read Parts I and IV of this book before you start your ride.

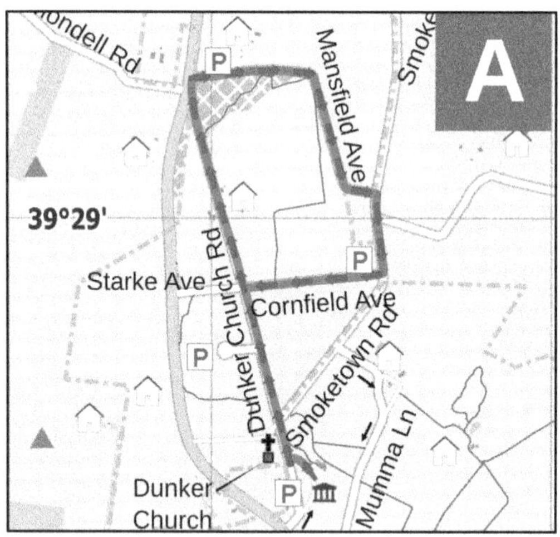

Segment A is a 2.4-mile ride. It begins at the Visitor Center and ends at the intersection of Cornfield Avenue and Dunker Church Road. Segment A is a mostly flat loop around The Cornfield. It covers much of the northern section of the battlefield. All roads are smoothly paved and have double-yellow lines. Car traffic is light (but shoulders are almost non-existent).

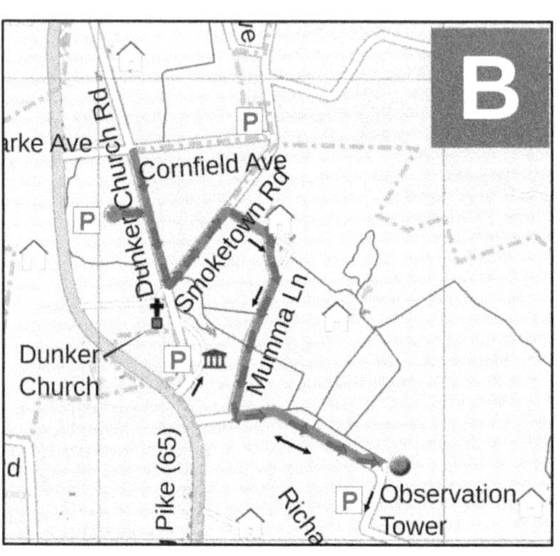

Segment B is a 1.7-mile ride. It begins at Dunker Church Road (at Cornfield Avenue), and continues south briefly to tour the West Woods by taking a right into Philadelphia Brigade Park. Next, you will turn around and continue south to turn left on Smoketown Road, and then ride through the Mumma and Roulette farms. Segment B ends at the east side of The Sunken Road.

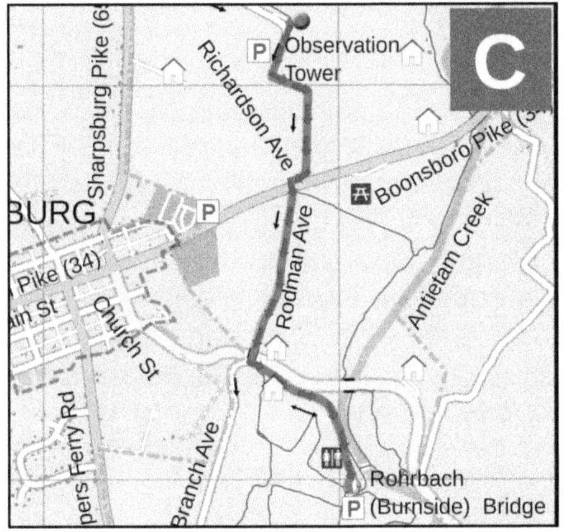

Segment C is a very hilly, 1.7-mile ride that runs roughly parallel to Antietam Creek, heading south. The segment begins on Richardson Avenue at the Observation Tower (built in 1897) and continues south through a hilly section of the Antietam battlefield. It ends at the parking lot above Rohrbach (Burnside) Bridge, near the entrance to a maze of hiking trails.

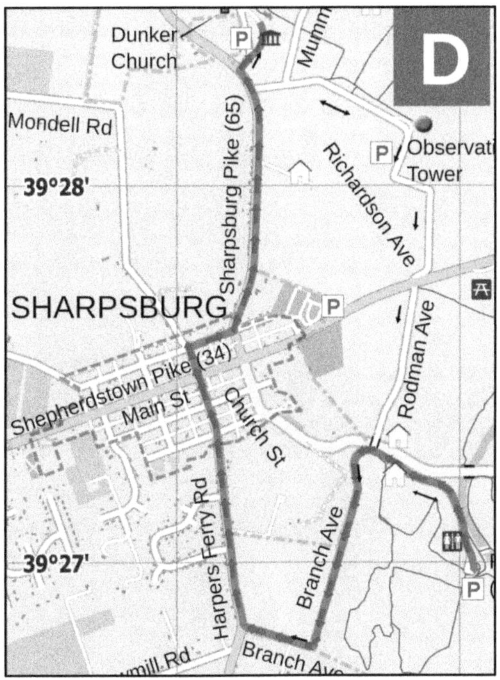

Segment D is a 3.4-mile ride from the Burnside Bridge area back to the Visitor Center. The ride on Branch Avenue cuts through the west edge of The Final Attack. However, once you turn right turn on Harpers Ferry Road and exit the park, the roads are heavily trafficked. There are no bicycle lanes or shoulders until you connect to Sharpsburg Pike, which offers wide shoulders (and a long but gradual incline). Sharpsburg has very limited dining and retail options, but if you plan ahead, your needs can be met.

Many bicyclists think that a 9.2-mile ride is relatively short. If you share that perspective, you may want to tour the battlefield twice in one day—the first time exclusively to enjoy the landscape (without stops); and the second time to learn more about the battlefield history. This touring approach can also help to bridge the varied and sometimes conflicting interests within a riding group.

Start at the Visitor Center

If this is your first visit to Antietam National Battlefield, you are encouraged to tour the Visitor Center before your bicycle tour. Your park admission includes a thirty-minute introductory video presentation about the Battle of Antietam. Next, you will want to walk to a few sites around the Visitor Center, including the New York State Monument, the Maryland State Monument, Dunker Church, and (for those tourists who want a deep-dive into Maryland soldiers at Antietam), the 3rd MD Infantry Monument. These four sites are listed as pre-steps on the Segment A cue table on p. 95.

On your walk and upcoming ride, you will find monuments and cast iron tablets that are not mentioned in this guidebook. Although Route 1 covers the entire battlefield park, a bicyclist will not have time (or the desire to stop) to visit every Antietam monument. Instead, this guidebook provides complete coverage of the following categories of monuments: all state monuments; all Maryland regimental and artillery battery monuments; and all mortuary cannons.

Park Your Bicycle (Across from Dunker Church)

Segment A (Loop Around The Cornfield)

Segment A is a 2.4-mile, mostly flat (65 feet up, 50 feet down) loop around The Cornfield. There are a few intense but very short hills. You will begin at the Visitor Center and end at the intersection of Cornfield Avenue and Dunker Church Road. If you skipped reading "The Northern Portion of the Battlefield" on p. 58, please do that now. For a visual reminder of battlefield geography, see Map 6 on p. 36.

The battle started when Maj. Gen. Joseph Hooker's 1st Corps marched south from the North Woods to D.R. Miller's cornfield. The fight pitted Hooker—and later, Maj. Gen. Joseph K.F. Mansfield's 12th Corps—against Maj. Gen. Thomas J. Jackson's Confederate division.

Confederate View—Col. Stephen D. Lee's Artillery Fired North

Looking Southeast into The Cornfield from Dunker Church Road

Note: Segment maps include green-boxed numbers that identify "stops" that correspond to numbered entries in a cue sheet. Each cue sheet identifies the exact location of the stop and a page reference to lookup photos, GPS coordinates, and historical summaries in Part IV.

Segment A Map and Cue Sheet

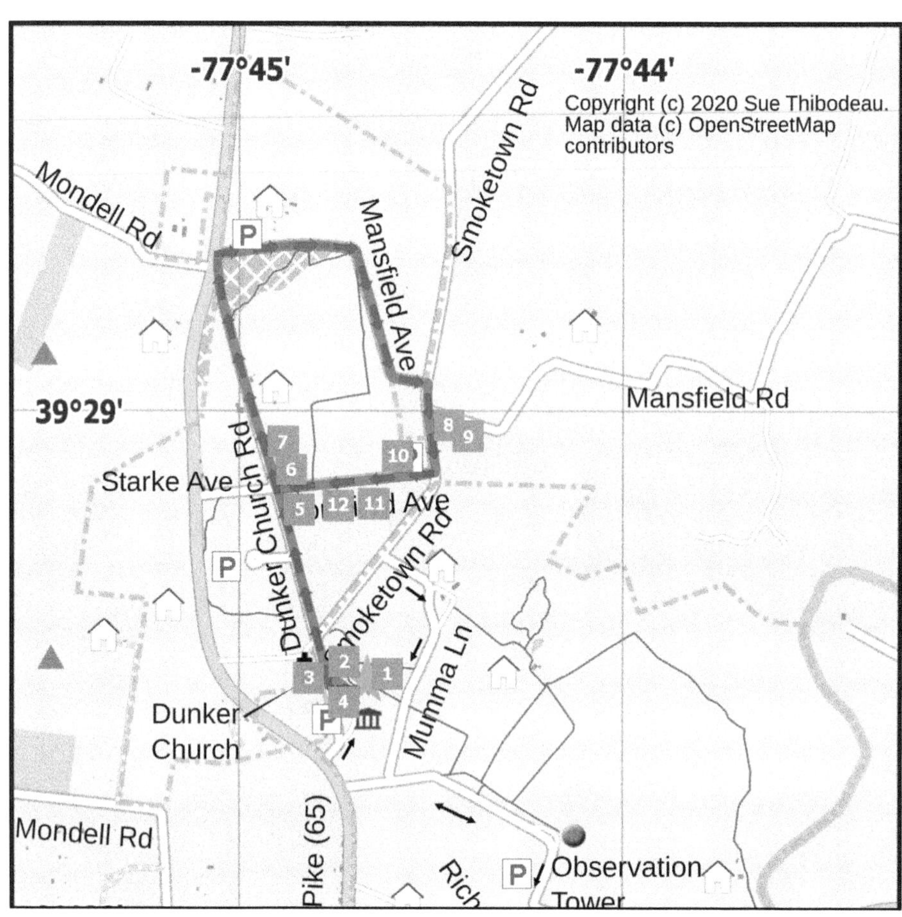

Map 18. Segment A Map (Loop Around The Cornfield)

The first four stops are part of an introductory walking tour suggested in "Start at the Visitor Center," p. 92. Although this guidebook intends to offer an orderly sequence of touring stops, you are encouraged freely to explore the park in whatever way and at whatever cadence that you want. When you are ready to ride, turn right on Dunker Church Road. Although your first mile is on a 35 mph paved road that has no shoulder and double-yellow lines, cars tend to give bicyclists a wide berth here. You will see cast-iron historical signs that stand low to the ground the full length of Dunker Church Road. At the 0.7-mile mark, you will pass the D.R. Miller farm house on your right. The Miller cornfield was a site of intense and prolonged fighting.

A	**Segment Cue Sheet (Loop Around The Cornfield)**			
Start	Visitor Center. See cue key, p. 87.			End
		[1] New York State Monument	p. 146	
		[2] Maryland State Monument	p. 41, 143	
		[3] Dunker Church	p. 40	
		[4] 3rd MD Infantry	p. 155	
0.0	R	Dunker Church Road		0.2
0.2	PoR	Smoketown Road		0.4
0.4	PoL	West Woods and slightly uphill		0.5
	PoR	[5] Massachusetts State Monument	p. 144	
0.5	PoR	Cornfield Avenue		1.0
	PoR	[6] New Jersey State Monument	p. 145	
	PoR	[7] Indiana State Monument	p. 142	
	CS	Slightly downhill		
1.0	BR	Mansfield Avenue		1.2
1.2	PoR	Cornfield Trail and start downhill		1.5
1.5	BR	Mansfield Avenue, up and down		1.6
1.6	BL	Steep up then down		1.8
1.8	R	Smoketown Road		
	PoL	[8] Joseph F.K. Mansfield Monument	p. 165	
Detour	Or L	Mansfield Road		
	PoR	[9] Joseph F.K. Mansfield Cannon	p. 165	
	U	Mansfield Road		
	L	Smoketown Road		
2.0	R	Cornfield Avenue		2.4
		[10] 1st MD Light Artillery Battery B	p. 152	
		[11] Georgia State Monument	p. 141	
		[12] Texas State Monument	p. 147	
2.4		Stop Dunker Church Road		

Table 7. Segment A Cue Sheet (Loop Around The Cornfield)

At the 1.0-mile mark the road will bend sharply right and up a steep but short hill where the Poffenberger farm will be on the left and the North Woods on the right. Your reward for making this climb will come in 0.4 miles when the road glides smoothly down East Woods.

At the 2.0-mile mark, turn right onto Cornfield Avenue to ride back to Dunker Church Road. There are many monuments along this stretch. The road is slightly uphill at 2.2-miles on the way to the top of a modest ridge on which the Visitor Center also sits, 0.5 miles south.

Looking West on Cornfield Avenue

The above photo shows your view after having passed Stop 10. The first monument honors the 27th Indiana. Next, you see the 137th and then the 128th Pennsylvania monuments. The shorter monument with a rounded cap is the 104th New York. In the distance and faintly visible are two tall monuments, the New Jersey and Indiana State Monuments; they are on the east side of Dunker Church Road.

While riding west on Cornfield Avenue, notice that Union monuments are on the north (right) side and Confederate monuments on the south (left) side. Their placement is deliberate, since Union infantry under Hooker attacked from your right (the D.R. Miller cornfield), and Confederate infantry under Jackson attacked from your left. Look for the Georgia and Texas State Monuments on your left (Stops 11 and 12, respectively) after passing the 104th New York monument.

Segment B (West Woods to Sunken Road)

Segment B is a 1.7-mile, modestly up and down ride (65 feet up, 35 feet down) with one nice downward glide on Mumma Lane. You will begin at the intersection of Cornfield Avenue and Dunker Church Road, and ride south to tour the West Woods, the Mumma farm area, and finally the full length of The Sunken Road. Segment B ends at the Observation Tower. If you skipped reading "The Center Portion of the Battlefield" on p. 64, please do that now.

By mid-morning, Union Maj. Gen. Edwin V. Sumner's 2nd Corps joined the battle, moving from the East Woods to the West Woods. At around 9:30 a.m., Brig. Gen. John Sedgwick's division attacked at the West Woods but they suffered devastating fire from Confederate artillery and an assault by Confederate infantry. Union soldiers withdrew after losing more than 2,200 men in about twenty minutes.

At The Sunken Road, Union Maj. Gen. William H. French battled Confederate Maj. Gen. Daniel Harvey Hill. With the support of Union Maj. Gen. Israel B. Richardson, and after almost four hours of fighting, French's men drove the Confederates back west. There were about 5,500 casualties. Today, The Sunken Road is a pedestrian trail that runs parallel to Richardson Avenue on its north side.

View from Mumma Lane, Looking Southeast to Observation Tower

The previous photo was taken while standing on Mumma Lane, northwest of the Observation Tower. You can see the continuation of Mumma Lane as it bends to meet Richardson Avenue (not visible). The Observation Tower marks the east boundary of the farm lane, known as The Sunken Road, which separates the Roulette and Piper farms. Map 8 on p. 46 identifies the 1862 families who worked Sharpsburg's farmland. In the photo's distance is the section of South Mountain that includes Crampton's gap (see Map 2 on p. 16).

Segment B Map and Cue Sheet

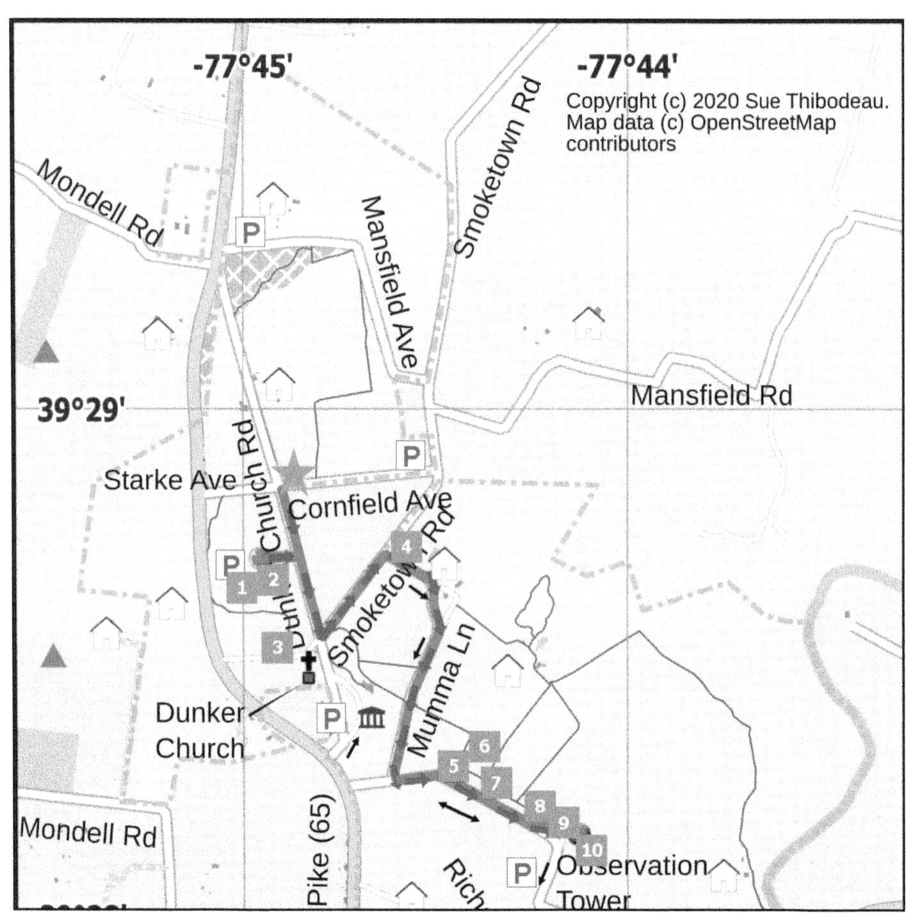

Map 19. Segment B Map (West Woods to Sunken Road)

Segment B includes 10 stops. Stops 1 and 2 are in West Woods, a 0.1-mile paved road that ends in a circular grassy area on which stands the Philadelphia Brigade Monument. Although the Philadelphia monument is an important historic structure, we do not label the monument as a "stop." Here we have our first example of this guidebook's rubric for keeping the number of stops manageable. The intent is to cover these complete categories of monuments: state monuments; Maryland regimental and artillery monuments; and mortuary cannons (see Part IV). Monuments or structures that do not fit into those three categories may be highlighted briefly in Segment overview pages.

B	**Segment Cue Sheet (West Woods to Sunken Road)**			
Start	West end of Cornfield Avenue. See cue key, p. 87.			End
0.0	L	Dunker Church Road, 35 mph		0.1
0.1	R	Philadelphia Brigade Park (West Woods)		0.2
		Note the Philadelphia Brigade Monument		
		[1] Baltimore Light Artillery Battery	p. 157	
		[2] William B. Starke Cannon	p. 169	
0.2	U	Back to Dunker Church Road, shaded		0.3
0.3	R	Dunker Church Road, slightly downhill		0.6
0.6	L	Smoketown Road, slightly uphill, 25 mph		0.8
Detour	or R	Gravel road before Dunker Church		
	PoR	[3] Purnell Legion Infantry	p. 153	
	U	Back to Dunker Church Road		
	X	Smoketown Road, slightly uphill, 25 mph		
0.8	R	Mumma Lane		1.0
		[4] 1st MD Light Artillery Battery A	p. 151	
	CS	Long, winding downhill glide		
1.0	CS	Mumma Lane, hilly		1.3
1.3	L	Richardson Avenue		1.7
		[5] 5th MD Infantry	p. 156	
		[6] 5th MD Companies A&I	p. 156	
		[7] George B. Anderson Cannon	p. 163	
		[8] Israel B. Richardson Cannon	p. 166	
		[9] Irish Brigade Monument	p. 167	
1.7		[10] Observation Tower		

Table 8. Segment B Cue Sheet (West Woods to Sunken Road)

With the exception of the West Woods, your tour of the northern half of ANB will not have much shade, because most roads cut through open fields. That is one good reason to begin your ride early in the morning during the hot months of June—September.

Entrance to West Woods

Cannons Near Mumma Lane

Philadelphia Brigade Monument

Stop 3 is an optional detour to visit the Purnell Legion Infantry Monument along a rough gravel road behind Dunker Church. Although the monument's location is inconvenient, it is part of Segment B so that you have an opportunity to visit *all* Maryland regimental and artillery monuments.

The desire to visit complete categories of monuments is also the reason that Segment B features six monuments all within a small area along The Sunken Road. There are no bicycle racks nearby. One option is to chain together your bicycles, but even in safe places, theft prevention is not guaranteed. Generally speaking, walking your bicycle does not damage the battlefield; but if you want official clarification or guidance on this topic, please consult a park ranger.

Segment C (South to Burnside Bridge)

Segment C is a challenging 1.7-mile ride over hilly countryside (160 feet up, 70 feet down) that begins at the Observation Tower on Richardson Avenue and continues south to end at the Burnside Bridge parking lot. If you skipped reading "The Southern Portion of the Battlefield" on p. 67, please do that now.

Also called the Lower (or Rohrbach) Bridge, the Burnside Bridge is one of three Sharpsburg area structures that span Antietam Creek. For reference, Map 2 on p. 16 shows the location of each bridge. Union Gen. McClellan set up his army headquarters at the Pry house on a hill between the Upper and Middle bridges. From there, Gen. McClellan could not see Maj. Gen. Burnside's three attempts to cross the Lower Bridge, downstream. At Antietam, Burnside's 9th Corps was the left flank of McClellan's federal army. The corps struggled for hours to advance west with the goal of crushing Confederate Gen. James Longstreet's division, the Confederate right flank.

View of Antietam National Cemetery from Rodman Avenue

While riding south on Rodman Avenue, look right to see the high ground. Confederate artillery fired from that hill. The area enclosed by stone walls is Antietam National Cemetery, which was dedicated on September 17, 1867 for the burial of Union soldiers.

Segment C Map and Cue Sheet

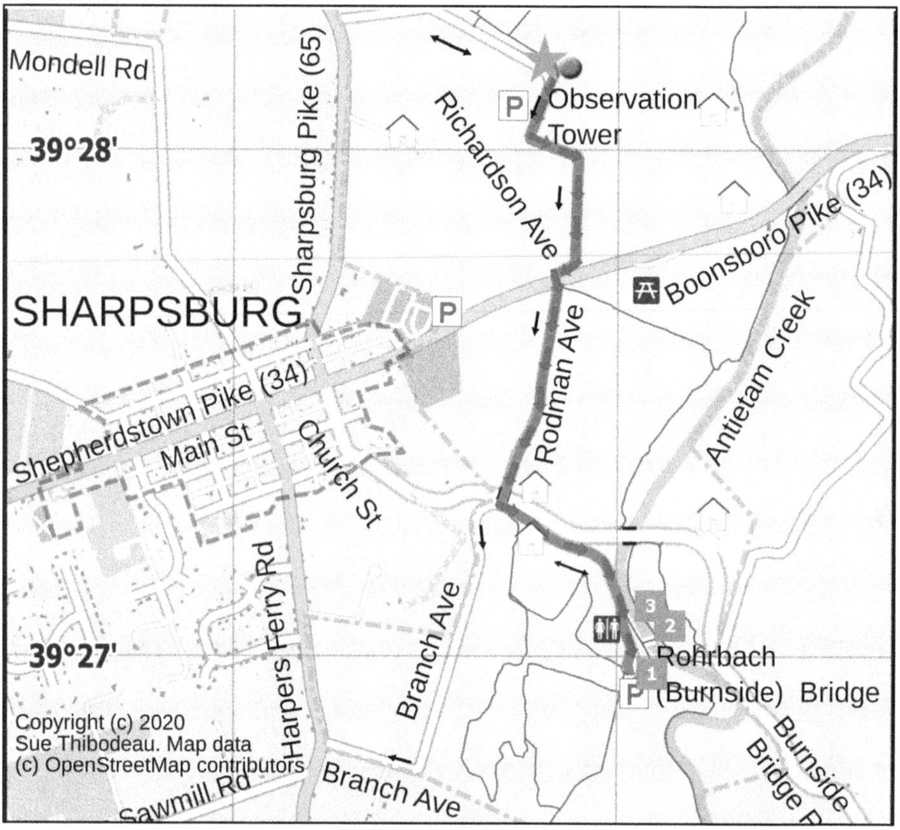

Map 20. Segment C Map (South to Burnside Bridge)

Future U.S. President William McKinley (1843-1901) served as a commissary sergeant for the 23rd Ohio. The president's monument (see 1, above) was dedicated in October, 1903—one month after an assassin killed him in Buffalo, New York. The inscription says that he "personally and without orders served 'hot coffee' and 'warm food' to every man in the Regiment, on this spot and in doing so had to pass under fire."

C	Segment Cue Sheet (South to Burnside Bridge)		
Start	Observation Tower. See cue key, p. 87.		End
0.0	S	Richardson Avenue	
		Winding and steep up and down terrain	0.2
0.2	BL	Sharp	
	BR	Sharp and hilly	0.3
0.3	CS	Begin steep downhill	0.5
0.5	CS	Uphill climb	0.6
0.6	CS	Down again, stop sign	
	X	Boonsboro Pike onto Rodman Avenue	0.7
0.7	CS	Gradual then sharp incline	0.9
0.9	CS	Top of hill (50th PA), then down again	1.1
1.1	PoL	Sherrick farm	
1.15	X	Modern bridge	1.2
1.2	L	At dead-end	
	PoR	Otto farm	
	CS	Down, then steep incline	1.7
1.7		Arrive Burnside Bridge Parking Lot	
		[1] McKinley Monument	
		[2] Burnside Bridge	
		[3] 2nd MD Infantry p. 154	

Table 9. Segment C Cue Sheet (South to Burnside Bridge)

At the 0.6-mile mark, you could detour down Boonsboro Pike (MD 34) to visit Antietam National Cemetery on the east edge of Sharpsburg. But since as of this writing there are no bicycle racks near the cemetery, this guidebook recommends that you return by car and park in the lot across the street. Perhaps most importantly, Main Street is a bumpy, hilly, and heavily trafficked town road with no shoulders; so, we will avoid it. Instead, Segment C crosses the pike to follow Rodman Avenue.

After crossing the modern-day bridge at the south end of Rodman Avenue, the road up to the Burnside Bridge narrows and its winding nature compromises visibility. There are no shoulders (only gullies and trees). The last 0.5 miles of Segment C is the most difficult climb of your entire ride. Fortunately, touring vehicles tend to drive slowly in this area and most bicyclists manage quite well, even if they are walking their bikes.

Union View of the Burnside Bridge (From East Bank)

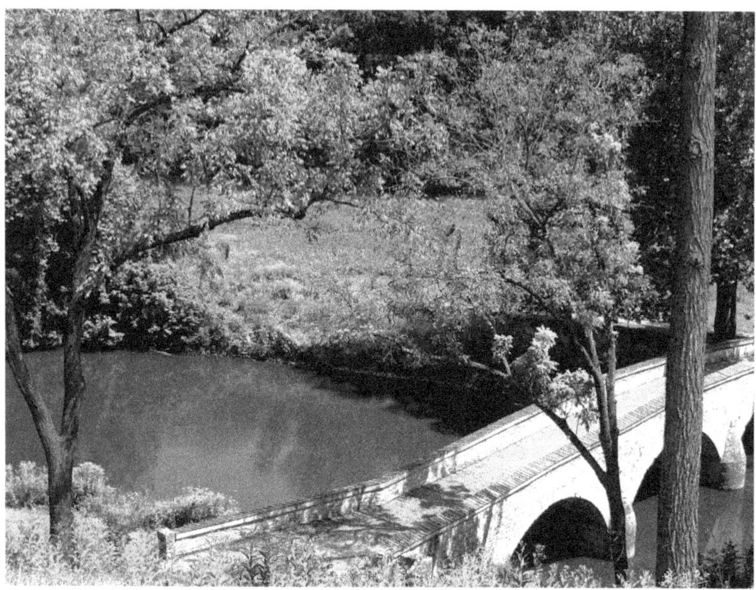

Confederate View of the Burnside Bridge (From West Bank)

Segment D (The Final Attack and Back)

Segment D is a 3.4-mile hilly ride (100 feet up, 200 feet down) through the southern half of the battlefield, mostly along Branch Avenue, which bisects the fields on which The Final Attack occurred. The last 1.9 miles, however, are the return trip to the Visitor Center on heavily trafficked public roads into and out of downtown Sharpsburg.

After more than three hours of deadly fighting, Maj. Gen. Ambrose E. Burnside's 9th Corps began crossing the Rohrbach Bridge over Antietam Creek, struggling to pull wagons and artillery to support four divisions into the fields southeast of Sharpsburg. In the meantime, with his right flank seriously threatened, Gen. Robert E. Lee scrambled to reinforce his line with artillery but was ultimately saved by the timely arrival of Maj. Gen. A.P. Hill's division (from Harpers Ferry) to blunt the Union assault.

Segment D covers "The Final Attack," when from 3:00-5:30 p.m., the two armies squared off in the hilly fields southeast of Sharpsburg. When the Union left flank collapsed, the battle was over.

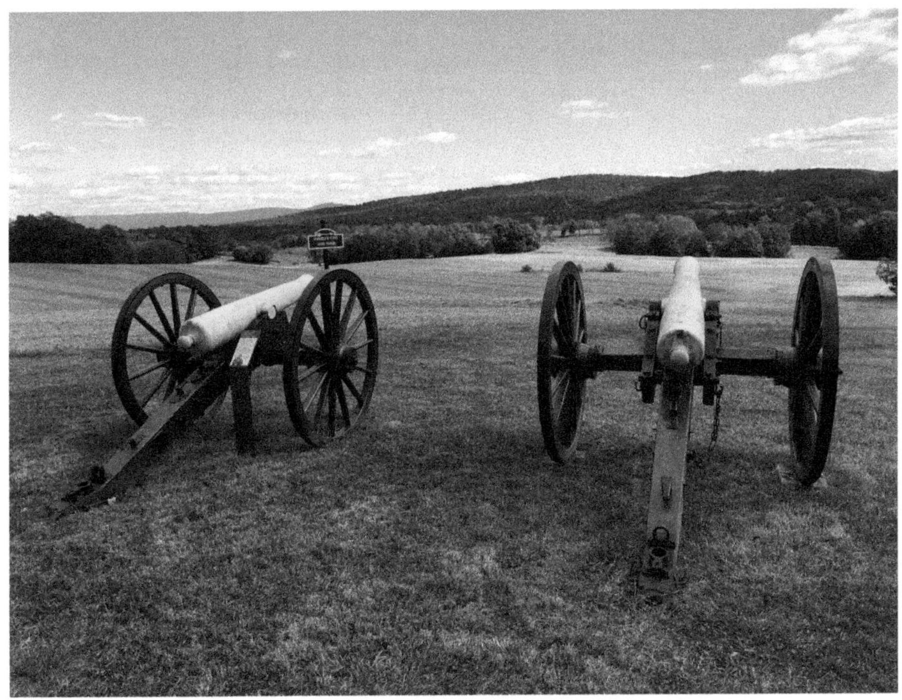

Pegram's (Confederate) Artillery Battery Facing Antietam Creek

Segment D Map and Cue Sheet

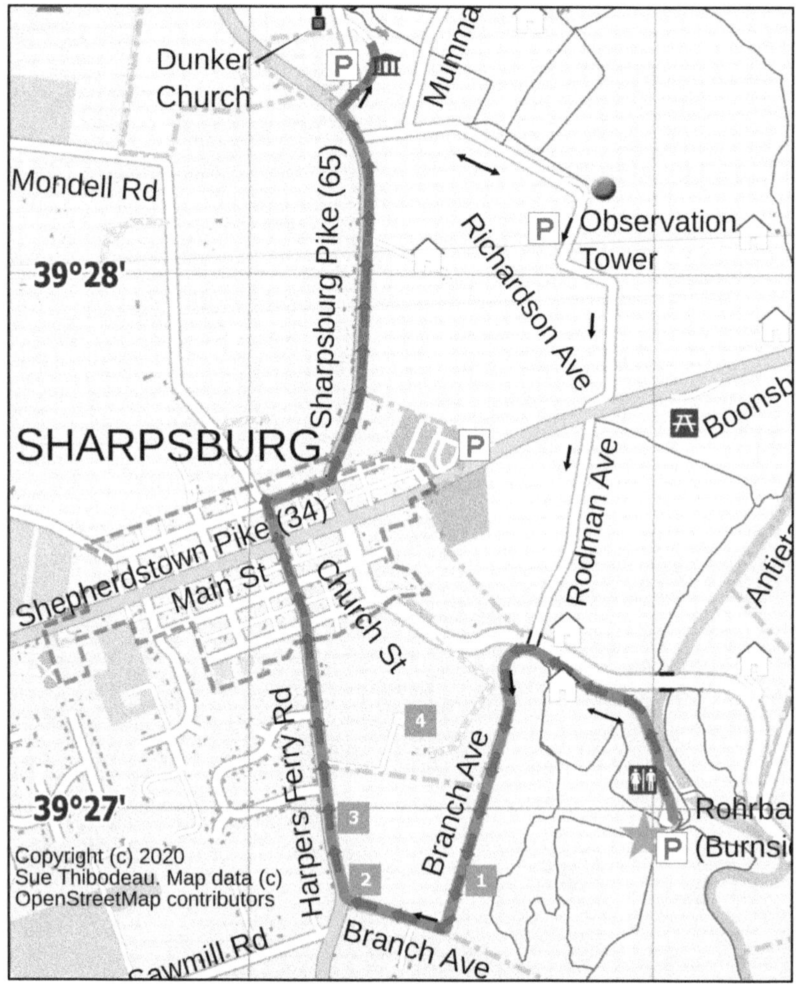

Map 21. Segment D Map (The Final Attack and Back)

Note that the Segment D Cue Sheet (below) offers you an opportunity to walk your bike on a pedestrian pathway that leads to the Rodman Mortuary Cannon (number 4 in the map above). The 9th NY and 8th CT regimental monuments are nearby. This is a good spot to look east to appreciate the rough terrain on which The Final Attack was waged. And if you look northeast toward Antietam National Cemetery, you will understand why that high ground was a powerful position for Confederates to post artillery.

D	Segment Cue Sheet (The Final Attack and Back)		
Start	Burnside Bridge Parking Lot. See cue key, p. 87.		End
0.0	CS	Downhill	0.2
0.2	BL	And continue up and down (note guardrails)	0.5
0.5	Stop		
	CS	Branch Avenue, uphill, 25 mph	0.7
0.7	CS	To top of hill; down and sharply up	0.8
0.8	CS	Branch Avenue	0.9
0.9	CS	Downhill	1.0
1.0	CS	Uphill, near 30th OH	1.1
1.1	CS	Downhill	1.25
		[1] Lawrence O'Bryan Branch Cannon p. 164	
1.25	BR	Branch Avenue, uphill	1.5
1.5	Stop	[2] On right, Pegram's Virginia Battery	1.5
1.5	R	Harpers Ferry Road (public road, 25 mph)	1.7
1.7	CS	Harpers Ferry Road	1.9
1.9	PoR	[3] 1st MD Artillery Battery (CSA) p. 158	
Detour	R	At first right on 0.3-mile hiking trail (dismount)	
		[4] Isaac P. Rodman Cannon p. 168	
		Note 9th NY and 8th CT monuments	
	U	Return to Harpers Ferry Road	
	CS	At all stop signs in town	
2.3	R	West Chapline Street	2.5
2.5	L	Maryland Route 65 (40 to 50 mph)	
	CS	Wide shoulders, uphill	2.6
2.6	PoR	Convenience store	
3.2	PoR	Richardson Avenue	
3.3	R	Dunker Church Road, then BR	3.4
3.4		Arrive Visitor Center	

Table 10. Segment D Cue Sheet (The Final Attack and Back)

7. Route 2–From C&O Canal South

After describing the Chesapeake & Ohio Canal from Sharpsburg south to Harpers Ferry, this chapter outlines the options for extending your ride to include a tour of Antietam National Battlefield. If you are riding south on the C&O Canal Towpath, this chapter is for you; if you are riding north, please turn to Chapter 8.

Chapter 7 discusses the trade-offs for two different points from which to exit the towpath and connect to the battlefield. For your health and safety, please study your options carefully before selecting a route. The chapter concludes with touring maps and cue sheets for two routes:

Route 2.1—Exit at M80.9, Taylors Landing (p. 116)

Route 2.2—Exit at M76.6, Snyders Landing (p. 120)

Notably, these touring directions focus exclusively on the steps required to exit and return to the canal towpath. This is to avoid the redundant inclusion of maps, tables, and text. Therefore for both routes, you will refer to Chapter 6 for maps and cue sheets to navigate Antietam National Battlefield. (See p. 20 for a key to map symbols and abbreviations).

Safety Note

This guidebook does not cover the topic of how to bicycle the C&O Canal Towpath, or how to bicycle safely on public roadways, both of which require a very different set of skills than riding on smoothly paved park roads.[78]

All routes to and from the C&O Canal are on rural, public roads that have fast-moving motor vehicle traffic. Please wear a helmet and bright clothing, turn on your blinkies, and use your mirror. A ride to Sharpsburg is not the time to learn how to ride safely on winding, hilly, and no-shoulder country roads. If you are not an experienced road bicyclist, please consider transporting your bicycle between the canal and the battlefield park.

And finally, always check ahead for NPS alerts about canal flooding, downed trees, detours, and closures.

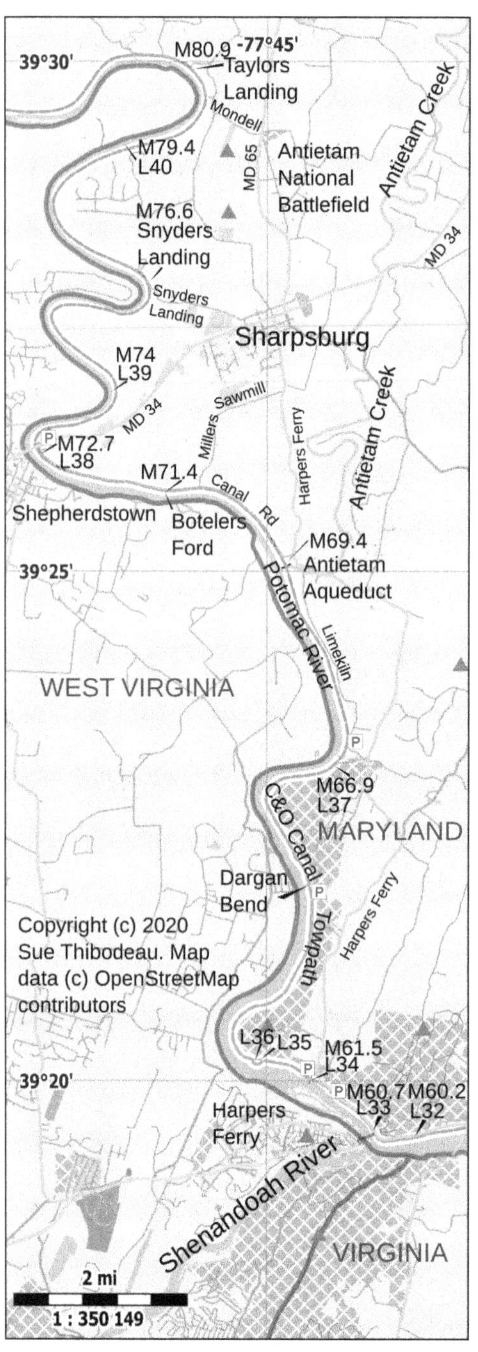

Map 22. C&O Canal, M60.2 to M80.9

The C&O Canal

The Chesapeake & Ohio Canal runs along the Potomac River on the Maryland (and Washington, DC) side. In this map, the canal towpath is orange, the river is blue, and the state border is purple.

Although the canal does not have water at all locations along its length, the canal towpath is a continuous, mostly fine gravel and dirt trail that extends 184.5 miles north from Washington, DC, to the small town of Cumberland, Maryland. Sometimes the canal towpath is on the canal's east side and sometimes it is on the west side. Occasionally, a paved public road follows the towpath, e.g., Canal Road from Lock 38 to the Antietam Aqueduct.

For the history buff who wants a touring excursion to Antietam National Battlefield, there are many good online resources that identify Taylors Landing, Snyders Landing, and Canal Road at Millers Sawmill Road as good exits for Sharpsburg. This guidebook makes it easy for you to select a route that is specific to your touring needs and educational interests. You will find zoomed in maps of towpath access points later in this chapter.

Harpers Ferry, West Virginia, the location of an important garrison during the Civil War, is about 13 miles south of Shepherdstown (Lock 38). On September 15, 1862, Union Brig. Gen. Dixon S. Miles surrendered to Maj. Gen. Thomas "Stonewall" Jackson. It was the largest surrender of a U.S. military force in the country's history.[79]

Bicyclists who want to enter Harpers Ferry from the canal towpath must carry their bikes up a steep stairway to the footbridge that connects Maryland to West Virginia. It is highly recommended that you check trail conditions when planning your trip. You will want to know about things like this: A train derailment in December 2019 destroyed a section of the bridge when two freight cars fell into the Potomac River. To plan your Harpers Ferry adventure, start here to read park alerts: https://www.nps.gov/hafe/index.htm. Unlike Sharpsburg, Harpers Ferry has many bicycle racks, although most of them are just over the footbridge and at the Visitor Center. Many people prefer not to bicycle in town and opt to walk or hike instead.

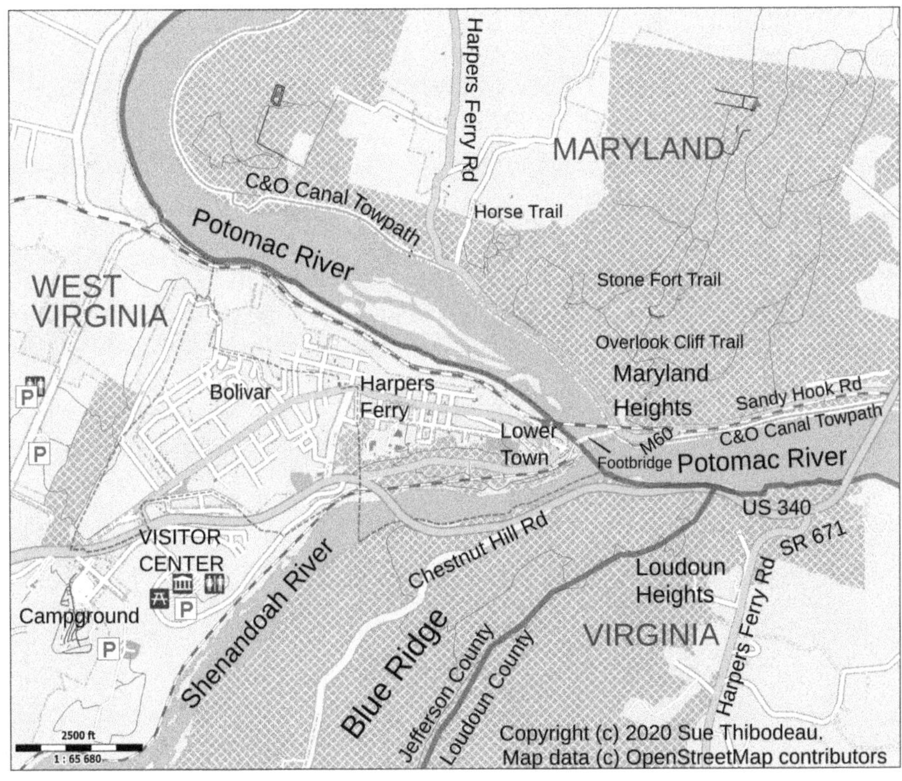

Map 23. Harpers Ferry Area

Two Options for Exiting the Canal Towpath

If you are riding south on the C&O Canal Towpath, you have two good options for connecting to Antietam National Battlefield. These are marked with arrows on Map 24, p. 114. The first option is to exit at Taylors Landing (M80.9) and the second is to exit at Snyders Landing (M76.6). Both options minimize backtracking for the southbound bicyclist.

The following comparison table will help you to decide where to leave the canal towpath to begin your excursion to Antietam National Battlefield. Once you select your exit point, you will have effectively selected your overall route from the canal to ANB and back again. The return is described at a high-level on p. 115. Once you select your route, you will find maps and cue sheets starting on p. 116 for Route 2.1, and on p. 120 for Route 2.2.

Table 11. Rt. 2 Southbound C&O Canal Towpath Options

Two Options:	**Rt. 2.1–Exit at M80.9 Taylors Landing (9.5 total miles)**	**Rt. 2.2–Exit at M76.6 Snyders Landing (11.9 total miles)**
Thumbnail images	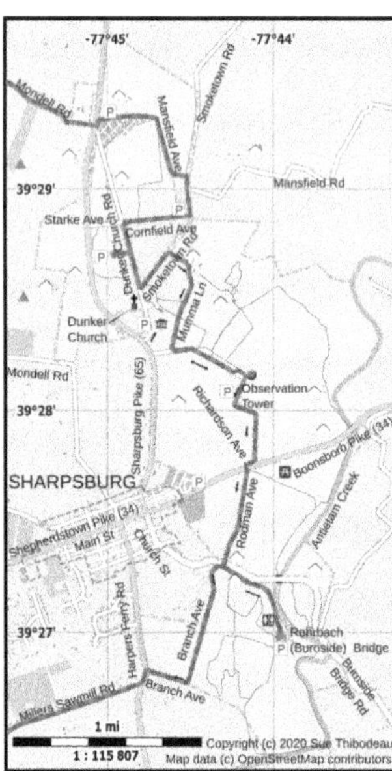	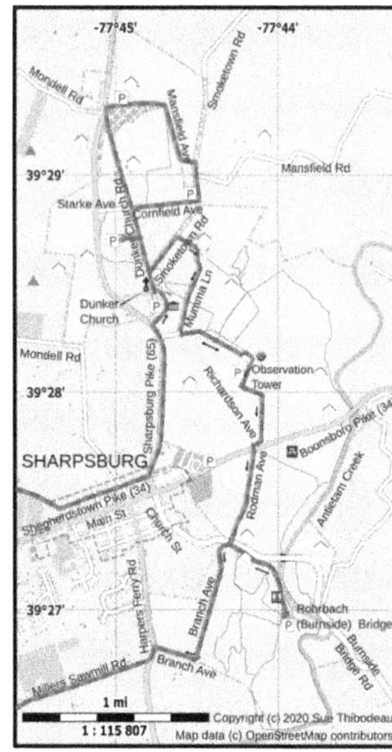

Two Options:	**Rt. 2.1–Exit at M80.9 Taylors Landing (9.5 total miles)**	**Rt. 2.2–Exit at M76.6 Snyders Landing (11.9 total miles)**
Your Goal	Ride through battlefield without stopping at the Visitor Center or any place downtown.	Complete a battlefield tour that includes a stop at the Visitor Center (downtown optional).
Park Roads	6.3 miles (out of 9.5 total miles)	7.3 miles (out of 11.9 total miles)
Public Roads	3.2 miles M80.9 to ANB: 1.4 miles ANB to M71: 1.8 miles	4.6 miles M76.6 to ANB: 2.8 miles ANB to M71: 1.8 miles
C&O Canal Exit Point	**M80.9** RIDE AT YOUR OWN RISK – Boat ramp and parking at landing – Extremely narrow, rural "lanes" – Poor visibility, many turns – One long and very steep climb – To ANB: 200 ft. up Hauser Ridge – No shoulders, fast-moving cars – 35 mph to North Woods	**M76.6** REQUIRES ROAD SKILLS – Boat ramp and parking at landing – Rural, town, and major roads – Good visibility, mostly straight – A few short, modest hills – To ANB: 190 ft. up, 30 ft. down. – No shoulders, fast-moving cars – 35 mph into town
Touring Directions	Begin on p. 116	Begin on p. 120

In summary, if you exit at Taylors Landing (M80.9), you are committing to a very steep (200 feet), 1.4-mile climb on single-lane roads that have two-way car traffic, no shoulders, and low visibility. This is the shortest route to the battlefield and bypasses downtown Sharpsburg. On the other hand, if you exit at Snyders Landing (M76.6), you will ride 1.4 miles to downtown Sharpsburg and then 1.4 miles to the battlefield Visitor Center. The hills are shorter and less severe (190 feet up, 30 feet down) than the Taylors Landing option. Like all roads into Sharpsburg, shoulders are intermittent.

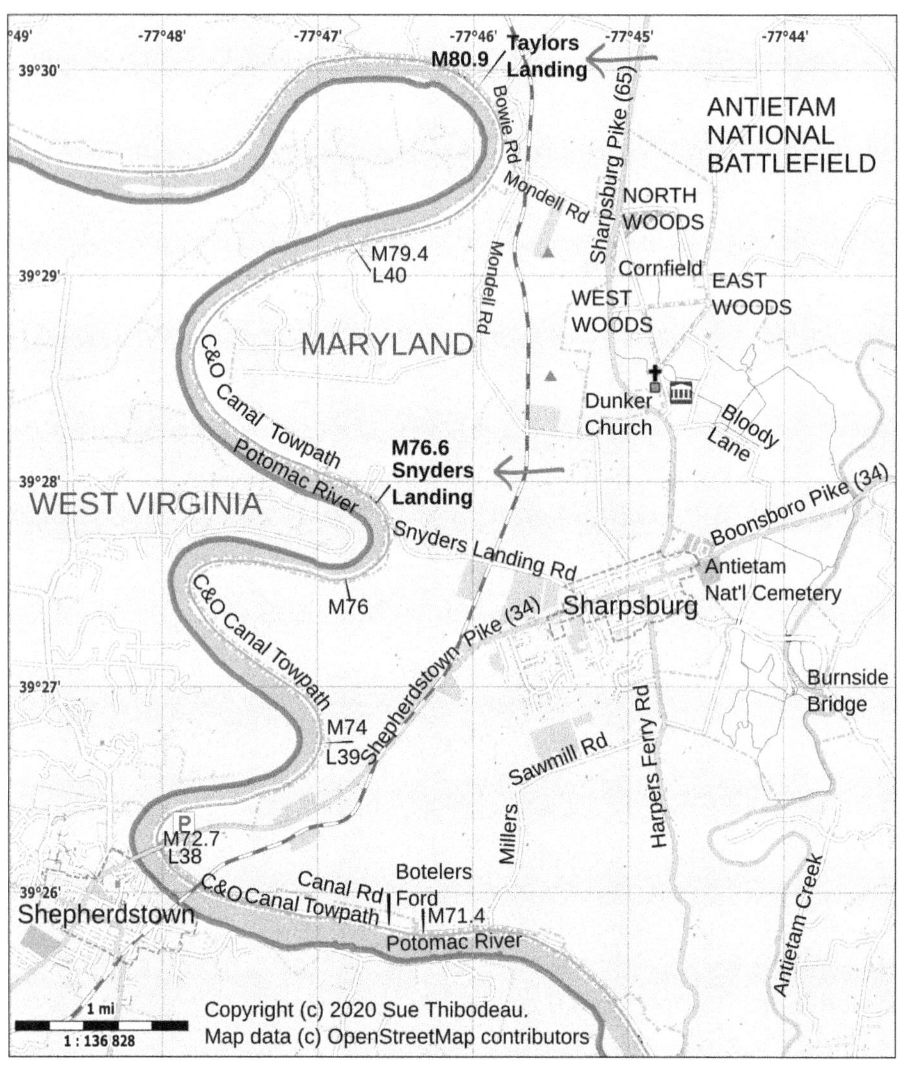

Map 24. Rt. 2 Options for a Southbound Exit

Your Return to the Canal Towpath (South)

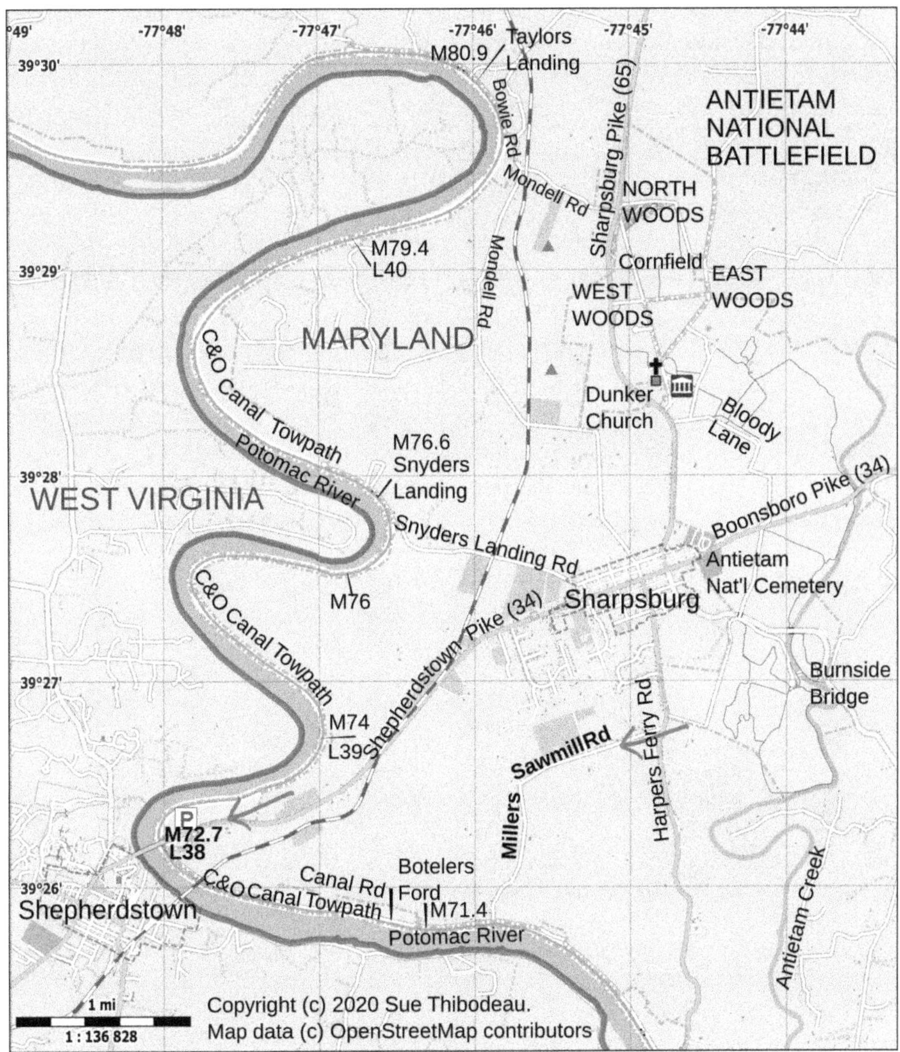

Map 25. Rt. 2 Options for a Southbound Return

Having discussed two options for exiting the towpath, we turn to the question of where to return. This guidebook recommends that southbound bicyclists return to the canal towpath via Millers Sawmill Road to M71 (at Canal Road). This is convenient, because your battlefield tour ends nearby on Harpers Ferry Road. Turn right on

Millers Sawmill Road. Use caution as you enjoy a mostly flat, slightly downhill, 1.8-mile ride on a public road that is not heavily trafficked.

An alternative is to use the maps in this book to take Harpers Ferry Road north to downtown Sharpsburg. Then turn left onto MD 34, and ride about 3 miles (mostly double-yellow lines) to Shepherdstown to eat or spend the night. Of course, Sharpsburg also offers traveling accommodations, and for both towns, pre-trip research planning is recommended.

Route 2.1—Your Battlefield Tour from M80.9

[CAUTION] If you want to minimize the number of extra miles riding on public roads—especially downtown—then exiting at Taylors Landing is a very attractive option. However, not only is the ride physically demanding to the point that you will likely need to walk your bicycle, local car traffic poses unavoidable hazards for bicyclists. Most bicyclists will prefer to exit at Snyders Landing instead (see p. 120).

Segment A—Exit at Taylors Landing (M80.9)

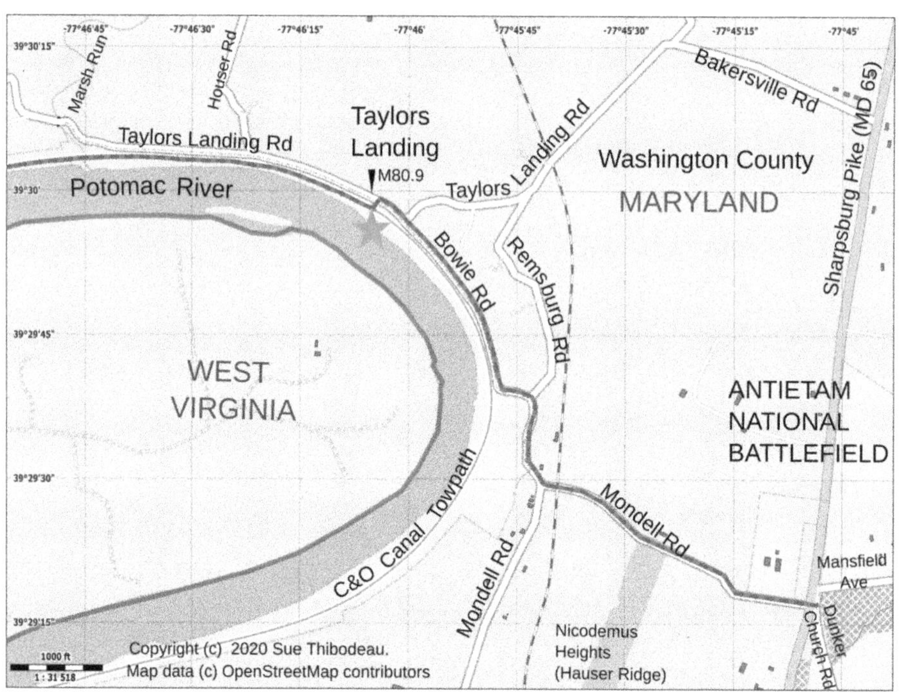

Map 26. Rt. 2 M80.9, Exit South at Taylors Landing

A	Segment Cue Sheet (Exit at Taylors Landing)		
Start	M80.9 (39.49943, -77.76809). See cue key, p. 87.		End
0.0	CS	Pass through 1st (not 2nd) set of swing gates	
	L	Over small bridge	
	QR	Taylors Landing Road. CS for 350 ft. to fork	
0.55	R	Bowie Rd (narrow, 20 mph); up then down	0.75
0.75	BL	Down at fork, to Mondell Road; then under bridge into wooded area, and begin uphill	0.9
0.9	CS	Uphill	1.3
1.3	PoL	Driveway	1.3
1.4	Stop	At MD 65. Totals: 200 ft. up, 70 ft. down	1.4
1.4	X/L	Dunker Church Road (to Mansfield Ave)	

Table 12. Rt. 2 Cue Sheet—Exit at Taylors Landing

Segment B—Tour Battlefield from North Woods

Map 27 on the next page will help you to navigate a 6.3-mile ride from the northern half of the battlefield to Branch Avenue at Harpers Ferry Road in the southern end of the battlefield park. That is where you will pickup Segment C (p. 119) to return to the C&O Canal Towpath (M71) via Millers Sawmill Road.

Brown's Virginia Battery[80]
(Facing East over Branch Avenue)

However, if you want to visit specific battlefield sites or monuments, you will likely need turn-by-turn directions. With one slight change, you can follow the touring directions for Route 1 (in Chapter 6). Start Route 1 at the 1.0-mile point of Segment A, and then complete your battlefield tour normally, as follows:

1. Start Rt. 1 Segment A at Mile 1.0 (Table 7, p. 95).
2. Follow Rt. 1 Segment B (Table 8, p. 99).
3. Follow Rt. 1 Segment C (Table 9, p. 103).
4. Follow Rt. 1 Segment D to Mile 1.5. (Table 10, p. 107).

This map shows that the only difference between Route 1 and Route 2.1—with respect to the battlefield tour—is its starting point:

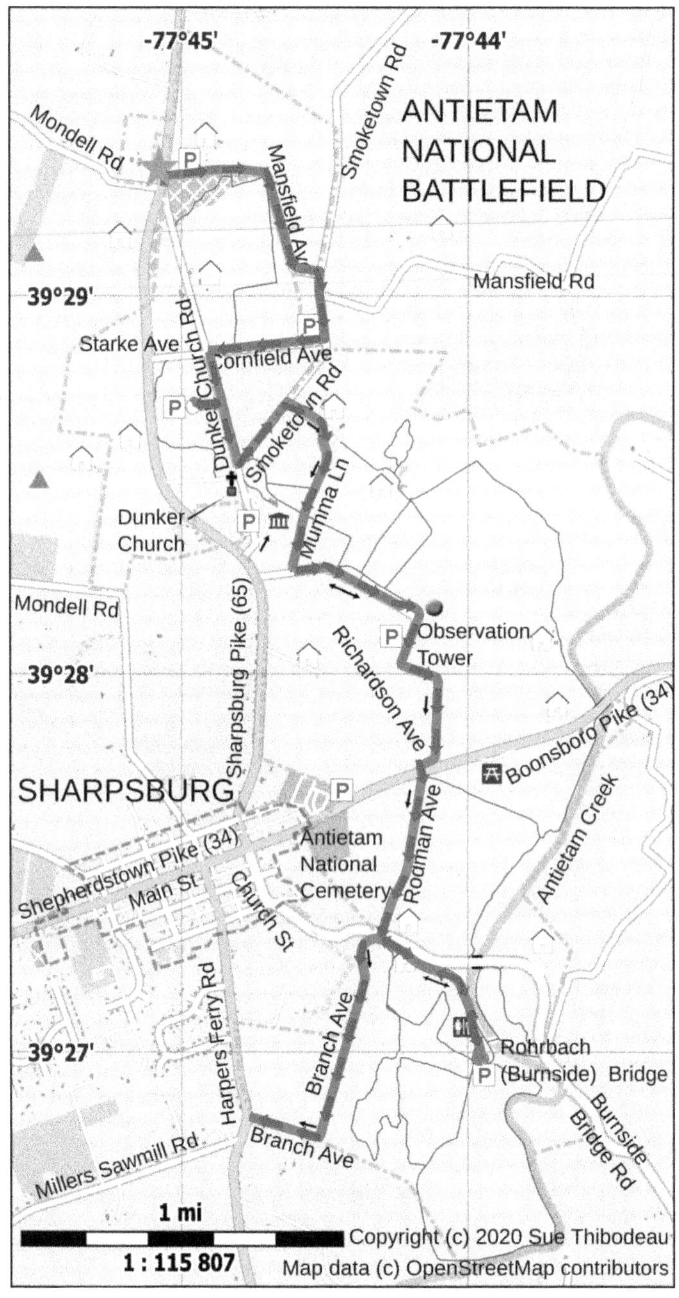

Map 27. Rt. 2 M80.9, Battlefield Tour from North Woods

Segment C—Return to Canal via Millers Sawmill Road

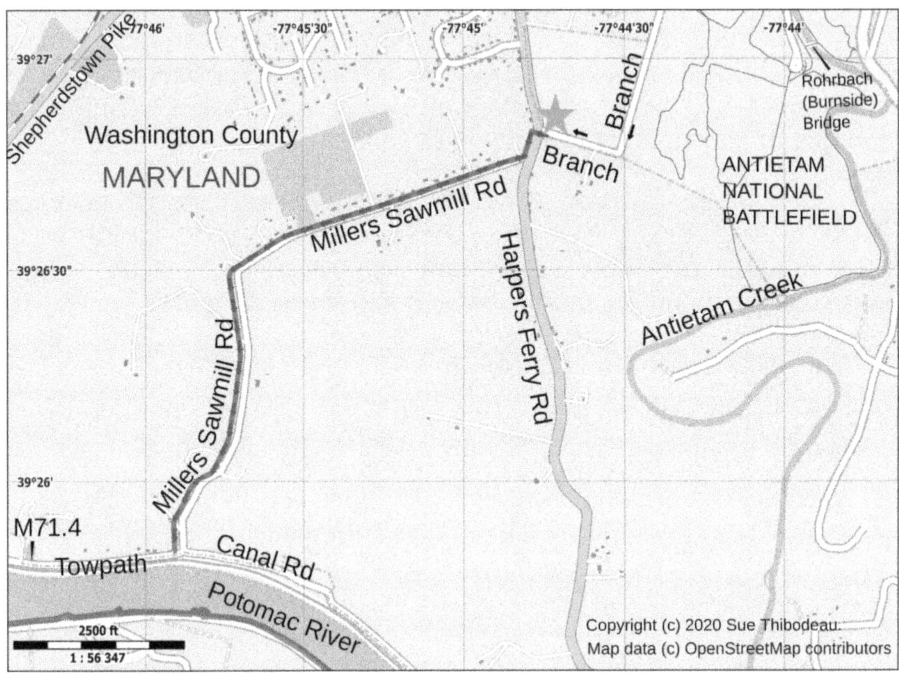

Map 28. Rt. 2 M80.9, Return to M71 via Millers Sawmill Road

C	**Segment Cue Sheet (Return via Millers Sawmill Rd.)**		
Start	39.44716, -77.74601. See cue key, p. 87.		End
0.0	From Branch Avenue at Harpers Ferry Road:		
	L	For 400 feet on Harpers Ferry Road	
	R	Millers Sawmill Road, mostly flat	1.0
1.0	BL	Millers Sawmill Road, slightly down, then bigger decline starting at 1.4	1.8
1.8	Arrive	Canal Road. Totals: 40 ft. up, 200 ft. down	

Table 13. Rt. 2 Cue Sheet—Return via Millers Sawmill Road

When you arrive at Canal Road, stop and look straight ahead to see the canal, the canal towpath, and then the Potomac River. Turn left to continue your southbound ride. Antietam Creek Campsite is about one mile south of here. Although not recommended, you could also take Harpers Ferry Road south to Antietam Aqueduct.

Route 2.2—Your Battlefield Tour from M76.6

While riding south on the canal towpath, once you pass Taylors Landing (M80.9), your next option for exiting the towpath is Snyders Landing (M76.6). For most bicyclists, exiting at Snyders Landing is the safest and most comfortable riding option.

Although the ride from Snyders Landing to the battlefield is longer than Taylors Landing (2.8 miles versus 1.4 miles), the incline is far more gradual and less severe than on Mondell Road. And most importantly, you will be more visible to motor vehicle traffic.

Segment A—Exit at Snyders Landing (M76.6)

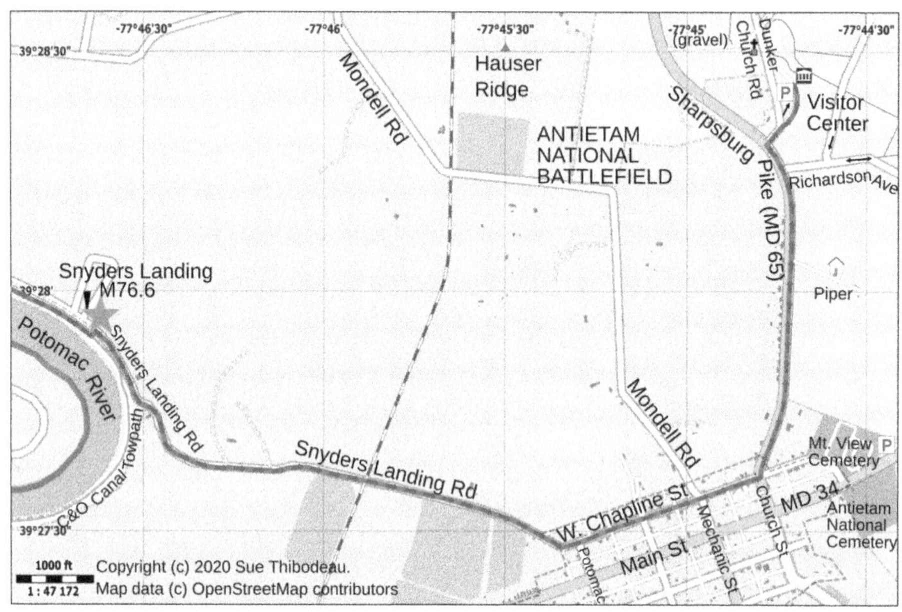

Map 29. Rt. 2 M76.7, Southbound Exit at Snyders Landing

Snyders Landing Road will take you into the north end of downtown Sharpsburg. For a map of downtown, see Map 16 on p. 79. Most of the town is residential. Check online for the latest information on places to eat, since your options are limited and some places (like Nutter's Ice Cream) have limited hours and payment options. As of this writing, a convenience store and grill is located on the right side of Sharpsburg Pike, 0.1 miles after turning left from West Chapline Street.

A	Segment Cue Sheet (Exit at Snyders Landing)		
Start	M76.6 (39.46511, -77.77744). See cue key, p. 87.		End
0.0	CS	Through gates	
	L	Over bridge	
	QR	Snyders Landing Road (20 mph, mostly pavement, mostly flat to 0.3-mile mark)	0.3
0.3	CS	Slightly uphill, narrow, no shoulders, wooded, residential	0.4
0.4	CS	Up to 0.6 peak, then up again at 1.0	1.4
1.4	L	West Chapline Street. Totals: 120 ft. up, 0 ft. down	1.9
1.9	L	Sharpsburg Pike, slightly uphill, wide shoulders, 25 to 40 mph	2.0
2.0	PoR	Convenience store and grill	2.4
2.4	PoR	Piper farm	
2.65	PoR	Richardson Avenue	
2.7	R	Dunker Church Road	
2.8	BR	Arrive at Visitor Center	

Table 14. Rt. 2 Cue Sheet—Exit at Snyders Landing

Segment B—Tour Battlefield from Visitor Center

Map 30 on p. 122 is enough to guide your 7.3-mile ride from the Visitor Center to the intersection of Branch Avenue and Harpers Ferry Road. That is where you would pick up Segment C to return to the C&O Canal Towpath. However, if you want to visit specific battlefield sites or monuments, you will need to follow a slightly modified version of Route 1's Segment bicycle cues, in order:

1. Follow Rt. 1 Segment A (Table 7, p. 95).
2. Follow Rt. 1 Segment B (Table 8, p. 99).
3. Follow Rt. 1 Segment C (Table 9, p. 103).
4. Follow Rt. 1 Segment D to Mile 1.5 (Table 10, p. 107).

Segment C—Return to Canal (Millers Sawmill Road)

Follow the map and directions for "Segment C—Return to Canal via Millers Sawmill Road" on p. 119.

This map shows that the only difference between Route 1 and Route 2.2—with respect to the battlefield tour—is how it ends:

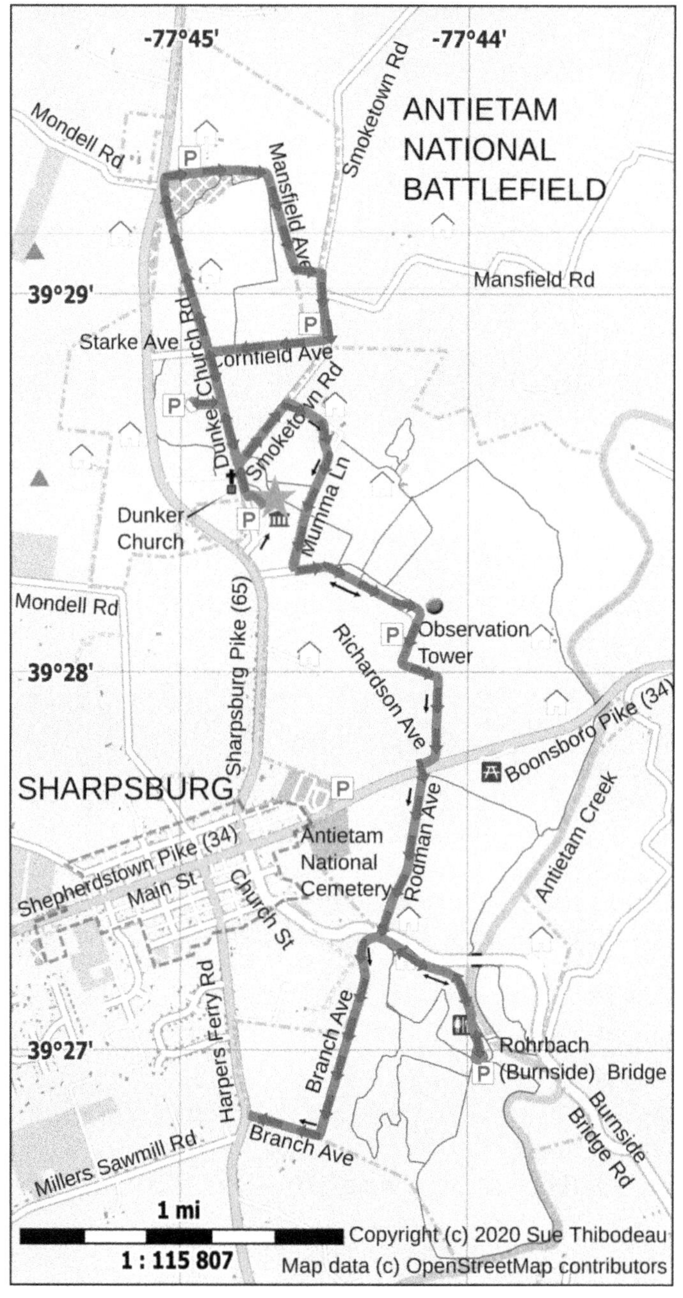

Map 30. Rt. 2 M76.7, Battlefield Tour from Visitor Center

8. Route 3–From C&O Canal North

If you are bicycling north on the Chesapeake & Ohio Canal Towpath, this chapter outlines the options for extending your ride to include a tour of Antietam National Battlefield. (If you are riding south, refer to Chapter 7 instead).

Chapter 8 discusses the trade-offs for two different points from which to exit the towpath and connect to the battlefield. For your health and safety, please study your options carefully before selecting a route. The chapter concludes with touring maps and cue sheets for two routes:

Like Chapter 7, these touring directions focus exclusively on the steps required to exit and return to the C&O Canal Towpath. In other words, regardless of which touring route you select, you will refer to Chapter 6 for maps and cue sheets to navigate Antietam National Battlefield. (See p. 20 for a key to map symbols and abbreviations).

These comments from Chapter 7 bear repeating: All routes to and from the C&O Canal are on rural, public roads that have fast-moving motor vehicle traffic. Please wear a helmet and bright clothing, turn on your blinkies, and use your mirror. A ride to Sharpsburg is not the time to learn how to ride safely on winding, hilly, and no-shoulder country roads. If you are not an experienced road bicyclist, please consider transporting your bicycle between the canal and the battlefield park. And finally, always check ahead for NPS alerts about canal flooding, downed trees, detours, and closures.

On the Way to Antietam Creek

During the U.S. Civil War, Union and Confederate soldiers crossed the Potomac River and C&O Canal. Three major crossings were invasions by Gen. Lee's Army of Northern Virginia—the Maryland Campaign in 1862; the Gettysburg Campaign in 1863; and Jubal Early's 1864 attempt to take Washington, DC. With respect to the Maryland Campaign, the following maps show three important canal sites: Point of Rocks, Monocacy Aqueduct, and White's Ford.

On the 4th and 9th of September, 1862, Confederate Maj. Gen. D.H. Hill and Brig. Gen. John Walker each tried (and failed) to destroy the aqueduct over the Monocacy River (M42.2). Walker moved six miles farther north in an effort to disrupt the railroad at Point of Rocks, Maryland (M48.2).

On Sugarloaf Mountain, Union signalmen saw Gen. Lee's army cross the Potomac River near White's Ford.

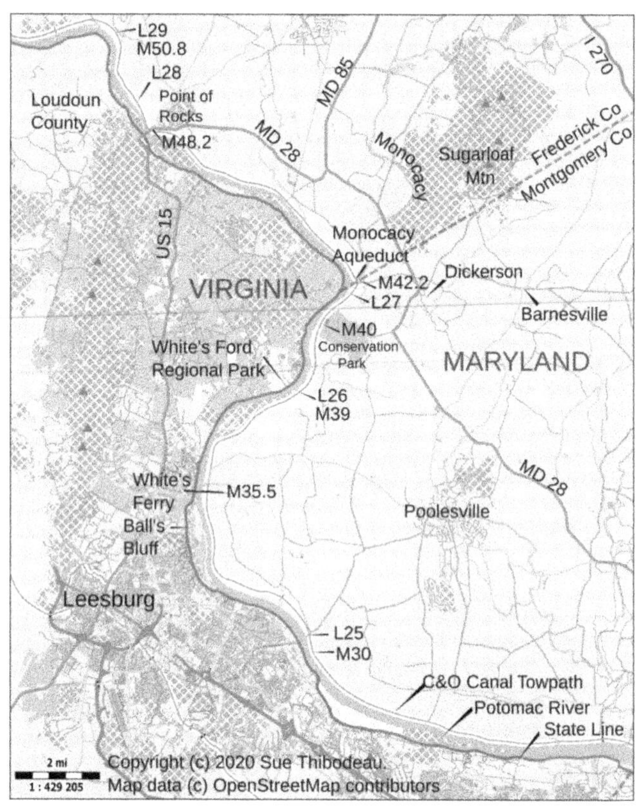

Map 31. White's Ford to Point of Rocks (M39–48.2)

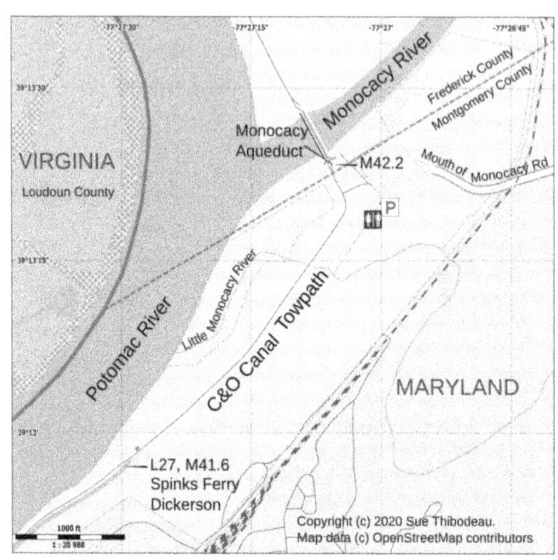

Map 32. Monocacy Aqueduct (M42.2)

Maj. Gen. Stuart's Confederate cavalry passed through Barnesville and there was skirmishing in Poolesville. By September 5–6, Confederate Maj. Gens. Longstreet and Jackson were on their way to Frederick from which the Monocacy River flows. Along the way, a courier accidentally dropped a copy of Gen. Lee's battle plans (Special Order 191), which was found by Union soldiers who delivered it to Gen. McClellan.[81]

Harpers Ferry was surrendered to Confederate Maj. Gen. Jackson on September 15, 1862. Harpers Ferry is at M60.7.

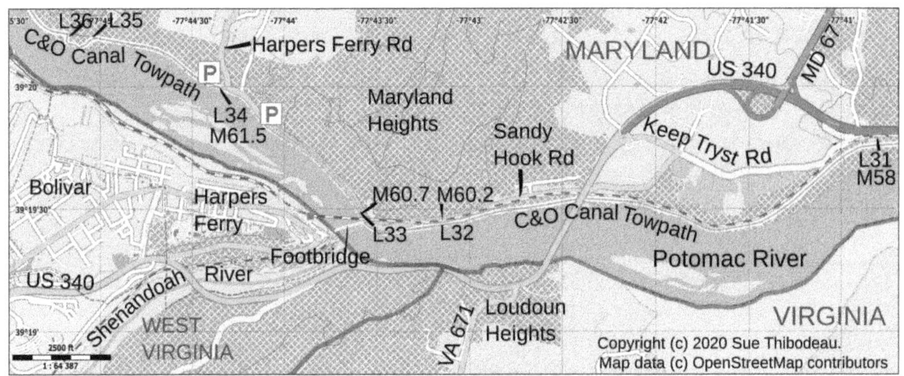

Map 33. Approach to Harpers Ferry (M58–60.7)

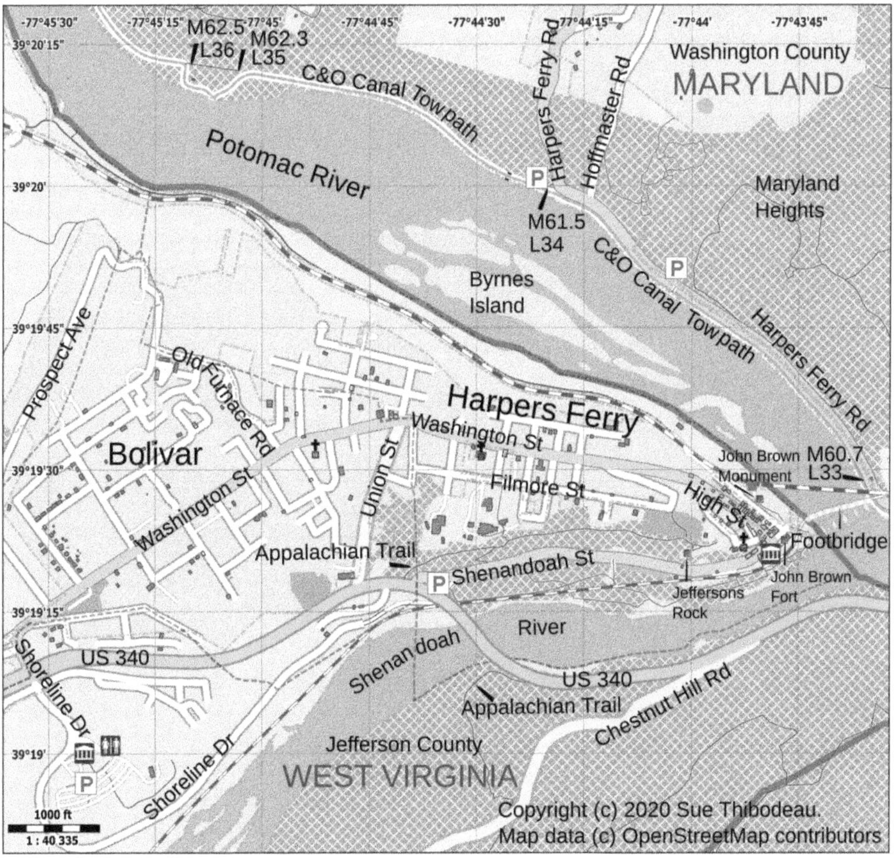

Map 34. Harpers Ferry (M60.7–62.5)

Two Options for Exiting the Canal Towpath

If you are riding north on the C&O Canal Towpath, you have two good options for connecting to Antietam National Battlefield. These are marked with arrows on Map 35, p. 128. The first option is to exit near M71 to take Canal Road to Millers Sawmill Road. The second option is to exit at Snyders Landing (M76.6). Both options minimize backtracking and road riding, while also ensuring that you will ride the full length of the towpath that is west of the battlefield.

The following comparison table will help you to decide where to leave the canal towpath to begin your excursion to Antietam National Battlefield. Once you select your exit point, you will have effectively selected your overall route from the canal to ANB and back again. The return is described at a high-level on p. 115. Once you select your route, you will find maps and cue sheets starting on p. 130 for Route 3.1, and on p. 133 for Route 3.2.

Table 15. Rt. 3 Northbound C&O Canal Towpath Options

Two Options:	**Rt. 3.1–Exit at M71 to Millers Sawmill Road (12.8 total miles)**	**Rt. 3.2–Exit at M76.6 Snyders Landing (12.7 total miles)**
Thumbnail images	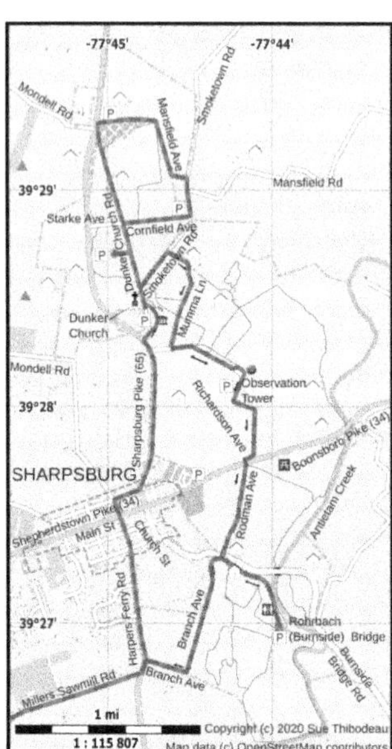	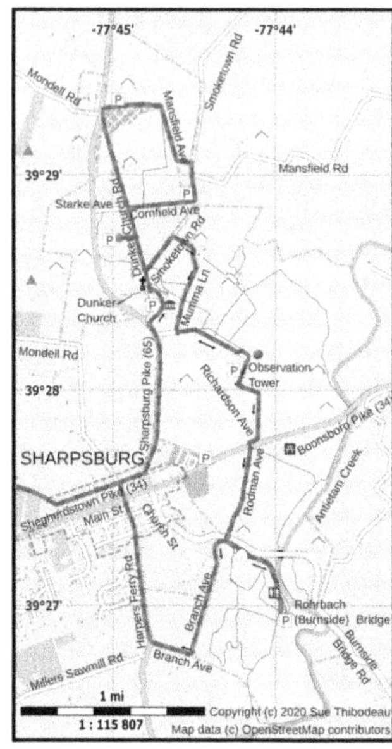

Two Options:	**Rt. 3.1–Exit at M71 to Millers Sawmill Road (12.8 total miles)**	**Rt. 3.2–Exit at M76.6 Snyders Landing (12.7 total miles)**
Your Goal	Ride through town once, at the beginning of your ANB excursion.	Ride through town at beginning and end of your ANB excursion.
Park Roads	7.3 miles (out of 12.8 total miles)	7.3 miles (out of 12.7 total miles)
Public Roads	5.5 miles M71 to ANB: 3.7 miles ANB to M71: 1.8 miles	5.4 miles M76.6 to ANB: 2.8 miles ANB to M76.6: 2.6 miles
C&O Canal Exit Point	**Near M71 (to Millers Sawmill Road)** REQUIRES ROAD SKILLS Canal Road runs on the east side of the canal towpath. You can connect at the Antietam Aqueduct (M69.4), or wait until M71, where you will take a right onto Millers Sawmill Road. – To ANB: 200 ft. up, 40 ft. down – No shoulders – Less traffic than the Harpers Ferry Road alternative – 35 mph into town	**M76.6 (Snyders Landing)** REQUIRES ROAD SKILLS – Boat ramp and parking at landing – Rural, town, and major roads – Good visibility, mostly straight – A few short, modest hills – To ANB: 190 ft. up, 30 ft. down – No shoulders – Fast-moving cars – 35 mph into town
Touring Directions	Begin on p. 130	Begin on p. 133

Your two best options for exiting and returning to the C&O Canal Towpath are marked with red arrows on the next map. Both options are very similar in terms of mileage, elevation, and road quality. Which option you choose will largely depend on when and how you want to ride through downtown Sharpsburg. As noted in Table 15, Route 3.1 will take you into downtown Sharpsburg once (before you tour the battlefield); but Route 3.2 will take you downtown twice (before and after your battlefield tour).

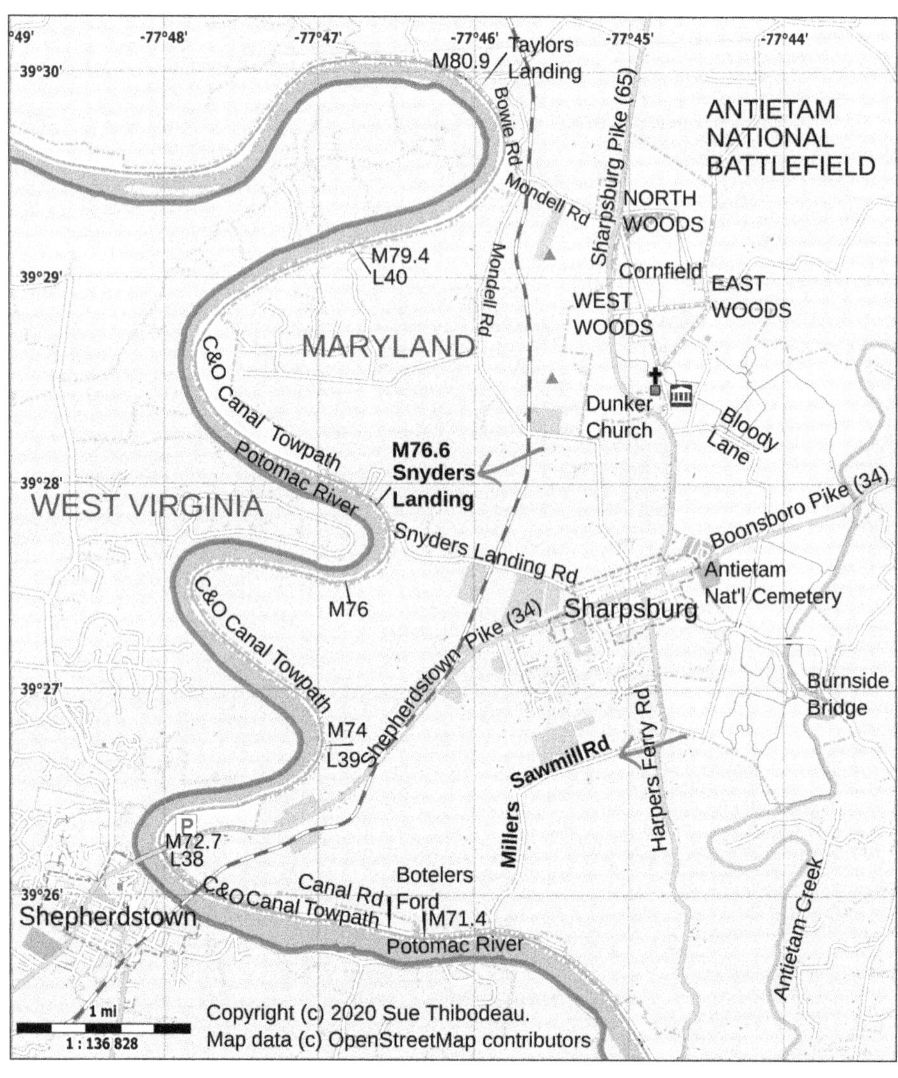

Map 35. Rt. 3 Options for a Northbound Exit

Your Return to the Canal Towpath (North)

If you exit the towpath at M71, you will return to M71 to continue your ride north on the towpath. If you exit at M76.6, you will return to M76.6. From Sharpsburg, many roads connect to the canal towpath:

1. M69.4 (Antietam Aqueduct) to Harpers Ferry Road (Map 36)
2. M71 (Canal Road) to Harpers Ferry Road
3. M72.7 (Lock 38) to Shepherdstown Pike
4. M76.6 (Snyders Landing) to Snyders Landing Road
5. M80.9 (Taylors Landing) on the way to Mondell Road

Tip: Map 36 shows the approach from Lock 37 to Antietam Aqueduct, which you will pass on your way to M71 or M76.6. Due to car traffic, we do not recommend getting on Harpers Ferry Road here. But note that picnic tables and portable toilets are nearby.

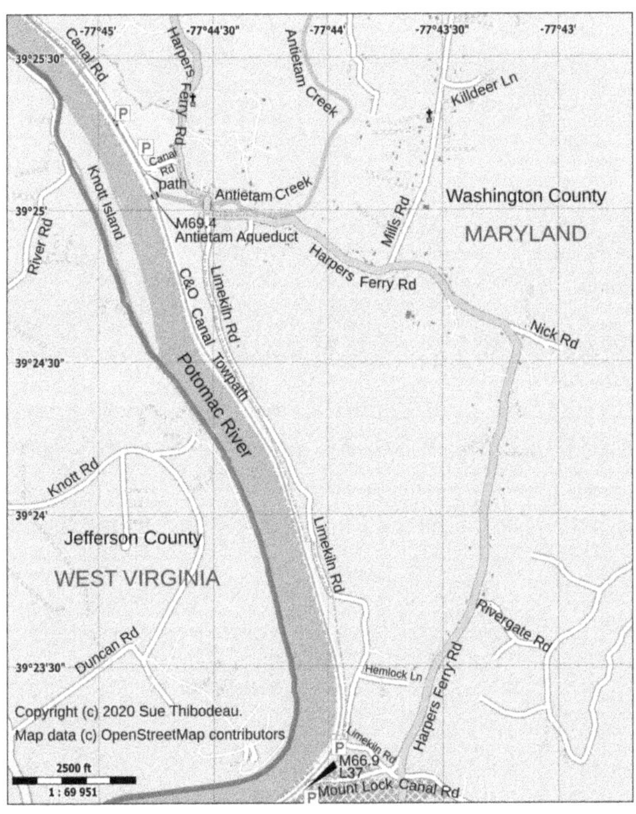

Map 36. Harpers Ferry Road at Antietam Aqueduct

Route 3.1—Your Battlefield Tour from M71

When riding north on the towpath, Millers Sawmill Road is a good exit and return point for an excursion to Antietam National Battlefield.

Segment A—Exit at Canal Road (M71)

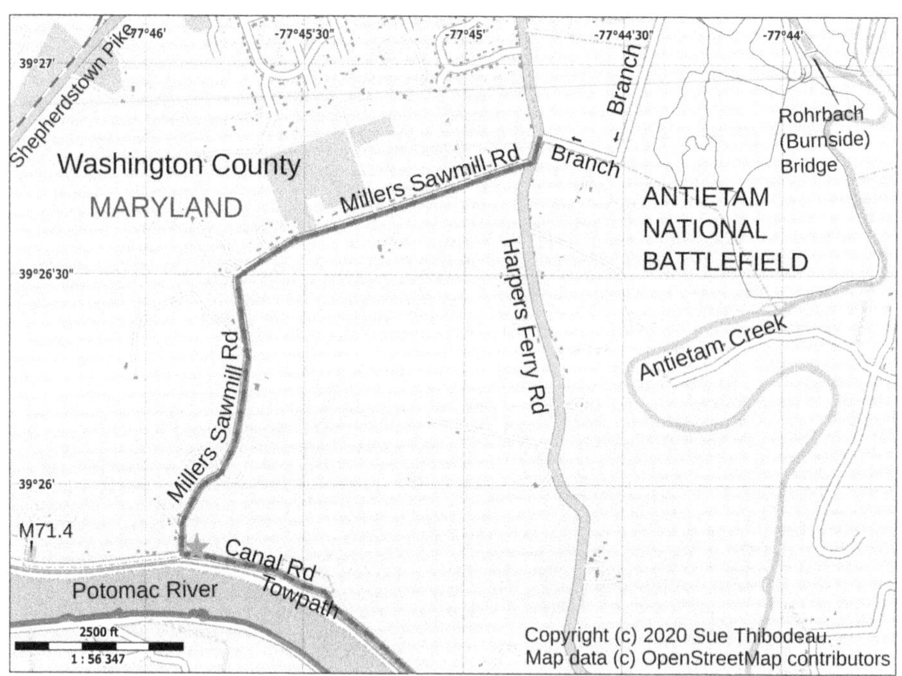

Map 37. Rt. 3 M71, Exit North at Canal Road to Millers Sawmill

These directions start 0.1 miles north of the Antietam Aqueduct (M69.4), at a path to Canal Road near Millers Sawmill Road.

A	Segment Cue Sheet (Exit Near M71, Canal Road)		
Start	M71 (39.41888, -77.74687). See cue key, p. 87.		End
0.0	R	To path	
	R	Millers Sawmill Road, mostly flat	0.8
0.8	BR	Millers Sawmill Rd and uphill	1.8
1.8	Arrive	Harpers Ferry Rd. Totals: 230 ft. up, 40 ft. down.	

Table 16. Rt. 3 Cue Sheet—Exit at Canal Road (Millers Sawmill)

Segment B—Harpers Ferry Road to Visitor Center

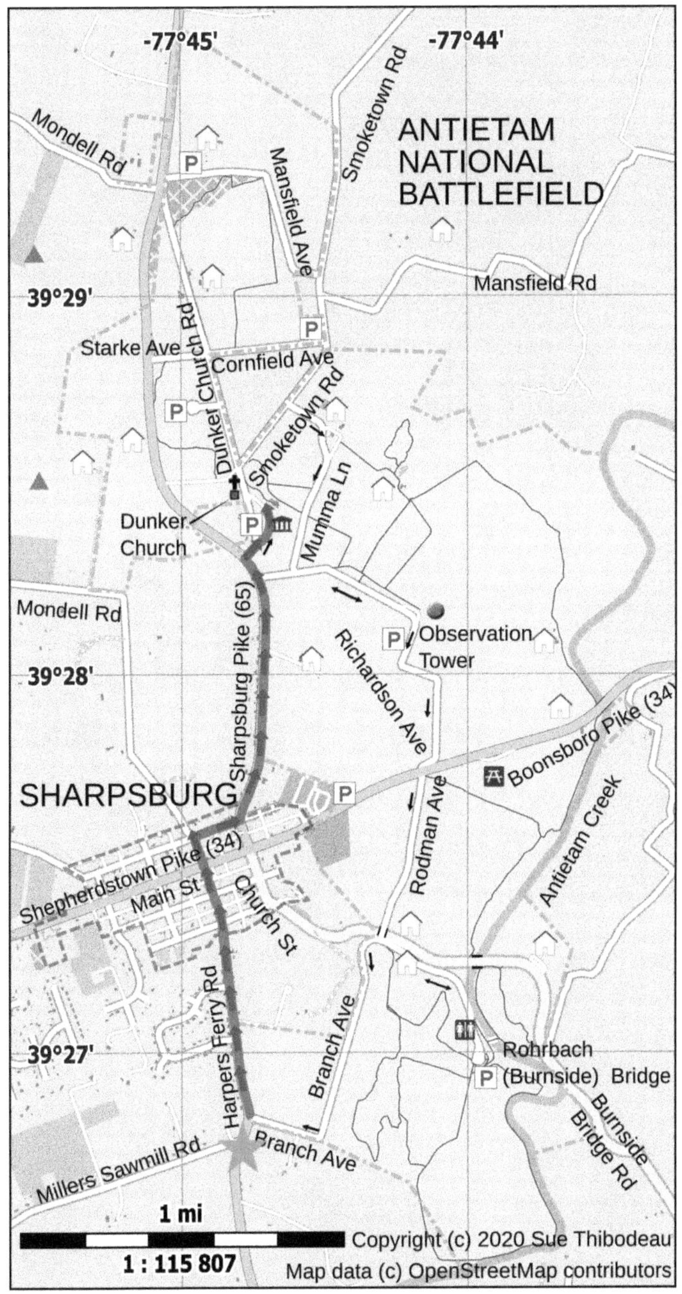

Map 38. Rt. 3 M71, Harpers Ferry Road to Visitor Center

B	Segment Cue Sheet (Harpers Ferry Rd. to ANB)		
Start	39.44716, -77.74601. See cue key, p. 87.		End
0.0	Millers Sawmill Road at Harpers Ferry Road		
	L	Harpers Ferry Rd., no shoulders, major road	0.1
0.1	PoR	1st MD Artillery (CSA) Monument, p. 158	
	CS	Mostly flat	0.5
0.5	CS	Slight incline	0.65
0.65	X	High Street	
0.7	X	Antietam Street	
0.8	X	Main Street, slight incline	
0.9	R	West Chapline Street. Totals: 3 ft. up, 60 ft. down	1.0
1.0	L	Sharpsburg Pike, slightly uphill, wide shoulders, 25 to 40 mph	1.1
1.1	PoR	Convenience store and grill	
1.5	PoR	Piper farm	
1.75	PoR	Richardson Avenue	
1.8	R	Dunker Church Road	1.9
1.9	BR	Arrive at Visitor Center	

Table 17. Rt. 3 Cue Sheet—Harpers Ferry Road to Visitor Center

Segment C—Tour Battlefield from Visitor Center

Follow the map and directions for "Segment B—Tour Battlefield from Visitor Center" on pp. 121-122.

Segment D—Return to Canal (Millers Sawmill Road)

Follow the map and directions for "Segment C—Return to Canal via Millers Sawmill Road" on p. 119.

Route 3.2—Your Battlefield Tour from M76.6

For bicyclists riding north on the C&O Canal Towpath, a second option for an excursion to Antietam National Battlefield is to exit and return to the towpath via Snyders Landing (M76.6).

Segment A—Exit at Snyders Landing (M76.6)

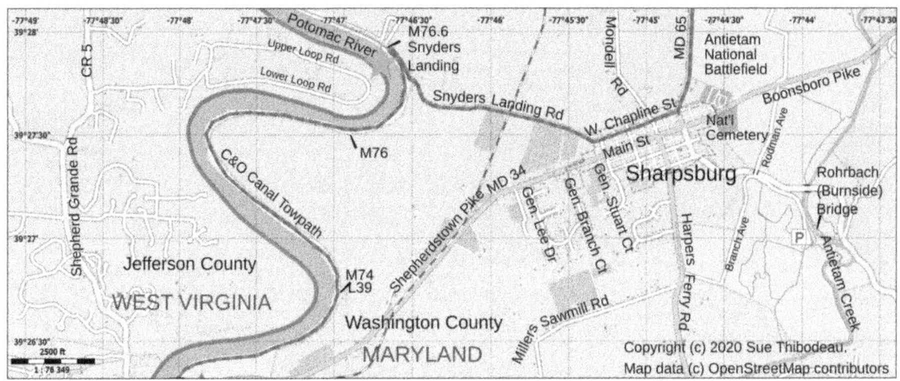

Map 39. Rt. 3 M76.6, Exit North at Canal Road to Millers Sawmill

A	Segment Cue Sheet (Exit at Snyders Landing)		
Start	M76.6 (39.46511, -77.77744). See cue key, p. 87.		End
0.0	R	Over bridge	
	QR	Snyders Landing Rd (20 mph, mostly flat and mostly pavement to 0.3)	0.3
0.3	XS	Slightly up (narrow, no shoulders, wooded, residential)	0.4
0.4	XS	Up to 0.6 peak, then up again at 1.0	1.4
1.4	L	West Chapline Street. Totals: 120 ft. up, 0 ft. down	1.9
1.9	L	Sharpsburg Pike, slightly uphill, wide shoulders, 25 to 40 mph	2.0
2.0	PoR	Convenience store and grill	
2.4	PoR	Piper farm	
2.65	PoR	Richardson Avenue	
2.7	R	Dunker Church Road	2.8
2.8	BR	Arrive at Visitor Center	

Table 18. Rt. 3 Cue Sheet—Exit at Snyders Landing

Segment B—Tour Battlefield from Visitor Center

Follow the map and directions for "Segment B—Tour Battlefield from Visitor Center" on pp. 121–122.

Segment C—Return to M76.6 (Snyders Landing)

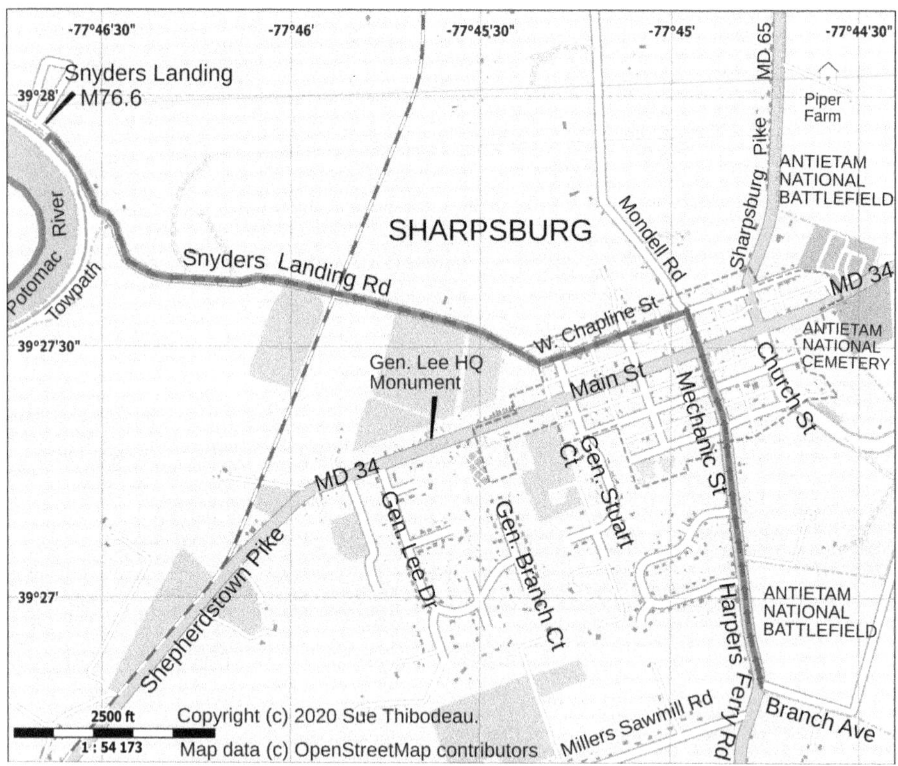

Map 40. Rt. 3 M76.6, Return North at Snyders Landing

If you want one more historical diversion while riding in downtown Sharpsburg, you might want to consider visiting a small monument on the north side of Main Street approaching the west edge of town. The Gen. Robert E. Lee's Headquarters Monument stands on a small patch of federal land. The monument is difficult to visit by car because there are no nearby parking areas, but on a bicycle a visit is a little easier to manage. See Map 40, above.

C	Segment Cue Sheet (Exit at Snyders Landing)		
Start	39.44716, -77.74601. See cue key, p. 87.		End
0.0	Branch Avenue at Harpers Ferry Road		
	R	Harpers Ferry Road, slightly down	0.6
0.6	X	High Street onto South Mechanic Street	
	CS	South Mechanic Street	0.8
0.8	X	Main Street (MD 34), mostly flat	
0.9	L	West Chapline Street, slightly up	1.3
1.3	BR	Snyders Landing Road (20 mph)	
	CS	Mostly down	
2.6	L	Over bridge. Arrive at M76.6. Totals: 30 ft. up, 180 ft. down.	

Table 19. Rt. 3 Cue Sheet—Return North at Snyders Landing

PART IV: MONUMENTS AND STRUCTURES

Chapter 9 Listing

You can visit all of the above monuments while riding Route 1, Segment A (p. 93). For easy reading before or after your ride, Chapter 9 provides a centralized and inter-connected set of monument summaries.

9. State Monuments

Of the ninety-six monuments on Antietam National Battlefield, seven are dedicated specifically to honor soldiers who hailed from a common state: Georgia, Indiana, Maryland, Massachusetts, New Jersey, New York, or Texas. This chapter provides an overview of those seven monuments, since you will see all of them on your bicycle tour.

Thirteen Union and eight Confederate states did not install and dedicate a state monument on Antietam National Battlefield. Lack of funding and competing priorities were the most pressing factors in a state's decision to forego a design and development project. The Confederate states suffered severe economic challenges in the wake of war; and whereas Union states may have had greater financial resources, in many cases that was not enough to offset the time and cost constraints of higher priority projects. For example, it should not be surprising that Pennsylvania chose to direct more of its resources to the development of Gettysburg National Military Park.

On the other hand, Pennsylvania erected more monuments at Antietam than any other state, for a total of nineteen monuments that together represent the state's significant contribution to the Union's battlefield strength. (New York and Maryland tied for second, having ten monuments each). Pennsylvania's Philadelphia Brigade Monument, which stands seventy-three feet tall in West Woods, is not only the tallest structure on the battlefield, but also one of the oldest, having been dedicated on September 17, 1896. Pennsylvania, New York, and Ohio together installed about one-third of all monuments at Antietam, but of those three, only New York erected a state monument.[82]

In summary, this chapter categorizes and describes Antietam's state monuments for tourists who will quickly note that these structures are among the largest on the battlefield, and perhaps for that reason alone, the most visually impressive. For a more complete history in terms of the participation of soldiers from other states, you are encouraged to explore the park to find Antietam's eighty-nine other, mostly regimental monuments.[83]

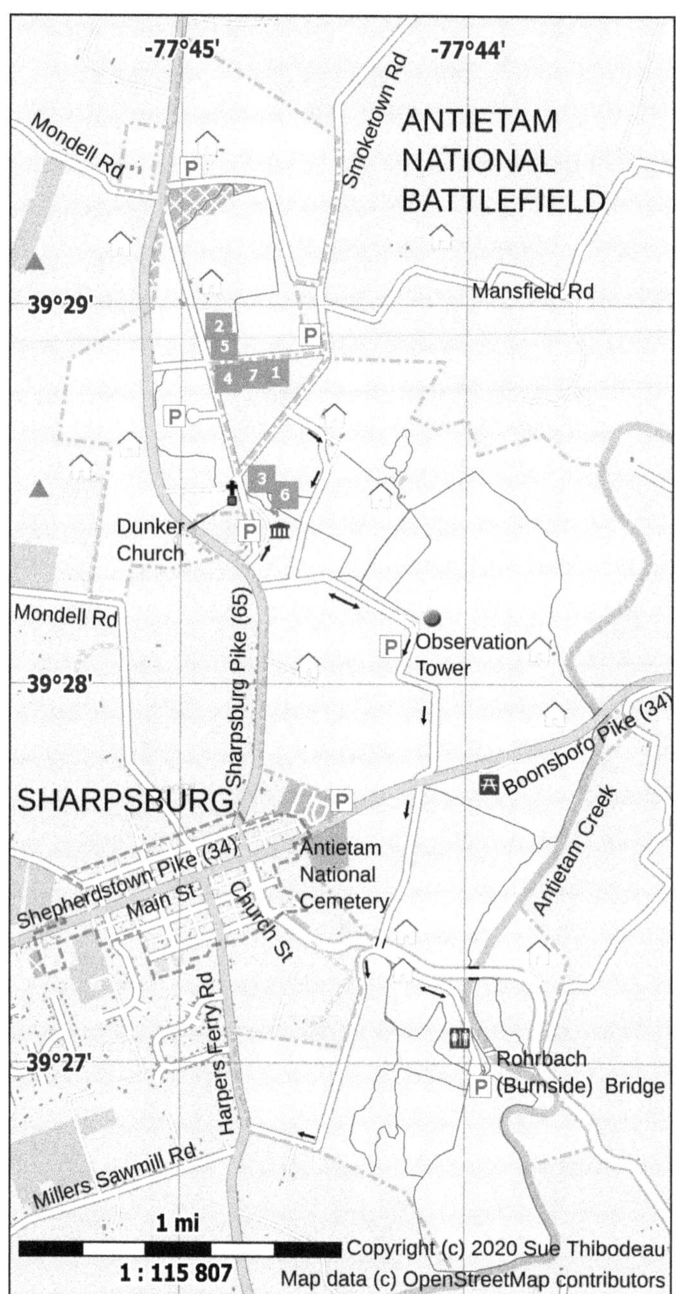

Map 41. State Monuments at Antietam

The green numbers on Map 41 correspond to an alphabetized listing and description of Antietam's state monuments, below.

1. Georgia State Monument (CSA)

Dedication: September 20, 1961 (Civil War Centennial)
Designer: Harry Sellers (Marietta Memorials)
Location: Cornfield Avenue (south side)
GPS (lat, lon): 39.48089, -77.74589

Georgia State Moment

"We sleep here in obedience to law;

When duty called, we came

When country called, we died."

Georgia erected near identical, blue granite monuments at Antietam, Gettysburg, Vicksburg, and Kennesaw Mountain—all of which include the somber inscription quoted above. This twelve-foot-high,[84] art deco style monument stands on the south side of Cornfield Avenue, and its placement identifies where Georgian soldiers attacked at the D.R. Miller cornfield (behind the camera). Thirty-nine regiments, seven artillery batteries, and one cavalry battalion served as Georgians in Gen. Robert E. Lee's army at Antietam.[85] One of the thirteen original colonies and the fourth state to be admitted into the Union, Georgia was the fifth Confederate state to secede.

2. Indiana State Monument (USA)

Dedication:	September 17, 1910 (48th battle anniversary)
Rededication:	September 9, 1962 (Civil War Centennial)
Sculptor	John K. Lowe (J.N. Forbes Company)[86]
Location:	Dunker Church Road at Cornfield Avenue (north)
GPS (lat, lon):	39.48102, -77.74834

The Indiana State Monument is a thirty-five-foot-high granite obelisk that stands on a square, parapeted platform with granite minié balls decorating its perimeter.[87] The monument honors the service of the 7th, 14th, 19th, and 27th Indiana Infantry and the 3rd Indiana Cavalry.

The 27th Indiana fought with the Union 12th Corps in the D.R. Miller cornfield, near where the Indiana State Monument is located. The regiment suffered nearly 50 percent casualties at Antietam.[88]

About the fighting at The Sunken Road, Col. William Harrow of the 14th Indiana Regiment, wrote these words in his report to Brig. Gen. Nathan Kimball (1st Brigade, Third Division, 2nd Corps):

> We ascended the hill in our front and occupied the crest, from which position we engaged the enemy, sheltered under ditches, rocks, and fences, with a large reserved force in a field of corn in their rear. The contest here continued for near four hours, during all which time the enemy poured upon us a terrific and murderous fire from infantry ... [89]

Indiana State Monument

The J.N. Forbes Company also manufactured battlefield markers for the five Indiana military units who served at Antietam.

3. Maryland State Monument (USA, CSA)

Dedication: May 30, 1900 (Memorial Day)
Rededications: September 2, 1962; July 1, 1989; June 3, 2006[90]
Designer: State of Maryland
Location: Dunker Church Road at Smoketown Road
GPS (lat, lon): 39.47597, -77.74606

Maryland State Monument

The Maryland State Monument is a forty-foot-high octagonal structure that has eight columns, eight bronze tablets, four bas-relief battle scenes, and a copper dome that is topped with a female figure that holds a wreath and a sword.[91] A stone bench is on the west side of monument.

The monument is unique in that it is a gazebo that honors all eight Union and Confederate military units that fought at the Battle of Antietam. For a unit listing and a brief history of presidential visits, see p. 41; for detailed descriptions of each unit and their markers, see Chapter 10.

"Antietam Battlefield Commission of Maryland

Benjamin F. Taylor, Second Maryland Infantry, U.S.A
Joseph M. Sudsburg, Third Maryland Infantry, U.S.A.
George R. Graham, Fifth Maryland Infantry, U.S.A.
William Gibson, Purnell Legion, Maryland Infantry, U.S.A.
William H. Parker, Battery 'A' First Md. Light Artillery, U.S.A.
Theodore J. Vanneman, Battery 'B' First Md. Light Artillery, U.S.A.
Henry Kyd Douglas, Staff Gen. Thomas J. Jackson, C.S.A.
Osmun Latrobe, Staff Gen. James Longstreet, C.S.A.
William F. Dement, First Maryland Battery, C.S.A.
Lloyd Lowndes, Governor of Maryland"[92]

4. Massachusetts State Monument (USA)

Dedication: September 17, 1898 (36th battle anniversary)[93]
Rededication: September 9, 1962 (Civil War Centennial)
Designer: Commonwealth of Massachusetts
Location: Dunker Church Road at Cornfield Avenue (south)
GPS (lat, lon): 39.48059, -77.74814

One of the oldest monuments erected at Antietam National Battlefield, the Massachusetts State Monument is an altar-like granite structure that stands on a prominent hill near the southwest corner of The Cornfield. The 2nd, 12th, 13th, 19th, and 20th Massachusetts infantry occupied the hill that veterans considered "sacred."[94] The 12th Massachusetts suffered 67 percent killed, wounded, or missing / captured casualties—the highest Union regimental percentage casualty rate for the battle.[95] Notably, future Associate U.S. Supreme Court Justice Oliver Wendell Holmes (1841–1935) served as a first lieutenant in the 20th Massachusetts at Antietam.

In the monument's center is a bas-relief of the state seal. The two flanking tablets list the names of one cavalry and fifteen infantry regiments, three artillery batteries, and two companies of sharpshooters. Beyond the state monument, three Massachusetts regiments were also honored with monuments in the West Woods (15th MA) and on the east side of Antietam Creek at Burnside Bridge (21st and 35th MA).

Massachusetts State Monument

5. New Jersey State Monument (USA)

Dedication:	September 17, 1903 (41st battle anniversary)
Rededication:	September 9, 1962 (Civil War Centennial)
Sculptor:	Giuseppe Moretti (1857–1935)[96]
Designer:	John L.W. Passmore Meeker, James Wallings[97]
Location:	Cornfield Avenue, near Dunker Church Road
GPS (lat, lon):	39.48090, -77.74826

New Jersey State Monument

The six sides of the New Jersey State Monument represent each of six regiments that fought at Antietam: the 1st, 2nd, 3rd, 4th, and 13th infantry and Hexamer's Battery A.[98] The sculpture that tops the monument is Capt. Hugh C. Irish, Company K, 13th New Jersey, who was shot through the heart and died on the field near this location.[99] New Jersey also installed seven separate infantry and artillery monuments on the Antietam Battlefield (plus one in Crampton's Gap).

6. New York State Monument (USA)

Dedication:	September 17, 1920 (58th battle anniversary)[100]
Rededication:	September 2, 1962 (Civil War Centennial)
Sculptors:	Ricci & Zari (architecture firm)[101]
Designer:	Edward Pearce Casey (1864–1940)[102]
Location:	Ridge east of Dunker Church, near Visitor Center
GPS (lat, lon):	39.47513, -77.74499

The New York State Monument stands on high ground across from Dunker Church. At fifty-eight-feet-high, you can see it from most points in the northern half of the park, and as far away as the Pry House on the east bank of Antietam Creek. John W. Schildt wrote that the monument marks "the southern edge of the bloodiest square mile in American History."[103] In 1907, New York State purchased this seven-acre parcel to honor 27,000 New Yorkers who fought at Antietam.[104] The tablet on the south side of the monument lists sixty-three New York officers who were killed or mortally wounded at Antietam. About 250 veterans attended the dedication in 1920.[105]

In total, New York erected ten monuments at Antietam, the first of which was in 1887, a monument to the 20th New York regiment, also known as the "Turner Rifles," a largely German military unit.

New York State Monument

7. Texas State Monument (CSA)

Dedication:	November 11, 1964 (Veteran's Day)
Sculptor:	Harold B. Simpson (1917–1989)
Location:	Cornfield Avenue (south side)
GPS (lat, lon):	39.48081, -77.74698

Texas State Monument

Texas erected identically shaped and styled red granite monuments on eleven Civil War battlefields. The Texas Brigade:

> ...Almost alone during this powerful federal onslaught, the Texas Brigade sealed a threatening gap in the Confederate line. In so doing the 1st Texas Infantry Regiment suffered a casualty rate of 82.3 percent, the greatest loss suffered by an infantry regiment, North or South, during the war.[106]

Texas and Georgia are the only Confederate state monuments at Antietam. There is one Confederate regimental monument, the 11th Mississippi; two markers (the A.N.V. marker on Piper farm and Gen. Lee's headquarters marker on Route 34); and one controversial equestrian statue of Gen. Lee near the Newcomer house.[107]

Chapter 10 Listing

Maryland's regimental and artillery battery monuments are located throughout the battlefield park, which means that you can visit all of them in the course of riding Route 1, Segments A (p. 93), B (p. 96), C (p. 101), and D (p. 105). For easy reading before or after your ride, Chapter 10 provides a centralized and inter-connected set of monument summaries.

10. Maryland Monuments

Having covered the general topic of state participation at the Battle of Antietam—specifically, the monuments built by states to commemorate their unique contributions to the battle—we now consider Maryland's six infantry regiments and two artillery batteries. At Antietam, these military units are honored by eight similarly styled four-foot-high granite blocks (plus one company monument that is styled differently).

Located throughout the battlefield park to mark the locations from which the soldiers fought, and to which veterans of the battle attached memories and significance, all eight monuments display the Maryland State Seal. Most of the seals are oxidized bronze, as in this photo (5th MD Infantry Monument).

Rather than try to describe all of Antietam's ninety-six monuments, this guidebook takes a thematic approach. Maryland monuments receive spotlight attention, because in their own home state Marylanders fought in opposing armies. This chapter will summarize the battlefield actions of native Marylanders who fought against each other in the countryside of western Maryland. The stories of these soldiers are told through monument inscriptions and official reports written by the unit commanders.

Since the Maryland regimental and artillery monuments are relatively small, they are easy to miss while bicycling the battlefield. Monument inscriptions are extremely brief. This chapter provides background material on each military unit so that it is easier to visualize what happened here on the battlefield on September 17, 1862.

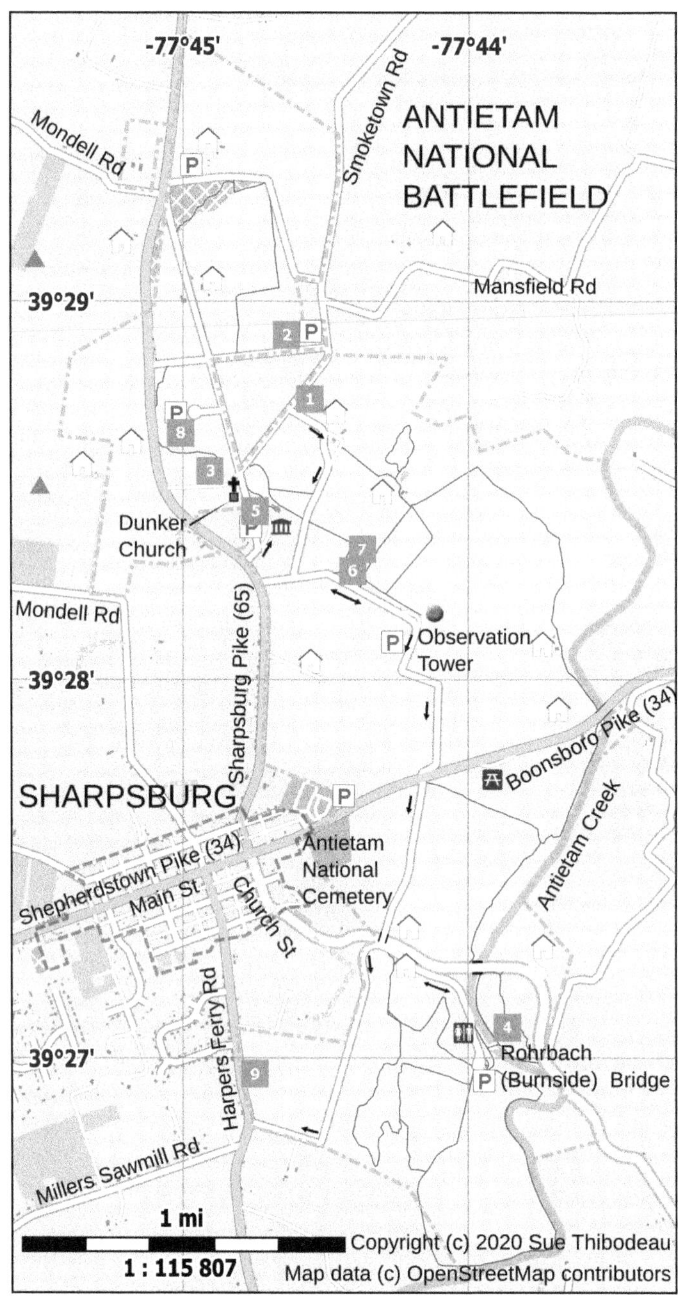

Map 42. Maryland Monuments at Antietam

The green numbers on Map 42 correspond to the following Maryland regimental and artillery monuments.

1. First Maryland Light Artillery Battery A

USA—Wolcott's Battery

Dedication:	May 30, 1900 (Memorial Day)
Location:	Mumma Farm (Mumma Lane)
GPS (lat, lon):	39.47861, -77.74360

Battery A	Capt. John W. Wolcott
Artillery Battalion	Capt. Emory Upton
1st Div. Infantry	Maj. Gen. Henry W. Slocum
6th Corps	Maj. Gen. William B. Franklin

Organized in	Baltimore and Pikesville (Baltimore County)
Artillery	Six 3" Ordnance Rifles[108]
Loss	14 — 1 Killed, 11 Wounded, 2 Missing[109]

"The battery under the command of Capt. John W. Wolcott occupied a line 100 feet in rear of this marker and facing Dunkard Church." ~ From the monument inscription.

After late afternoon fighting at the farm lane called The Sunken Road, and around 4:30 p.m., Battery A moved into "Mumma's swale," an area west of the lane and Mumma's cornfield. The 7th Maine was in their front, facing southwest. Wolcott's Battery A was behind the infantry regiment. Within thirty minutes, Confederate fire from Piper's farm hit twelve of Wolcott's men.[110]

According to the division artillery chief, Capt. Emory Upton, in his written report to Maj. Gen. Slocum, three Union batteries under Upton's command were placed facing Dunker Church. Wolcott's Battery A was positioned between Lt. Edward B. Williston's Battery D (2nd US) and Capt. Josiah Porter's Battery A (1st MA). Upton commended his officers, which included a fourth battery—that of Capt. William Hexamer, 1st New Jersey, Battery A—in his report:

"The commanders of batteries, Captains Hexamer and Wolcott and Lt. Williston, displayed great coolness and judgement in maneuvering their batteries and delivering their fire. They all speak in the highest terms of the conduct of their officers and men."[111]

2. First Maryland Light Artillery Battery B

USA—Snow's Battery

Dedication:	May 30, 1900 (Memorial Day)
Location:	East Woods (Cornfield Avenue)
GPS (lat, lon):	39.48115, -77.74399

Battery B	1st Lt. Theodore J. Vanneman (for Capt. Alonzo Snow)[112]
Artillery Battalion	Capt. Romeyn Beck Ayres
2nd Division	Maj. Gen. William F. Smith
6th Corps	Maj. Gen. William B. Franklin

Organized in	Port Deposit (Cecil County)
Artillery	Eight 3" Ordnance Rifles[113]
Loss	0

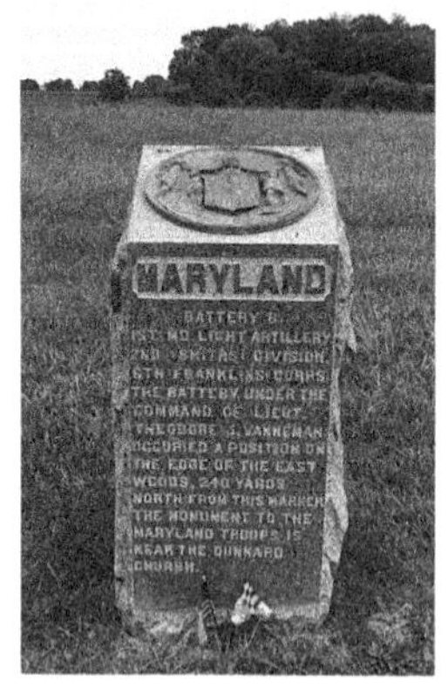

"The battery under the command of Lieut. Theodore J. Vanneman occupied a position on the edge of the East Woods 240 yards north from this marker." ~ From the monument inscription.

Lt. Theodore J. Vanneman's report to Capt. Romeyn Beck Ayres noted that Battery B was placed by Maj. Gen. Franklin in a cornfield and ordered to shell the woods in front of them (near Dunker Church). According to Ezra A. Carman, Battery B was positioned to the left of the 1st New York Battery, which was on a "grass field east of D.R. Miller's and north of the cornfield."[114] On the way there, moving through East Woods toward Hagerstown (Sharpsburg) Pike, the battery cut through the regimental line of the 33rd New York. It was around Noon–1:00 p.m.[115]

Once positioned, Battery B returned fire "from 2 1/2° to 3° elevation, using from 3 1/2 to 4 second fuses, and expended during the engagement about 300 rounds of ammunition." One horse was killed by a six-pound shot.[116] In the end, Union guns silenced two Confederate batteries near the West Woods.[117] When it was over, Vanneman wrote this about Battery B's engagement: "The officers and men during the action behaved with commendable bravery."[118]

3. Purnell Legion Maryland Infantry

USA

Dedication: May 30, 1900 (Memorial Day)
Location: Northwest of Dunker Church (West Woods)
GPS (lat, lon): 39.47528, -77.74809

Purnell Legion Lt. Col. Benjamin L. Simpson
3rd Brigade Capt. William B. Goodrich
2nd Division Brig. Gen. George S. Greene
12th Corps Maj. Gen. Joseph K.F. Mansfield

Organized in Pikesville (Baltimore County)
Loss 26 — 3 Killed, 23 Wounded, 0 Missing[119]

In September, 1862, the Purnell Legion no longer included cavalry companies or artillery batteries, the latter of which had split to become Maryland Light Artillery Battery A and Battery B. At Antietam, the legion consisted of nine companies of infantry totaling 204 men.[120] Its monument is located on the north end of a gravel road behind Dunker Church. According to the monument inscription, the Purnell Legion "occupied a line running north from this marker." By this time, Maj. Gen. Mansfield had been killed in the East Woods.

Around 8:15 a.m., the legion marched down Hagerstown (Sharpsburg) Pike behind the 124th Pennsylvania, thus detached from Goodrich's brigade. Goodrich was killed and his brigade—along with Confederate Col. Grigsby's Virginians, whom they fought—suffered heavy losses. The legion's commander reported that they remained with the Pennsylvanians "until the enemy appeared in overwhelming numbers and compelled [them] to retire."[121]

A few hours later, on the northwest side of Dunker Church (near where the Purnell Legion monument stands), several Union regiments, including the 13th New Jersey, turned back to Smoketown Road. The Purnell Legion withdrew to the Mumma farm. With this final action in the northern portion of the battlefield, Confederates from North Carolina and Arkansas secured Dunker Church.[122]

4. Second Maryland Infantry

USA

Dedication:	May 30, 1900 (Memorial Day)
Location:	East bank of Burnside Bridge (Union Advance Trail, Horseshoe Bend)
GPS (lat, lon):	39.45069, -77.73150
2nd MD	Lt. Col. J. Eugene Duryea
1st Brigade	Brig. Gen. James Nagle
2nd Division	Brig. Gen. Samuel D. Sturgis
9th Corps	Maj. Gen. Ambrose E. Burnside
Organized in	Baltimore
Loss	67 — 17 Killed, 47 Wounded, 3 Missing[123]

S.G. Elliott's 1864 "Map of the Battlefield of Antietam" indicates that Pvt. W. Kelly, Company H, died and was temporarily buried on the east bank of Antietam Creek (see below).[124] The cross marks identify Union graves. Kelly was one of 187 soldiers in the 2nd Maryland who fought at Antietam.[125] The regiment suffered 44 percent casualties, down to less than 100 men.[126] From the monument inscription: "At 9:30 a.m. advanced on the stone bridge, defended by Toombs' Brigade and two batteries on the high ground beyond. Charged to within 100 yards of the bridge when, checked by the severity of the enemy's fire, it took shelter along the bank of the stream and was engaged until 1:30 p.m. The bridge being carried, it crossed to the hills and the battle beyond."

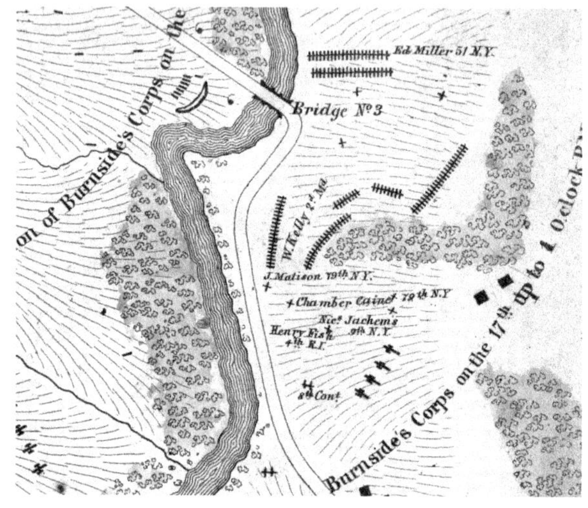

5. Third Maryland Infantry

USA

Dedication:	May 30, 1900 (Memorial Day)
Location:	East side of Dunker Church Road
GPS (lat, lon):	39.37326, -77.74603
3rd MD	Lt. Col. Joseph M. Sudsburg[127]
2nd Brigade	Col. Henry J. Stainrook
2nd Division	Brig. Gen. George S. Greene
12th Corps	Maj. Gen. Joseph K.F. Mansfield
Organized in	Baltimore
Loss	29 — 1 Killed, 25 Wounded, 3 Missing[128]

With the Purnell Legion (p. 153), the 3rd Maryland participated in the final action at Dunker Church. On a hill, the church was a strategic military position. From early morning and through the brutal fighting in D.R. Miller's cornfield, Union Gen. Hooker focused on Dunker Church. But Hooker's corps was weakened, and Mansfield's corps (now led by Brig. Gen. Alpheus S. Williams), and especially Greene's division, took the lead trying to capture Dunker Church.

The 3rd Maryland monument stands near the Visitor Center on the east side of Dunker Church Road. The monument inscription points you to the opposite side of the road; it says that the regiment "advanced to the corner of the Dunker Church, in front of this marker." Lt. Col. Joseph M. Sudsburg described the action of the 3rd Maryland in his official written report to Lt. Col. James C. Lane (Stainrook's 2nd Brigade):

"Arriving behind the crest of a little elevation, we were ordered to lie down ... We were ordered up, fixed bayonets ... We drove the enemy, who flew before us across the fields and across the road ... On the other side of the road is a church or school-house, surrounded by woods. Charging through this piece of woods, we drove the enemy out, and held possession nearly two hours. ... In this woods I lost most of my men. I took 148 into action."[129]

6, 7. Fifth Maryland and Companies A&I

USA

Dedication:	May 30, 1900	Regiment
Dedication:	September 17, 1890	Company A & I
Location:	Sunken Road Area (Richardson Avenue)	
GPS (lat, lon):	39.47140, -77.74069	Regiment
GPS (lat, lon):	39.47211, -77.73995	Company A & I

5th MD	Maj. Leopold Blumenberg
3rd Brigade	Brig. Gen. Max Weber
3rd Division	Brig. Gen. William H. French
2nd Corps	Maj. Gen. Edwin V. Sumner

Organized in	Baltimore
Loss	163 — 25 Killed, 123 Wounded, 15 Missing[130]

In 1862, a farm lane connected Hagerstown Pike to Boonsboro Pike. On September 17, Brig. Gen. George B. Anderson's North Carolinians lined the east side of road. On the west side, before the road's bend, Brig. Gen. Robert E. Rode's Alabamians dug in. The 5th Maryland attacked from the north. Maj. Blumenberg was wounded.

Brig. Gen. Max Weber's brigade (1,798 men) led the attack. On the left was the 1st Delaware (708 men); on the right, the 4th New York (450 men); and in the center, the 5th Maryland (550 men).[131] Col. Dwight Morris' brigade and then Brig. Gen. Nathan Kimball's brigade attacked next. Brig. Gen. William H. French praised Weber: "The gallantry and coolness of General Max Weber excited the admiration of the whole command. With consummate skill and judgment he led the attack, and left the field reluctantly, severely wounded."[132]

Two monuments honor the 5th Maryland; one for the regiment (pictured on p. 149) and the other for Companies A&I (pictured here). The A&I monument was the first Maryland monument erected at Antietam. It marks the regiment's farthest point of advance, about 300 feet north of The Sunken Road.

8. Baltimore Light Artillery Battery

CSA—Brockenbrough's Battery

Dedication:	May 30, 1900 (Memorial Day)
Location:	West Woods (west of Philadelphia Brigade circle)
GPS (lat, lon):	39.47801, -77.75031
Baltimore Battery	Capt. John B. Brockenbrough[133]
Artillery Battalion	Maj. Lindsay M. Shumaker
Infantry Division	Brig. Gen. John R. Jones (Jackson's Division)
Command	Maj. Gen. Thomas J. Jackson
Organized in	Richmond, Virginia
Artillery	One 3" Ordnance Rifle, One 12# Howitzer, One Rifled Blakely, One 10# Parrott[134]
Loss	8 — 0 Killed, 8 Wounded[135]

"The battery, under the command of Capt. J.B. Brockenbrough, occupied a position near this marker at daybreak, and opened the battle on the Confederate side." ~ From the monument inscription.

According to Confederate Brig. Gen. John R. Jones' official written report, the Confederate response to a "storm of shell and grape" from Union guns on their front (North Woods) and extreme right (near the Upper Bridge) came from the artillery batteries of Jackson's Division, namely those of Poague, Carpenter, Brockenbrough, Raine, Caskie, and Wooding.[136]

In the West Woods, the guns of Brockenbrough's Battery fired into D.R. Miller's cornfield and also at Union men moving down Hagerstown (Sharpsburg) Pike toward Dunker Church. Later, and from a location farther west at Hauser Ridge, the battery fired on Union Maj. Gen. John Sedgwick's division as they attacked the West Woods.

9. First Maryland Artillery Battery

CSA—Dement's Battery

Dedication: May 30, 1900 (Memorial Day)[137]
Rededication: September 20, 1961
Location: Southeast Sharpsburg (Harpers Ferry Road)
GPS (lat, lon): 39.44881, -77.74643

1st MD Artillery: Capt. William F. Dement
Artillery Battalion: Maj. Alfred R. Courtney
Infantry Division: Ewell's Division (Brig. Gen. Alexander Lawton)
Command: Maj. Gen. Thomas J. Jackson

Organized in: Fredericksburg, Virginia
Artillery: Four 12# Napoleons[138]
Loss: 0

"The battery under the command of Capt. Wm. F. Dement occupied a position in the field, in the rear of this marker." ~ From monument inscription.

Capt. Dement's battery was positioned at Loudoun Heights (Harpers Ferry) on September 16, 1862. Although there is no evidence that the battery actively participated in the Battle of Antietam—when in the late afternoon they might have supported Confederate Maj. Gen. A.P. Hill on the Confederate army's right flank—a 1908 map published by the Antietam Battlefield Board clearly shows Dement's battery marching east along modern-day Millers Sawmill Road.[139]

The monument inscription indicates that the battery "occupied a position" in the fields near Harpers Ferry Road. The structure, which includes a four-foot-high fieldstone retaining wall, stands on the east side of Harpers Ferry Road and north of Millers Sawmill Road.

The Sunken Road Viewed from the Observation Tower

Dunker Church Viewed from Cornfield Avenue

Chapter 11 Listing

Antietam's mortuary cannons are located throughout the battlefield park, which means that you can visit all of them in the course of riding Route 1, Segments A (p. 93), B (p. 96), C (p. 101), and D (p. 105). For easy reading before or after your ride, Chapter 11 provides a centralized and inter-connected set of monument summaries.

11. Mortuary Cannons

At the Battle of Antietam, six generals died from their battlefield wounds—two died within the day (k, killed) and four died of mortal wounds (mw): [140]

Army of the Potomac (USA):

	Rank	Life	Burial
Joseph K.F. Mansfield (mw)	Maj. Gen.	1803–62	Connecticut
Israel B. Richardson (mw)	Maj. Gen.	1815–62	Michigan
Isaac P. Rodman (mw)	Brig. Gen.	1822–62	Rhode Island

Army of Northern Virginia (CSA):

	Rank	Life	Burial
George B. Anderson (mw)	Brig. Gen.	1831–62	North Carolina
Lawrence O. Branch (k)	Brig. Gen.	1820–62	North Carolina
William E. Starke (k)	Brig. Gen.	1814–62	Virginia

In 1898, the U.S. War Department installed six mortuary cannons as memorials to the three Union and three Confederate generals who were mortally wounded at the Battle of Antietam. These inverted "Napoleon" cannons—smoothbore weapons named for French Emperor Louis Napoleon III—are mounted on four-foot-square fieldstone foundations. Their green color is due to bronze oxidation. The U.S. War Department placed each cannon at the approximate location of the general's wounding (not necessarily the place of death, and certainly not the place of burial).

Notably, twelve other generals (six Union, six Confederate) survived their Antietam wounds. Although no monuments were erected on the battlefield to commemorate their sacrifice, you will recognize their names as part of the battle narrative. For the Union, they are: Samuel W. Crawford; Napoleon J.T. Dana; George L. Hartsuff; Joseph Hooker; John Sedgwick; Max Weber. For the Confederacy, they are: Richard H. Anderson; Maxcy Gregg; John R. Jones; Alexander R. Lawton; Roswell S. Ripley; Ambrose R. Wright.

As you tour Antietam National Battlefield, refer to this chapter for an overview of the stories of the generals whose lives were lost here. Map 43 marks the location of each mortuary cannon, numbered alphabetically according to the general's last name.

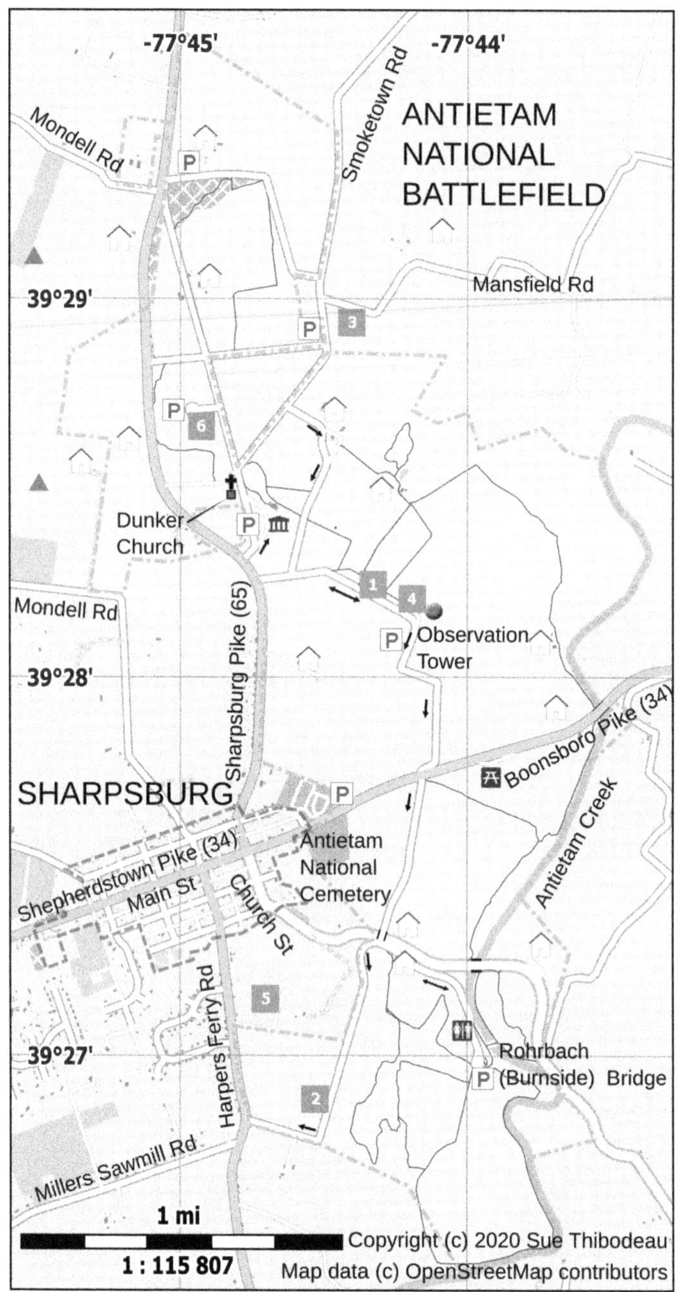

Map 43. Mortuary Cannons at Antietam

The green numbers on Map 43 correspond to an alphabetized listing and description of Antietam's mortuary cannons, below.

1. George B. Anderson (CSA)

Anderson Mortuary Cannon

Location:	Sunken Road (Richardson Avenue area)
GPS (lat, lon):	39.47041, -77.73825
Command:	Brigade in D.H. Hill's Division (T.J. Jackson)
Life:	1831–62. Mortally wounded.
Birthplace:	Hillsboro, North Carolina
Burial:	Oakwood Cemetery, Raleigh, NC

Brig. Gen. George B. Anderson Mortuary Cannon

While fighting with his fellow North Carolinians in The Sunken Road, Brig. Gen. George B. Anderson was struck in the foot by a bullet. He was taken to Shepherdstown and then Virginia to heal, but after finally making it back to Raleigh, Anderson died from complications associated with a surgery to amputate his infected foot. The general died on October 16, 1862.[141]

2. Lawrence O'Bryan Branch (CSA)

Branch Mortuary Cannon

Location:	Branch Avenue (west side)
GPS (lat, lon):	39.44803, -77.74136
Command:	Brigade in A.P. Hill's Division (T.J. Jackson)
Life:	1820–62. Killed.
Birthplace:	Enfield, North Carolina
Burial:	Old City Cemetery, Raleigh, NC

In the late afternoon, while standing in the fields west of Antietam Creek and in the south end of the battlefield, Brig. Gen. Lawrence O'Bryan Branch was conferring with three other brigadier generals (Gregg, Pender, and Archer). During that conversation, a federal bullet ripped through Branch's face and head, killing him instantly. His brigade of North Carolina soldiers had only recently arrived on the battlefield (after a seventeen-mile march from Harper's Ferry)—in time to repel the Union advance that threatened Gen. Lee's right flank.

The Branch mortuary cannon plaque (not visible) faces Branch Avenue. Its inscription is similar to the other memorials: "Brigadier General L. O'Branch C.S.A. Killed Here." The inverted cannon is a four-foot-high, twelve-pounder Napoleon with typical green oxidation.

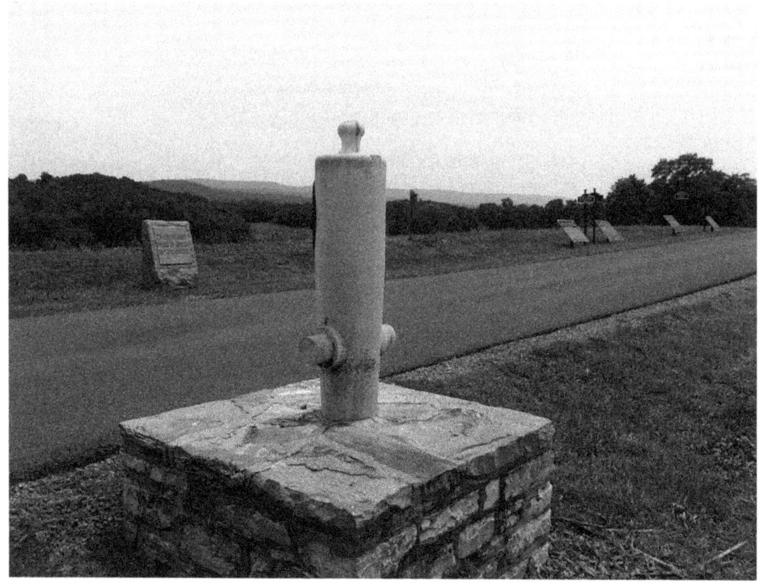

Brig. Gen. Lawrence O'Bryan Branch Mortuary Cannon

3. Joseph K.F. Mansfield (USA)

Mansfield Mortuary Cannon

Location:	East Woods (Mansfield Road)
GPS (lat, lon):	39.48313, -77.74092
Command:	12th Corps, Army of the Potomac
Life:	1803–62. Mortally wounded.
Birthplace:	New Haven, Connecticut
Burial:	Indian Hill Cemetery, Middletown, Connecticut

Maj. Gen. Joseph F.K. Mansfield Mortuary Cannon

Maj. Gen. Joseph King Fenno Mansfield was nearly sixty years old at Antietam[142] and recently assigned by Gen. McClellan to lead the 12th Corps in support of Maj. Gen. Joseph Hooker's 1st Corps drive into The Cornfield. While Mansfield led from the front battle line in the East Woods, both "horse and rider were shot down" at about 7:35 a.m. He died the next day at a nearby farm.[143]

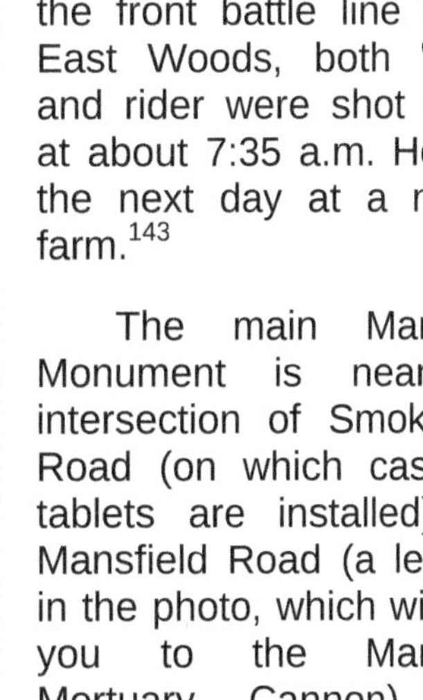

The main Mansfield Monument is near the intersection of Smoketown Road (on which cast iron tablets are installed) and Mansfield Road (a left turn in the photo, which will take you to the Mansfield Mortuary Cannon). The main monument was dedicated on May 24, 1900.

Mansfield Monument

Maj. Gen. Joseph K.F. Mansfield died after having served for forty-five years in the military, starting as a West Point cadet.

4. Israel B. Richardson (USA)

Richardson Mortuary Cannon

Location:	Sunken Road (near the Observation Tower)
GPS (lat, lon):	39.46946, -77.73608
Command:	1st Division, 2nd Corps (Edwin V. Sumner)
Life:	1815–62. Mortally wounded.
Birthplace:	Fairfax, Vermont
Burial:	Oak Hill Cemetery, Pontiac, Michigan

Maj. Gen. Israel B. Richardson commanded a division composed of three brigades, one of which was the famous Irish Brigade. With support from William H. French's 3rd Division, Richardson drove Confederates under Daniel H. Hill out of "The Bloody Lane." In this nearly four-hour fight, enfilading artillery fire hit Richardson. Although the wound did not appear to be life threatening, and Richardson received care at the Pry House, he died on November 3, 1862.[144]

Maj. Gen. Israel B. Richardson Mortuary Cannon

Irish Brigade

Brig. Gen. Thomas F. Meagher (1823–67) was an Irish nationalist who, after the British government convicted him of sedition, escaped to the U.S. before the outbreak of the Civil War. Under Maj. Gen. Richardson, Meagher led the Irish Brigade (one Massachusetts and three New York regiments at Antietam). In his official report, Meagher described the actions of his brigade in The Sunken Road:

"[T]he brigade poured in an effective and powerful fire upon the column... Despite a fire of musketry, which literally cut lanes through our approaching line, the brigade advanced under my personal command within 30 paces of the enemy..."[145]

Irish Brigade Monument

Dedication:	October 25, 1997
Location:	Sunken Road (near the Observation Tower)
Sculptor:	Ron Tunison (1946–2013)
GPS (lat, lon):	39.46937, -77.73609

The granite for this monument came from Ireland. Rev. William Corby (1833–97), Irish Brigade chaplain at Antietam, would become the President of the University of Notre Dame in 1866.

Irish Brigade Monument (and Richardson Cannon)

5. Isaac P. Rodman (USA)

Rodman Mortuary Cannon

Location:	Field east of Harpers Ferry Road
GPS (lat, lon):	39.45292, -77.74396
Command:	3rd Division, 9th Corps (Ambrose E. Burnside)
Life:	1822–62. Mortally wounded.
Birthplace:	South Kingston, Rhode Island
Burial:	Peace Dale, Rhode Island

While the rest of Maj. Gen. Ambrose E. Burnside's corps struggled to cross the Lower (Rohrbach) Bridge over Antietam Creek, Burnside sent Brig. Gen. Isaac P. Rodman's 3rd Division downstream to find a passable ford. About three hours later, Rodman crossed at Snavely's Ford, a two-mile hike from the bridge. The Union flanking maneuver on the Confederate right (south of Sharpsburg) was forcefully checked by the 4:00 p.m. arrival of Confederate Maj. Gen. Ambrose P. Hill's Light Division.

When Rodman spotted Hill's men, he galloped through the field to warn and reorganize his brigades. It was around this time that Rodman received a fatal bullet to his chest. He died thirteen days later, on September 30.

The Rodman Mortuary Cannon is a 0.3-mile walk along a pedestrian path from Harpers Ferry Road. Two regimental monuments in Rodman's division (9th NY and 8th CT) are nearby.

Brig. Gen. Isaac P. Rodman Mortuary Cannon

6. William B. Starke (CSA)

Starke Mortuary Cannon

Location:	West Woods (Philadelphia Brigade Park)
GPS (lat, lon):	39.47832, -77.74892
Command:	Brigade in Thomas J. Jackson's Division
Life:	1814–62. Killed.
Birthplace:	Brunswick County, Virginia
Burial:	Hollywood Cemetery, Richmond, Virginia

Brig. Gen. William B. Starke Mortuary Cannon

In the West Woods, Brig. Gen. William E. Starke was shot three times and died within the hour. Brig. Gen. John R. Jones described the event in his report to Maj. Pendleton dated January 21, 1863:

> At the dawn of day on the 17th the battle opened fiercely. A storm of shell and grape fell upon the division from several batteries in front, and at very short range, and from batteries of heavy guns on the extreme right, which enfiladed the position of the division and took it in reverse. ... I was rendered unfit for duty, and retired from the field, turning over the command to Brigadier-General Starke, who a half an hour afterward advanced his lines to meet the infantry of the enemy, which was approaching. The infantry became at once engaged, and the gallant and generous Starke fell, pierced by three balls, and survived but a few moments.[146]

Acknowledgements

For help completing this book, there is no one who deserves more heartfelt thanks than my husband, Timothy M. Thibodeau. Tim is my bicycling companion, sounding board, proof-reader, and "resident historian." Although Tim's expertise is medieval Europe, he has taught me a great deal about research methods, publishing mechanics, and the importance of historical themes and inter-connections. Without Tim's support, neither this book nor my previous one, *Bicycling Gettysburg National Military Park*, would ever have seen the light of day.

PART V: RESOURCES

Glossary

Term	Definition
AIC	Art Inventories Catalog. A database of historic art maintained by the Smithsonian Institution as part of the Smithsonian Institution Research Information System (SIRIS). Monument descriptions for United States National Parks are included.
AOP	Army of the Potomac. At Antietam, the Union (USA) army commanded by Gen. George B. McClellan. 87,000 AOP soldiers fought at Antietam Creek, Sharpsburg, Maryland.
ANB	Antietam National Battlefield.
ANV	Army of Northern Virginia. At Antietam, the Confederate (CSA) army commanded by Gen. Robert E. Lee. 45,000 ANV soldiers fought at Antietam Creek, Sharpsburg, Maryland.
Army	A military organization that is composed of corps. An army contains corps made up of divisions organized by brigade. Two armies fought at Antietam, the AOP and the ANV.
Artillery	Large-caliber, mounted guns often called cannons or ordnance weapons. Or, a military unit responsible for the operation, storage, and maintenance of large-caliber arms. Artillery units comprise one of three branches of an army, along with cavalry and infantry units.
Battalion	A battalion is similar to a regiment but smaller in size. Whereas a fully staffed regiment consists of ten companies, a battalion is four to eight companies. Artillery units are often battalions.

Term	Definition
Battery	An artillery unit that consists of four to six cannons and 100+ soldiers, called gunners.
Bicycle Cue	Bicycling directions formatted as text and often abbreviated for quick reading while riding a bicycle.
Border State	A state where slavery existed and yet the state government did not secede from the Union (Delaware, Kentucky, Maryland, and Missouri). Enslaved people in border states were exempt from President Abraham Lincoln's Emancipation Proclamation because those state governments were not at war with the Union.
Brigade	An infantry brigade consisted of four to six regiments, for a theoretical total of about 4,000 soldiers, although the numbers declined under the cumulative losses of each Civil War battle. Brigades were grouped into divisions. Generally, colonels or brigadier generals led infantry brigades. At Antietam, colonels and majors led AOP cavalry brigades attached to a single cavalry division (Alfred Pleasonton); and brigadier generals typically led ANV cavalry brigades attached to a single cavalry division (J.E.B. Stuart). At Antietam, captains often led AOP artillery brigades attached to divisions, whereas majors typically led ANV artillery brigades attached to divisions.
Caisson	An open horse-drawn carriage with two wheels that carries an ammunition chest.
Cannon	Also called a "gun," a large, heavy weapon that is mounted on wheels and manned by artillery units. Many types of cannons were used during the Civil War, including "Napoleon," Howitzer, Parrott rifle, and Ordnance rifle cannons.
Casualty	Killed, wounded, missing (or captured). According to American Battlefield Trust, the Battle of Antietam

Term	Definition
	produced 22,717 casualties and was the bloodiest day in U.S. military history. By the end of the war, there were 642,427 USA and 483,026 CSA casualties, categorized as follows: killed in action (110,100 and 94,000), wounded (275,174 and 194,026), diseased (224,580 and 164,000), and captured (30,192 and 31,000).[147]
Colors	A regimental flag that is carried into battle for the purpose of keeping a unit together during the chaos of battle. Also a symbol of regimental pride, the loss of one's colors was considered a disgrace (and the capture of an enemy flag was an honor).
Commander	A general term for an officer who leads a military unit.
Company	The smallest military unit, no larger than about 100 soldiers. Battlefield losses account for widely varying regimental sizes during the course of the war. Companies are identified by letter, A-K (omitting J). Usually commanded by captains, companies are grouped into regiments.
Corps	The highest level of military organization in an army, theoretically about 36,000 soldiers. A corps is composed of divisions. At Antietam, the AOP corps commanders were Maj. Gens. Hooker (1st corps), Sumner (2nd), Porter (5th), Franklin (6th), Burnside (9th), Mansfield (12th). The ANV corps commanders were Maj. Gens. Longstreet and Jackson.
CSA	Confederate States of America, also known as the Confederacy. The confederation of states that seceded from the United States of America. Jefferson Davis was President of the CSA.
Division	The second highest military unit, the building blocks of corps, theoretically about 12,000 soldiers.

Term	Definition
	The size of a division can vary widely over time and between armies. Divisions are composed of brigades. Divisions are led by major generals or brigadier generals, and are identified by number in the AOP, e.g., 1st Division (Doubleday) 1st Corps (Hooker), and by name in the ANV, e.g., McLaws' Division of Longstreet's Corps. At Antietam, both armies grouped cavalry together into a single division, whereas each division had its own artillery unit.
Federal	Referring to the government, laws, or armies of the United States of America. During the United States Civil War, federal troops represented the North in the conflict between North and South.
Flank	The end or side of a military line. For example, at Antietam, Maj. Gen. Thomas Jackson held the Confederate left flank and Maj. Gen., James Longstreet, the right flank. "Right" and "left" are used with respect to the army's orientation, which explains why the Confederate "right" was the Union "left," and vice versa.
ANB	Antietam National Battlefield was established on August 30, 1890. Battlefield management was transferred from the U.S. War Department to the NPS assumed in 1933.
GPS	Global Positioning System. A space-based navigation system that identifies locations in terms of longitude and latitude. GPS coordinates can be captured by GPS devices, including many cell phones.
HQ	Headquarters.
LCS	List of Classified Structures. A database of historic structures in United States National Parks. The database is maintained by the NPS.

Term	Definition
Minié ball	Named after inventor Claude-Étienne Minié, a grooved bullet that is loaded into a rifle's muzzle. The minié ball was the most common bullet used during the Civil War. Made of lead, the bullet turns white when it rusts.
NPS	National Park Service. An organization within the United States government that manages Antietam National Battlefield and the C&O Canal.
Order of Battle	An army's battle roster, including a listing of all military units deployed and their commanders.
Regiment	A military unit typically commanded by colonels, a regiment consists of about ten companies or about 1,000 soldiers (theoretically) when initially formed. Regiments are grouped into brigades. At Antietam, a Union regiment averaged 350 men, whereas a Confederate regiment consisted of about 200 men.[148]
Segment Map	In this book, a detailed map that is part of a bicycle route. Segment names are arbitrarily identified with a capital letter.
SIRIS	Smithsonian Institution Research Information System (owns the Art Inventories Catalog, or AIC).
USA	United States of America, or the Union. Abraham Lincoln was President of the USA from 1861–65.

Bibliography

This bibliography describes additional resources that you may want to consult while planning your tour. The references are categorized as follows: United States Civil War; Battle of Antietam (Sharpsburg); Civil War Maryland; and Tourism.

United States Civil War

Catton, Bruce. *The Civil War*. New York: Houghton Mifflin, 2005.

Davis, William C. *The Civil War: National Park Civil War Series*. Hatboro, PA: Eastern National, 2007.

McPherson, James M., ed. *The Atlas of the Civil War*. Philadelphia, PA: Running Press Book Publishers, 2010.

———. *Battle Cry of Freedom: The Civil War Era*. New York: Oxford University Press, 1988.

United States War Department. *The War of Rebellion: A Compilation of the Official Records of the Union and Confederate Armies*. Washington, DC: Government Printing Office, 1889.

Battle of Antietam (Sharpsburg)

Alexander, Ted. *The Battle of Antietam: The Bloodiest Day*. Charleston, SC: History Press, 2011.

Bailey, Ronald H., and Time-Life Books, eds. *The Bloodiest Day: The Battle of Antietam.* Alexandria, VA: Time-Life Books, 1984.

Banks, John. *Connecticut Yankees at Antietam.* Charleston, SC: History Press, 2013.

Carman, E.A. and E.B. Cope. *Atlas of the Battlefield of Antietam*. Washington, DC: Antietam Battlefield Board, 1908. https://www.loc.gov/item/2008621532/.

Carman, Ezra A. *The Maryland Campaign of September 1862, Volume II: Antietam*. Edited and annotated by Thomas G. Clemens. El Dorado Hills, CA: Savas Beatie, 2012.

Downey, Brian. *Antietam on the Web.* antietam.aotw.org.

Ernst, Kathleen A. *Too Afraid to Cry: Maryland Civilians in the Antietam Campaign*. Mechanicsburg, PA: Stackpole Books, 1999.

Frassanito, William A. *Antietam: The Photographic Legacy of America's Bloodiest Day*. New York: Charles Scribner's Sons, 1978.

Frye, Dennis E. *Antietam Revealed.* Collingswood, NJ: C.W. Historicals, 2004.

Gallagher, Gary W., ed. *The Antietam Campaign.* Chapel Hill: University of North Carolina Press, 1999.

———. *Antietam: Essays on the 1862 Maryland Campaign*. Kent, OH: Kent State University Press, 1989.

Gindlesperger, James, and Suzanne Gindlesperger. *So You Think You Know Antietam? The Stories Behind America's Bloodiest Day*. Winston-Salem, NC: John F. Blair Publisher, 2012.

Gottfried, Bradley M. *The Maps of Antietam.* El Dorado Hills, CA: Savas Beatie, 2012.

Harsh, Joseph L. *Sounding the Shallows: A Confederate Companion for the Maryland Campaign of 1862.* Kent, OH: Kent State University Press, 2000.

———. *Taken at the Flood: Robert E. Lee and Confederate Strategy in the Maryland Campaign of 1862.* Kent, OH: Kent State University Press, 1999.

Hartwig, D. Scott. *To Antietam Creek: The Maryland Campaign of September 1862.* Baltimore: Johns Hopkins University Press, 2012.

Hoptak, John David, and Keith B. Snyder. *The Battle of Antietam: September 17, 1862.* [Sharpsburg, MD?]: Western Maryland Interpretive Association, n.d.

Johnson, Curt, and Richard C. Anderson. *Artillery Hell: The Employment of Artillery at Antietam*. College Station: Texas A&M University Press, 1995.

Kalasky, Robert J. *Shadows of Antietam.* Kent, OH: Kent State University Press, 2012.

Large, George R., and Joe A. Swisher. *Battle of Antietam: The Official History by the Antietam Battlefield Board*. Shippensburg, PA: Burd Street Press, 1998.

Luvaas, Jay, and Harold W. Nelson, eds. *Guide to the Battle of Antietam: The Maryland Campaign of 1862*. Lawrence: University Press of Kansas, 1987.

McGrath, Thomas A. *Maryland September: True Stories from the Antietam Campaign.* Gettysburg, PA: Thomas Publications, 1997.

McPherson, James M. *Crossroads of Freedom: Antietam*. New York: Oxford University Press, 2002.

Mingus, Scott L., Sr. *Human Interest Stories from Antietam.* Orrtanna, PA: Colecraft Industries, 2007.

Murfin, James V. *The Gleam of Bayonets: The Battle of Antietam and Robert E. Lee's Maryland Campaign, September 1862.* Baton Rouge: Louisiana State University Press, 1993.

National Park Service. *Antietam National Battlefield*. nps.gov/anti.

Orrison, Robert, and Kevin R. Pawlak. *To Hazard All: A Guide to the Maryland Campaign, 1862.* El Dorado Hills, CA: Savas Beatie, 2018.

Pawlak, Kevin R. *Images of America: Antietam National Battlefield.* Charleston, SC: Arcadia Publishing, 2019.

Priest, John Michael. *Antietam: The Soldiers' Battle*. Shippensburg, PA: White Mane Books, 1989.

———. *Antietam: The Soldiers' Battlefield; A Self-Guided Mini-Tour*. Shippensburg, PA: White Mane Publishing, 1994.

Rafuse, Ethan S. *Antietam, South Mountain and Harpers Ferry: A Battlefield Guide*. Lincoln: University of Nebraska Press, 2008.

Reardon, Carol, and Tom Vossler. *A Field Guide to Antietam*. Chapel Hill: University of North Carolina Press, 2016.

Schildt, John W. *Hail to the Chief: Presidential Visits to Antietam*. Chewsville, MD: John W. Schildt, 2002.

———. *Monuments at Antietam*. Chewsville, MD: Antietam Publications, 1991.

Sears, Stephen W. *Landscape Turned Red: The Battle of Antietam.* Boston: Houghton Mifflin, 1983.

Stahl, Joseph, and Matthew Borders. *Faces of Union Soldiers at Antietam.* Charleston, SC: History Press, 2019.

Stotelmyer, Steven R. *Too Useful to Sacrifice: Reconsidering George B. McClellan's Generalship.* El Dorado Hills, CA: Savas Beatie, 2019.

Tilberg, Frederick. *Antietam*. Washington, DC: National Park Service, 1994.

Time-Life Books, eds. *Antietam: Voices of the Civil War.* Alexandria, VA: Time-Life Books, 1996.

Trail, Susan W. "Remembering Antietam: Commemoration and Preservation of a Civil War Battlefield." PhD diss., University of Maryland, 2005.

Vermilya, Daniel J. *That Field of Blood: The Battle of Antietam.* El Dorado Hills, CA: Savas Beatie, 2018.

Walker, Keven M., and K.C. Kirkman. *Antietam Farmsteads: A Guide to the Battlefield Landscape*. Sharpsburg, MD: Western Maryland Interpretive Association, 2010.

Civil War Maryland

Baker, Jean H. *The Politics of Continuity: Maryland Political Parties from 1859–1870.* Baltimore: Johns Hopkins University Press, 1973.

Bockmiller, Stephen R. *Hagerstown in the Civil War.* Images of America. Charleston, SC: Arcadia Publishing, 2011.

———. *Washington County in the Civil War*. Images of America. Charleston, SC: Arcadia Publishing, 2016.

Cottom, Robert I., Jr., and Mary Ellen Hayward. *Maryland in the Civil War: A House Divided.* Baltimore: Maryland Historical Society, 1994.

Cox, Richard P. *Civil War Maryland: Stories from the Old Line State.* Charleston, SC: History Press, 2008.

Fields, Barbara Jeanne. *Slavery and Freedom on the Middle Ground: Maryland during the Nineteenth Century*. New Haven, CT: Yale University Press, 1985.

Floyd, Claudia. *Maryland Women in the Civil War: Unionists, Rebels, Slaves and Spies*. Charleston, SC: History Press, 2013.

———. *Union-Occupied Maryland: A Civil War Chronicle of Civilians and Soldiers.* Charleston, SC: History Press, 2014.

Hedberg, Jacqueline Simmons. *Plantations, Slavery and Freedom on Maryland's Eastern Shore*. Charleston, SC: History Press, 2019.

Jacobs, Charles T. *The Civil War Guide to Montgomery County, Maryland.* Rockville, MD: Montgomery County Historical Society, 1996. First published 1983.

Mitchell, Charles W., ed. *Maryland Voices of the Civil War.* Baltimore: Johns Hopkins University Press, 2007.

Schildt, John W. *Frederick in the Civil War: Battle and Honor in the Spired City.* Charleston, SC: History Press, 2010.

Snyder, Timothy R. *Trembling in the Balance: The Chesapeake and Ohio Canal During the Civil War*. Boston: Blue Mustang Press, 2011.

Soderberg, Susan Cooke. *A Guide to Civil War Sites in Maryland: Blue and Gray in a Border State.* Shippensburg, PA: White Mane Books, 1998.

Swank, Mark A., and Dreama J. Swank. *Maryland in the Civil War.* Images of America. Charleston, SC: Arcadia Publishing, 2013.

Toomey, Daniel Carroll. *The Civil War in Maryland.* 4th ed. Baltimore: Toomey Press, 1990.

Tourism

Auto Tours

Blue and Gray Magazine. *History and Tour Guide of the Antietam Battlefield*. Columbus, OH: Blue and Gray Enterprises, 1995.

Luvaas, Jay, and Harold W. Nelson. *Guide to the Battle of Antietam: The Maryland Campaign of 1862*. Lawrence: University Press of Kansas, 1987.

Orrison, Robert, and Kevin R. Pawlak. *To Hazard All: A Guide to the Maryland Campaign, 1862*. El Dorado Hills, CA: Savas Beatie, 2018.

Parzych, Cynthia. *Antietam: A Guided Tour Through History*. Guilford, CT: Morris Book Publishing, 2009.

Priest, John Michael. *Antietam: The Soldiers' Battlefield; A Self-Guided Mini Tour*. Shippensburg, PA: White Mane Publishing, 1994.

Rafuse, Ethan S. *Antietam, South Mountain and Harpers Ferry: A Battlefield Guide*. Lincoln: University of Nebraska Press, 2008.

Readon, Carol, and Tom Vossler. *A Field Guide to Antietam*. Chapel Hill: University of North Carolina Press, 2016.

TravelBrains. *Antietam Expedition Guide*. N.p.: TravelBrains, 2004.

Hiking & Biking

Broadwell, Larry. *Hiker's Guide to Civil War Trails in the Mid-Atlantic Region*. Vienna, VA: Potomac Appalachian Trail Club, 2015.

Hahn, Thomas F. *Towpath Guide to the C&O Canal*. Harpers Ferry, WV: Harpers Ferry Historical Association, 2015.

High, Mike. *The C&O Canal Companion: A Journey through Potomac History*. 2nd ed. Baltimore: Johns Hopkins University Press, 2015.

Joyner, Leanna. *Hiking through History: Civil War Sites on the Appalachian Trail*. Harpers Ferry, WV: Appalachian Trail Conservancy, 2015.

Shelton, Napier. *Potomac Pathway: A Nature Guide to the C&O Canal*. Atglen, PA: Schiffer Publishing, 2011.

Snyder, Keith. *Antietam Remembered: A Walking Tour*. [Sharpsburg, MD?]: Western Maryland Interpretative Association, n.d.

———. *Bloody Lane Trail*. Ibid.

———. *The Cornfield Trail*. Ibid.

———. *The Final Attack Trail: September Harvest of Death*. Ibid.

———. *Union Advance Trail*. Ibid.

———. *West Woods Trail*. Ibid.

TrailGuide: Official Guide to the C&O Canal Towpath and the Great Allegheny Passage. 16th ed. Homestead, PA: Great Allegheny Press, 2020.

Trailhead Graphics. *Battlefield America: Antietam National Battlefield*. Civil War Map Series. Aurora, CO: Trailhead Graphics, 2012.

———. *Civil War Campaigns Across the Potomac*. Civil War Battlefield Series. Aurora, CO: Trailhead Graphics, 2006.

U.S. Department of the Interior. *Chesapeake and Ohio Canal: Official National Park Handbook; 142*. Washington, DC: U.S. Department of the Interior, 1991.

Notes

ABBREVIATIONS:

ABT	American Battlefield Trust	LCS	List of Classified Structures
AIC	Art Inventories Catalog	NPS	National Park Service
ANB	Antietam National Battlefield	OR	Official Records

SIRIS Smithsonian Institution Research Information System
U.S. Postal Abbreviations

For brevity when referencing a SIRIS AIC record, these notes identify records by Control Number. For web access to a record, substitute the Control Number for the "X" in this template:
https://siris-artinventories.si.edu/ipac20/ipac.jsp?term=X&index=.NW.

Similarly, when referencing the NPS LCS record, these notes identify records by Record Number (then Structure Number) for a search on Antietam structures, e.g., "LCS 491, 115A." For web access to a record, substitute the Record Number for the "X" in this template, e.g., "491":
https://hscl.cr.nps.gov/insidenps/report.asp?PARK=ANTI&RECORDNO=X.
Note, however, that in 2020 the NPS moved the LCS to the Cultural Resources Inventory System (CRIS) at https://apps.cr.nps.gov/CRIS. As of this writing, the Internet Archive Wayback Machine caches LCS data, here:
https://web.archive.org/web/20120528104835/http://www.hscl.cr.nps.gov/insidenps/summary.asp.

All web links were accessed July 14, 2020.

1. In 1862 the Battle of Antietam covered about 7,680 acres (twelve square miles), nearly three times the acreage of today's battlefield park. On August 30, 1890, the U.S. Congress approved funding for the purchase of land on which military positions and battle lines could be marked on the Antietam battlefield. To complete that work effort, the U.S. Secretary of War created the Antietam Battlefield Board, a group of Union and Confederate veterans. The board managed about twenty-two acres and five miles of roads in 1898, when the U.S. War Department took control. Then in 1933, President Roosevelt issued an executive order to transfer management of Antietam National Battlefield (and other Civil War sites) to the NPS. George R. Large and Joe A. Swisher, *Battle of Antietam: The Official History by the Antietam Battlefield Board* (Shippensburg, PA: Burd Street Press, 1998), 195.

2. According to the ABT, about 132,000 soldiers fought at the Battle of Antietam (also called the Battle of Sharpsburg): 87,000 under Gen. George B. McClellan (West Point Class of 1846), Army of the Potomac; and 45,000 under Gen. Robert E. Lee (West Point Class of 1829), Army of Northern Virginia. ABT, "Antietam," https://www.battlefields.org/learn/civil-war/battles/antietam. For a classic numerical study, see Ezra A. Carman, "Strength of the Union and Confederate Armies Engaged at Antietam, September 17, 1862," Appendix 2 in *The Maryland Campaign of September 1862, Volume II: Antietam*, ed. and ann. by Thomas G. Clemens (El Dorado Hills, CA: Savas Beatie, 2012), 569–600.

For an Order of Battle that includes regimental officers, see Carman, "Organization of the Union and Confederate Armies in the Maryland Campaign of September 1862," Appendix 1, 521–68. Also, James V. Murfin, "Organization of the Union and Confederate Armies at the Battle of Antietam (Sharpsburg), September 17, 1862," Appendix C in *The Gleam of Bayonets: The Battle of Antietam and Robert E. Lee's Maryland Campaign, September 1862* (Baton Rouge: Louisiana State University Press, 1993), 343–373. The NPS Antietam website includes Orders of Battle for Gen. McClellan's army, https://www.nps.gov/anti/learn/historyculture/army-of-potomac.htm, and Gen. Lee's army, https://www.nps.gov/anti/learn/historyculture/army-n-virginia.htm.

3. The ABT reports 22,717 Antietam casualties. Although seven other Civil War battles had higher overall casualties, no battle had as many casualties *in one day* as the Battle of Antietam. The top-ten battles ranked by total casualties (killed, wounded, captured or missing) are as follows:

1. 51,000 casualties – Gettysburg (July 1–3, 1863)
2. 34,624 casualties – Chickamauga (September 19–20, 1863)
3. 30,000 casualties – Spotsylvania Court House (May 8–21, 1864)
4. 29,800 casualties – The Wilderness (May 5–7, 1864)
5. 24,000 casualties – Chancellorsville (April 30–May 6, 1863)
6. 23,746 casualties – Shiloh (April 6–7, 1862)
7. 23,515 casualties – Stones River (December 31, 1862–January 2, 1863)
8. 22,717 casualties – Antietam (September 17, 1862)
9. 22,180 casualties – Second Manassas (August 28–30, 1862)
10. 19,233 casualties – Siege of Vicksburg (May 18–July 4, 1863)

ABT, "Civil War Facts," https://www.battlefields.org/learn/articles/civil-war-facts.

Based on reports from Gens. McClellan and Lee, James V. Murfin estimated 22,701 Antietam casualties (12,410 Union and 10,291 Confederate). James V. Murfin, *The Gleam of Bayonets*, 297–98. Stephen W. Sears estimated 22,719 Antietam casualties (12,401 Union and 10,318 Confederate). Stephen W. Sears, *Landscape Turned Red: The Battle of Antietam* (Boston: Houghton Mifflin, 1983), 296. Sears' count is very close to Carman, which is 22,717 Antietam casualties (12,401 Union and 10,316 Confederate). Carman, "Casualties in the Union and Confederate Armies at the Battle of Antietam (Sharpsburg), September 17, 1862," Appendix 3, 601–20. Finally, Thomas Leonard Livermore recorded 26,134 Antietam casualties (12,410 Union and 13,724 Confederate). Thomas Leonard Livermore, *Numbers and Losses in the Civil War in America 1861–65* (New York: Houghton, Mifflin and Co., 1901), 92.

4. President Lincoln's Emancipation Proclamation did not free 450,000 enslaved people living in Maryland, Delaware, Kentucky, and Missouri—known as Union "border states"—because their state governments did not secede from the Union. Nor did the proclamation free more than 300,000 people living in Union-occupied parts of some southern states, i.e., Tennessee. Eric Foner, *Reconstruction: America's Unfinished Revolution: 1863–1877* (New York: History Book Club, 1988), 1. For an accessible introduction to the argument that Maryland was "not allowed to secede," see Richard P. Cox, "Brother Against Brother," in *Civil War Maryland: Stories from the Old Line State* (Charleston, SC: History Press, 2008), 37–44. Also, Claudia Floyd, *Union-Occupied Maryland: A Civil War Chronicle of Civilians and Soldiers* (Charleston, SC: History Press, 2014). Jean H. Baker, *The Politics of Continuity: Maryland Political Parties from 1858 to 1870* (Baltimore: Johns Hopkins University Press, 1973). For a description of how western Maryland wrestled with the issue of slavery in 1862, see Kathleen A. Ernst, "When That Time Comes, All Hearts and Hands Will Unite," in *Too Afraid to Cry: Maryland Civilians in the Antietam Campaign* (Mechanicsburg, PA: Stackpole Books, 1999), 225–241.

Enslaved Marylanders were not officially free until Maryland passed a new state constitution in November, 1864, that prohibited slavery. For context, in 1860 Maryland's population was 515,918 "white" (75%); 83,942 "free black" (12%); and 87,189 "slave" (13%). See Jacqueline Simmons Hedberg, *Plantations, Slavery and Freedom on Maryland's Eastern Shore* (Charleston, SC: History Press, 2019), 123. For an insightful study of Maryland history on the topic of slavery, see Barbara Jeanne Fields, *Slavery and Freedom on the Middle Ground: Maryland during the Nineteenth Century* (New Haven, CT: Yale University Press, 1985). More broadly, and with greater emphasis on a history that begins with Lincoln's Gettysburg Address, see David W. Blight, *Race and Reunion: The Civil War in American Memory* (Cambridge, MA: Harvard University Press, 2001).

5. ABT, "Antietam," https://www.battlefields.org/learn/civil-war/battles/antietam. Total Killed: 3,654 (2,108 Union and 1,556 Confederate). Total Wounded: 17,292 (9,540 Union and 7,752 Confederate). Total Missing/Captured: 1,771 (753 Union and 1,018 Confederate). Total Casualties: 22,717 (12,401 Union and 10,316 Confederate). The NPS has posted slightly different counts, but these appear to be "rounded." See NPS, https://www.nps.gov/anti/learn/historyculture/casualties.htm. John Michael Priest collected brigade-level troop strengths and casualty counts in an

appendix to: John Michael Priest, *Antietam: The Soldiers' Battle* (Shippensburg, PA: White Mane Books, 1989).

6. There were nearly 2,600 Confederate and 3,000 Union casualties in the area around The Sunken Road. "Many Confederate casualties occurred not in The Sunken Road itself, but on the high ground south of the road. This resulted as the retiring Confederates were exposed to a murderous infantry fire from Union regiments on the paralleling ridge north of the road—some 200 yards distant." Dennis E. Frye, *Antietam Revealed* (Collingswood, NJ: C.W. Historicals, 2004), 109, 113.

7. Gen. Hooker's division consisted of about 8,600 men. His opponent, Gen. Jackson, had about 7,700 men. Frye, 76. With respect to artillery, Hooker's Union infantry was supported by thirty twenty-pounder Parrott rifles posted on the east bank of Antietam Creek. These guns had a superior firing range (3,000–3,500 yards) to anything that Jackson could field that day. Jackson's Confederate infantry was supported by Col. Stephen D. Lee's four batteries across from the Dunker Church, plus J.E.B. Stuart's horse artillery posted on Nicodemus Heights. Frye, 77–8.

8. See this book's bibliography for a listing of notable auto tours, 182.

9. In Map 1, most towns east of the Monocacy River and north of the Potomac River are in Montgomery County. Confederate and Union forces marched through this area or skirmished while maneuvering to fight according to the objectives of a larger campaign in 1862 (Maryland), 1863 (Gettysburg), or 1864 (Raid on Washington). For an interesting collection of stories associated with these marches and skirmishes, see Charles T. Jacobs, *Civil War Guide to Montgomery County, Maryland*, rev. ed. (1983; Rockville, MD: Montgomery County Historical Society, 1996). For a similar but larger geographic listing by town, see Susan Cooke Soderberg, *A Guide to Civil War Sites in Maryland: Blue and Gray in a Border State* (Shippensburg, PA: White Mane Books, 1998). For a similar but larger chronological listing by town, see Daniel Carroll Toomey, *The Civil War in Maryland*, 4th ed. (Baltimore: Toomey Press, 1990). For a listing of Maryland markers that include Civil War sites by county, see Joe A. Swisher and Roger Miller, *The Complete Guide to Maryland Historic Markers* (Baltimore: Image Publishing, 1996). Finally, for an excellent series of Civil War history articles about the C&O Canal, see the quarterly newsletter of the C&O Canal Association, *Along the Towpath* (2007–18), http://www.candocanal.org/articles/civwr0.html.

10. For an advanced but accessible study in geology, see John Means, *Roadside Geology of Maryland, Delaware, and Washington, DC* (Missoula, MT: Mountain Press Publishing, 2010). The section on "Maryland 34, Boonsboro—Sharpsburg," 90–92, briefly describes the geological rationale for Gen. Lee's decision to form his battle line in the Hagerstown Valley (because South Mountain protected Lee on his eastern side). It also discusses how the Elbrook Formation of layered limestone, shale, and

dolomite in the Burnside Bridge area may have contributed to a higher battle casualty rate than the more evenly weathered limestone layer of the Conococheague Formation in The Cornfield.

11. The 1863 Gettysburg Campaign was the second Confederate invasion into northern states. The third invasion was the 1864 Raid on Washington (by Maj. Gen. Jubal Early).

12. Mike High, *The C&O Canal Companion: A Journey through Potomac History*, 2nd ed. (Baltimore: Johns Hopkins University Press, 2015), 26–27. White's Ford is at C&O Canal mile point 38.9 and Cheek's Ford is farther north at mile point 43.6. On September 5 and 9, 1862, Confederate soldiers tried but failed to destroy the Monocacy Aqueduct at mile point 42.2. Gen. Robert E. Lee's Army of Northern Virginia retreated back to Virginia after the Battle of Antietam, crossing the Potomac River at Boteler's (Packhorse) Ford at mile point 71.4, about one mile south of Shepherdstown.

13. Frederick has a rich Civil War history and is home to the National Museum of Civil War Medicine at 48 East Patrick Street. See National Museum of Civil War Medicine, *Walking Tour of Wartime Frederick* (Frederick, MD: printed by author, 2016). John W. Schildt, *Frederick in the Civil War: Battle and Honor in the Spired City* (Charleston, SC: History Press, 2010). More broadly, for an interesting essay on why Confederate leaders considered Maryland a southern state in September, 1862, see William A. Blair, "Maryland, Our Maryland," in *The Antietam Campaign*, ed. Gary W. Gallagher (Chapel Hill: University of North Carolina Press, 1999), 74–100.

14. For a study of the Battle of South Mountain, see John David Hoptak, *The Battle of South Mountain* (Charleston, SC: History Press, 2011). Ethan S. Rafuse, *Antietam, South Mountain and Harpers Ferry: A Battlefield Guide* (Lincoln: University of Nebraska Press, 2008). For Harpers Ferry, see Chester G. Hearn, *Six Years of Hell: Harpers Ferry During the Civil War* (Baton Rouge: Louisiana State University Press, 1996).

15. ABT, "South Mountain: Crampton's, Turner's and Fox's Gaps," https://www.battlefields.org/learn/civil-war/battles/south-mountain. Forces engaged: 46,000 (28,000 Union and 18,000 Confederate). Casualties: 5,010 (2,325 Union and 2,685 Confederate). During the Battle of South Mountain, Gen. Lee's Army of Northern Virginia was divided. Maj. Gen. James Longstreet's division was in western Maryland, and Maj. Gen. "Stonewall" Jackson's division was in Harper's Ferry, (West) Virginia.

16. See this book's bibliography for resources on hiking trails associated with the 1862 Maryland Campaign near ANB, 183.

17. A modest monument on the north side of West Main Street and east of General Lee Drive marks Gen. Lee's headquarters. See Map 16 on p. 79, and look for the NPS plot on Shepherdstown Pike. The West Virginia Division of the United Daughters of the Confederacy funded the monument, which was dedicated on the seventy-fourth anniversary of the Battle of Antietam

(September 17, 1936). Modern-day Civil War atlases mark the same location as Map 16. For example, see James M. McPherson, *The Atlas of the Civil War* (Philadelphia, PA: Pepperbox Press, 2010), 80–81. However, according to S.G. Elliott's 1864 map, Gen. Lee's headquarters was farther to the southwest, on the property of S.P. Groves. See S.G. Elliott, "Map of the battlefield of Antietam," 1864, Lionel Pincus and Princess Firyal Map Division, The New York Public Library, New York Public Library Digital Collections, http://digitalcollections.nypl.org/items/185f8270-0834-0136-3daa-6d29ad33124f.

Gen. McClellan established his headquarters at the Pry family house and barn, now the Pry House Field Hospital Museum, 18906 Shepherdstown Pike. From this location in the winter, facing west, you can see the Samuel Mumma farm to the south (your left) and the Samuel Poffenberger farm to the north (your right); about mid-way between those two points is the D.R. Miller farm. The Pry House Field Hospital Museum opened in 2006 under the sponsorship of the National Museum of Civil War Medicine and NPS management. The museum is an easy 3.5-mile car ride from ANB. For hours of operation, see https://www.civilwarmed.org/pry. For a short but interesting introduction to the history of the Pry House, see National Museum of Civil War Medicine, "About the Pry House," https://www.civilwarmed.org/pry/about-the-pry-house. Although the National Museum of Civil War Medicine is about twenty-five highway miles from ANB, you may want to extend your Civil War tour to include a visit to 48 East Patrick Street, Frederick. For more information, see https://www.civilwarmed.org.

18. Clara Barton, "The Women Who Went to the Field," 1892, quoted by the ABT, https://www.battlefields.org/learn/primary-sources/women-who-went-field.

19. According to Frye, the D.R. Miller cornfield covered 30 acres, and mature corn at that time generally did not exceed a height of 6.5 feet, with stalks spaced about 3 feet apart. Frye, 75. The quote by Gen. Hooker is from the NPS Antietam website. NPS, "Tour Stop 4–The Cornfield," https://www.nps.gov/anti/learn/photosmultimedia/tour-stop-4.htm.

20. At the Battle of Antietam, between 286–302 Union guns were engaged and manned by 57 batteries. Of the Union total, there were 108 twelve-pounder Napoleons (accurate for up to one mile, and very deadly when firing canister at short range); 42 long-range rifled guns; and 30 ten- and twenty-pounder Parrott rifles. Ted Alexander, *The Battle of Antietam: The Bloodiest Day* (Charleston, SC: History Press, 2011), 36. On the Confederate side, about 246 guns were engaged and manned by 59 batteries. Of the Confederate total, there were 41 Model 1841 six-pounders; 27 twelve-pounder Napoleons; and 4 twenty-pounder and 36 ten-pounder Parrott rifles. Alexander, 37.

21. For a description of the works of mercy and battlefield cleanup by Sharpsburg's civilian population, see Ted Alexander, "One Vast Hospital," in

The Battle of Antietam, 100–113. Alexander includes a map by Steven Stanley that identifies the locations of twenty-one Union field hospitals in the Sharpsburg area. For a discussion of field hospitals in Shepherdstown, see Kevin R. Pawlak, *Shepherdstown in the Civil War: One Vast Confederate Hospital* (Charleston, SC: History Press, 2015).

22. According to the NPS, the selection of marble for the Barton monument is "thought to symbolize Barton's 'rock-like' qualities in treating the wounded." Gen. Alfred M. Gruenther, National Chairman of the American Red Cross, dedicated the monument on September 9, 1962, as part of the Civil War Centennial Commemoration. Clara Barton Monument, LCS 491, 115A.

The leftmost monument in the photo is the 7th PA Reserves Monument. The monument was dedicated on September 16, 1906, and marks the location from which the regiment marched about 600 yards south to fight Brig. Gen. John Bell Hood's Confederates in The Cornfield. The 7th PA Reserves was also known as the 36th PA Infantry regiment. Pennsylvania formed reserve regiments whenever its enlistment quota had already been met. But when the state called a reserve regiment to duty, the regiment received a new regimental number that was twenty-nine more than its reserve number (e.g., the 7th reserves regiment became the 36th regiment).

23. In 1862, Maryland Route 34 was called Shepherdstown Road (or "Pike") from Sharpsburg west to Shepherdstown. It was called Boonsboro Road (or "Pike") from Sharpsburg east to Boonsboro. S.G. Elliott's 1864 map labels this the road to Boonsboro as "Sharpsburg Turnpike." See S.G. Elliott, "Map of the battlefield of Antietam."

24. In 1862, Maryland Route 65 (Sharpsburg Pike) was called Hagerstown Road (or "Pike," "Turnpike"). When the Antietam Battlefield Commission designed the park road network, they redirected Hagerstown Road around the west side of Dunker Church, and the road that passes the church on its east side was renamed Dunker Church Road.

25. The monument in the photo honors the 12th PA Cavalry, a little known regiment that at the Battle of Antietam served as an arm of the provost marshal ("military police"). The 12th PA Cavalry participated in battles and skirmishes throughout Maryland, including (according to the monument's inscription): Clarksburg, Sugar Loaf Mountain, Monocacy, South Mountain, Frederick, Maryland Heights, Sharpsburg (Antietam), Crampton's Pass, and Boonsboro. See Larry B. Maier, *Leather and Steel: The 12th Pennsylvania Cavalry in the Civil War* (Shippensburg, PA: Burd Street Press, 2001).

26. The NPS website cites ninety-six as the number of monuments at Antietam. NPS, "Antietam Monuments," https://www.nps.gov/anti/learn/historyculture/monuments.htm. However, differences in what constitutes a "monument" can result in different counts. For example, NPS Chief Historian

(Retired) Dennis E. Frye indicates that the NPS "counts 103 monuments on the battlefield," which includes "two pillars at the entrance to Philadelphia Brigade Park and two small directional markers on Branch Avenue." Frye, 168.

27. Sue Thibodeau, *Bicycling Gettysburg National Military Park: The Cyclist's Civil War Travel Guide* (Victor, NY: Civil War Cycling, 2019).

28. Although Civil War Cycling does not recommend using a GPS exclusively to bicycle Gettysburg National Military Park, GPS use is far more workable at Antietam National Battlefield. A Gettysburg tour requires frequent turns, as often as every few hundred yards, that force one's eyes off the road; but the Antietam road network is not nearly so complicated or as heavily trafficked. Intermittent cellular service can be a problem, however, so it is always a good idea to have a backup plan, like paper maps or PDFs that you can consult on your mobile device.

29. In this guidebook, "L" is an abbreviation for a canal lock, and "M" is a "mile point." You will see "MP" on other maps. For reference, the Sharpsburg area roughly extends north from M69.4 (Antietam Aqueduct) to Taylors Landing (M80.9). As of this writing, the NPS "Chesapeake and Ohio Canal" map of the entire 184.5-mile towpath is available for download, here: https://www.nps.gov/choh/planyourvisit/upload/CHOHmap-full-140922-v7-accessible.pdf

30. The name "Dunker" is a nickname associated with full immersion Christian baptism. At the beginning of the battle, the Confederates controlled the church and surrounding area. It was a tactical target for the Union army, sitting as it does on a ridge that advantages artillery fire. After the battle, the church functioned as an embalming station. In 1921, the Dunker Church was destroyed in a thunder storm, but enough of its foundation remained that in 1960, the State of Maryland gave money to the NPS to rebuild the church that you see today. Other sources use the name "Dunkard Church."

31. For basic information on Antietam National Battlefield, see the NPS website, www.nps.gov/anti/planyourvisit/basicinfo.htm.

32. Col. Ezra A. Carman (1834–1909) organized the 13th NJ Volunteer Infantry, Army of the Potomac, and fought with his regiment at the Battle of Antietam. In 1894 the Antietam Battlefield Board hired Carman as its expert historian.

33. NPS, "Artillery at Antietam," https://www.nps.gov/anti/learn/historyculture/arty.htm. This short article includes photos of four different types of cannons fired at the Battle of Antietam: 1841 Model Gun (smoothbore, six-pound projectiles, range up to 1,523 yards); 1857 Model Napoleon (smoothbore, twelve-pound projectiles, range up to 1,619 yards); Parrott rifle (ten-pound projectiles, range up to 1,900 yards); and 3-Inch Ordnance rifle (ten-pound projectiles, range of 1830 yards at 5-degree elevation). At Antietam, an army captain would lead an artillery battery that

consisted of about 70–100 artillerymen and 4–6 cannons. According to Frye, there were 293 Union cannons and 246 Confederate cannons (for a total of 539) at the Battle of Antietam. Frye, 71. Johnson credits Carman for the following numbers: 301 Union cannons and 219 Confederate cannons (for a total of 520). Curt Johnson and Richard C. Anderson, *Artillery Hell: The Employment of Artillery at Antietam* (College Station: Texas A&M University Press, 1995), 84, 102.

34. For the first-time visitor to Antietam National Battlefield, especially bicyclists who may know very little about the battle, all military maps in this guidebook deliberately omit military detail. The maps intend to reduce the battle scene to the approximate positions of two armies—with blue blocks roughly corresponding to Union divisions and red blocks to Confederate divisions. Army divisions are not labeled in order to further emphasize that these military maps are impressionistic and designed for ease of learning while touring the park on a bicycle.

35. For a reference to the monuments at Antietam National Battlefield, see John W. Schildt, *Monuments at Antietam* (Chewsville, MD: Antietam Publications, 1991). James and Suzanne Gindlesperger, *So You Think You Know Antietam? The Stories Behind America's Bloodiest Day* (Winston-Salem, NC: John F. Blair Publisher, 2012). For a more general discussion of monuments at U.S. national military parks, see Denise D. Meringolo, *Museums, Monuments, and National Parks: Toward a New Genealogy of Public History* (Amherst, MA: University of Massachusetts Press, 2012). Timothy B. Smith, *The Golden Age of Preservation: The Decade of the 1890s and the Establishment of America's First Five Military Parks* (Knoxville, TN: University of Tennessee Press, 2008).

36. The NPS Order of Battle at https://www.nps.gov/anti/learn/historyculture/org-cht-12-corps.htm identifies the commander of the 3rd MD Infantry as "Joseph H. Sudbsurg," but Sudsburg's official report "concerning the action of the Third Maryland Regiment in the battle near Sharpsburg" has this closing: "J.M. SUDSBURG." See *OR* 19:1, 510–11.

37. Franklin D. Roosevelt, "Address at Antietam Battlefield, Maryland," September 17, 1937, online by Gerhard Peters and John T. Woolley, The American Presidency Project, https://www.presidency.ucsb.edu/node/208743.

38. John W. Schildt, "Hail to the Chief: Presidential Visits to Antietam" (Brunswick, MD: John W. Schildt, 2002). On the topic of presidential visits to Antietam (unless otherwise noted), Schildt is the primary source for information summarized in this guidebook.

39. NPS, "Presidential Visits to Antietam," https://www.nps.gov/anti/learn/historyculture/presidential-visits-to-antietam.htm. Grant's visit is not included in Schildt's listing.

40. There is no record that Maj. Gen. Joseph Hooker ordered his corps to attack Nicodemus Heights (and they did not).

41. Maj. Gen. J.E.B. Stuart commanded Gen. Lee's cavalry division at the Battle of Antietam. Stuart positioned Capt. John Pelham's horse artillery on Nicodemus Heights. For a comprehensive essay on the artillery on Nicodemus Heights, see Robert E. L. Krick, "Defending Lee's Flank," in *The Antietam Campaign*, ed. Gary W. Gallagher (Chapel Hill: University of North Carolina Press, 1999), 192–222.

42. The best printed study of Antietam farming households is Keven M. Walker and K.C. Kirkman, *Antietam Farmsteads: A Guide to the Battlefield Landscape* (Sharpsburg, MD: Western Maryland Interpretive Association, 2010). The Jacob Rohrbach Inn published an interesting web blog series called, "The Farmsteads at Antietam." The inn is located in downtown Sharpsburg (https://jacob-rohrbach-inn.com/the-inn/). It offers mountain bike rentals and a concierge service that, depending on your needs, may provide bike transportation or pickup.

43. Gary L. Miller, "Historical Natural History: Insects and the Civil War," Montana State University Entomology Group, http://www.montana.edu/historybug/civilwar2/buzz.html. Reprinted and adapted in part from G.L. Miller, "Historical Natural History: Insects and the Civil War," *American Entomologist*, 43 (1977): 227–245. The monument in the photo that stands in The Sunken Lane was dedicated to the 132nd PA regiment on September 17, 1904. It depicts a color bearer. AIC MD000376.

44. Walker and Kirkman, 83.

45. Steve A. Hawks, "Sherrick Farm," *Stone Sentinels: Antietam* (website), https://antietam.stonesentinels.com/places/sherrick-farm/.

46. Robert Gould Shaw, Shaw to Francis George Shaw, September 21, 1862, Letter. In *Blue-Eyed Child of Fortune: The Civil War Letters of Colonel Robert Gould Shaw*, ed. Russell Duncan (Athens: University of Georgia Press, 1992), 241. Less than one year after Capt. Shaw fought at Antietam, he was promoted to colonel of the first all-black regiment, the 54th MA Infantry. Shaw died leading his regiment in the federal attack on Fort Wagner near Charleston, South Carolina, July, 18, 1863.

47. A Hagerstown newspaper, *The Herald of Freedom and Torch Light*, reported the following: “From Hagerstown to the southern limits of the county wounded and dying soldiers are to be found in every neighborhood and in nearly every house. The whole region of country between Boonsboro and Sharpsburg is one vast hospital. ... In this town the Washington House, County Hall, and Lyceum Hall have been appropriated to the use of the wounded, and our citizens, especially the ladies, are untiring in their efforts to relieve them.” Quoted in https://www.nps.gov/anti/learn/historyculture/women-at-antietam.htm.

48. "Removal of Soldiers' Remains," *Alleghanian*, July 3, 1867, 3, compiled by William Bauman in "Canal Trade 1867," January, 2017, http://www.candocanal.org/histdocs/Newspapers-1867.pdf. The newspaper article indicates that the cargo of coffins arrived at Clarysville, Maryland from Washington, DC, via the C&O Canal.

49. The Private Soldier Monument, also known as "Old Simon," was the first monument to be dedicated on the Antietam battlefield. The sculptor, James W. Polette, was from Rhode Island. The sculpture was displayed at the Philadelphia Centennial in 1876 and later transported to Sharpsburg (from Washington, DC) via the C&O Canal. According to Frye, the sculpture weighs 250 tons and the entire monument (sculpture and pedestal) is 40.5 feet high. Frye, 168.

50. Even though Maryland was a Union "border state," the state owns the land in Hagerstown's Washington Confederate Cemetery. For background, it helps to remember which states seceded from the Union: South Carolina (December 20, 1860); Mississippi (January 9, 1861); Florida (January 10, 1861); Alabama (January 11, 1861); Georgia (January 19, 1861); Louisiana (January 26, 1861); Texas (February 1, 1861); Virginia (April 17, 1861); Arkansas (May 6, 1861); North Carolina (May 20, 1861); and Tennessee (June 8, 1861).

51. Elmwood Cemetery is a private cemetery in Shepherdstown, West Virginia. Most of the Confederate soldiers buried here had family roots in western Maryland and (West) Virginia. Col. Henry Kyd Douglas (staff officer for Maj. Gen. Thomas J. Jackson) fought at the Battle of Antietam and has a relatively large grave marker at Elmwood Cemetery. However, many of the Confederate men buried in the cemetery fought at other battles: Capt. Redmond Burke (a scout for J.E.B. Stuart); Lt. Andrew Leopold (a Virginia cavalryman who was hanged in 1864 "for shooting Union sympathizers at Shepherdstown"); Lt. William H. Hogan (a cavalry scout and courier); Alexander R. Boteler (staff officer for "Stonewall" Jackson and J.E.B. Stuart); Lt. Col. William F. Lee (mortally wounded at the Battle of First Manassas); Col. Isaac S. Tanner (surgeon); Col. William Augustine Morgan (Virginia cavalryman); Col. Isaac V. Johnson (Virginia infantryman); and Brig. Gen. William W. Kirkland (North Carolina infantryman). Elmwood Cemetery, http://elmwoodcemeteryshepwv.org/.

52. Washington Confederate Cemetery is part of Rose Hill Cemetery in Hagerstown, Maryland. In 1871, the State of Maryland purchased this land for the burial of Confederate soldiers who fought at the Battles of South Mountain and Antietam. Of the 2,468 Confederate soldiers buried here, 2,122 could not be identified. In 1877, Robert E. Lee's nephew, Fitzhugh Lee, gave a speech at the dedication of the nineteen-foot-high centerpiece statue, which symbolized Hope. Rose Hill Cemetery, "A Cemetery within a Cemetery," https://rosehillcemeteryofmd.org/rich-in-history/history-of-rose-hill/.

53. Mt. Olivet Cemetery is in Frederick, Maryland. Its Civil War graves include Union and Confederate burials from the Battles of Antietam, Gettysburg, and Monocacy. You can learn more about Civil War history by visiting the following graves: Barbara Fritchie, Gen. James Cooper, and the many graves along "Confederate Row." Mt. Olivet Cemetery, http://www.mountolivetcemeteryinc.com/.

54. Although Maryland never seceded from the Union, some of her citizens enlisted with Confederate regiments. At the Battle of Antietam, the following military units fought for the Army of the Potomac: 5th MD (Blumenberg), Weber's 3rd Brigade, French's 3rd Division, Sumner's 2nd Corps.; Battery A (Wolcott), MD Light Artillery, Slocum's 1st Division, Franklin's 6th Corps; Battery B (Vanneman), MD Light Artillery, Smith's 2nd Division, Franklin's 6th Corps; 2nd MD (Duryea), Nagle's 1st Brigade, Sturgis' 2nd Division, Burnside's 9th Corps; 3rd MD (Sudsburg), Stainrook's 2nd Brigade, Greene's 2nd Division, Mansfield's 12th Corps; 3rd MD (Simpson) "Purnell Legion," Goodrich's 3rd Brigade, Greene's 2nd Division, Mansfield's 12th Corps.

These Maryland military units fought for the Army of Northern Virginia: Chesapeake Artillery (Brown's Battery), Ewell's (Lawton) Division, Jackson's Command; 1st MD Battery (Dement's Battery), Ewell's (Lawton) Division, Jackson's Command; Baltimore Battery (Brockenbrough's Battery), Jackson's (J.R. Jones) Division, Jackson's Command.

55. Union Brig. Gen. Winfield S. Hancock started the battle as the commander of the 1st Brigade, 2nd Division (Smith), 6th Corps (Franklin).

56. Pennsylvania native Brig. Gen. A.A. Humphreys' division arrived at Sharpsburg on September 18. Concerned that he had been wrongly accused of arriving late to the battlefield, Humphreys defended his service in a letter to the U.S. Secretary of War, Edwin M. Stanton. *OR* 19:1, 368–74.

57. Massachusetts native Maj. Gen. Darius N. Couch's division, officially part of the 4th Corps, did not arrive from Harpers Ferry in time to fight at the Battle of Antietam. Arriving on September 18, Couch's division was attached to Franklin's 6th Corps.

58. Gen. Robert E. Lee's sixth youngest child (of seven), Robert E. Lee, Jr. (1843–1914), was a nineteen-year-old gunner in the Rockbridge Artillery, also known as Poague's Battery. At Antietam, the younger Robert fought on the west side of Hagerstown Pike, on the slopes of Nicodemus Heights.

59. At Antietam, there were two generals in the Army of Northern Virginia whose last name was Anderson: Maj. Gen. Richard H. Anderson, a division commander in Longstreet's command; and Brig. Gen. George B. Anderson, a brigade commander in D.H. Hill's division, Jackson's command.

60. At Antietam, there were two generals in the Army of Northern Virginia whose last name was Jones: Brig. Gen. David R. Jones, a division

commander under Longstreet; and Brig. Gen. John R. Jones, who commanded Jackson's Division.

61. At Antietam, there were two generals in the Army of Northern Virginia whose last name was Hill: Maj. Gen. Ambrose P. Hill and Maj. Gen. Daniel H. Hill. Both men were division commanders under Jackson.

62. Daniel Harvey Hill's sister-in-law, Mary Anna Morrison, married Thomas J. Jackson, which would make the two men brothers-in-law.

63. Sears, 198. At the Battle of Antietam, Rufus R. Dawes (1838–99) was a major in Brig. Gen. John Gibbon's brigade of mid-westerners attached to the 1st Division (Doubleday), 1st Corps (Hooker), Army of the Potomac (McClellan). Despite having picked up the regimental colors of the 6th Wisconsin during the fight in The Cornfield, Dawes survived the battle and the war. After the Battle of Antietam, Dawes fought at Chancellorsville; Gettysburg; the Mine Run Campaign; the Battle of the Wilderness; the Siege of Petersburg; and the Battles of Spotsylvania and Cold Harbor. Notably, his son Charles would serve as Vice President of the United States under Calvin Coolidge (1925–29).

64. John David Hoptak, and Keith B. Snyder, *The Battle of Antietam: September 17, 1862.* ([Sharpsburg, MD?]: Western Maryland Interpretive Association, n.d.), 33, 43, 46, 56. This 82-page, 8" x 11" paperback is a very helpful introduction to the Battle of Antietam. Hoptak worked as a Park Ranger at both the Antietam and Gettysburg battlefields.

65. Many historical references and military atlases were consulted while drawing these maps. Because the maps are designed to make it easier for bicyclists to understand park exhibits while touring, their creation inevitably involved a "visual averaging" of battlefield positions; the omission of small engagements on the field; and a lack of consideration for the timing intricacies of battle actions. For detailed military maps, see Bradley M. Gottfried, *The Maps of Antietam* (El Dorado Hills, CA: Savas Beatie, 2012). Also, Carol Reardon, and Tom Vossler, *A Field Guide to Antietam* (Chapel Hill: University of North Carolina Press, 2016).

No matter how detailed one draws a military map, it is also not possible to provide numbers about strength (engagement) and casualties, partly because "time" is a dynamic construct, and partly because competing analyses exist even for static tabulations. In any case, the Antietam Battlefield Board (1890s) conceptualized the battle as progressing in three phases whose strength and casualty numbers were estimated as follows:

	Strength		
Phase	Union	Confederate	Total
1. Morning	23,600	20.100	43,700
2. Mid-Day	10,000	6,800	16,800
3. Afternoon	13,800	7,150	20,950

Casualties (killed, wounded, captured, missing)

Phase	Union	Confederate	Total
1. Morning	7,280	6,580	13,860
2. Mid-Day	2,900	2,600	5,500
3. Afternoon	2,600	1,120	3,270

NPS, "Casualties of Battle," https://www.nps.gov/anti/learn/historyculture/casualties.htm. Although the casualty total in the above table (22,630) does not match the 22,717 figure from the ABT, which this guidebook adopts, the Antietam Battlefield Board numbers provide a helpful context with respect to general time of day.

66. In June, 2020, Timothy H. Smith and Andrew Dalton of the Adams County (PA) Historical Society found a recently digitized (New York Public Library) map by Simon Green Elliott. Once discovered, this 1864 map became known as the "Elliott Antietam Burial Map," because it identifies the (temporary) locations of more than 5,800 Union and Confederate graves. For a series of fourteen official military maps drawn under the direction of the U.S. Secretary of War, see E.A. Carman and E.B. Cope, *Atlas of the Battlefield of Antietam* (Washington, DC: Antietam Battlefield Board, 1908), https://www.loc.gov/item/2008621532/.

67. For fascinating background information about Elliott, see Andrew I. Dalton, "S.G. Elliott: A California Railroad Swindler Turned Civil War Cartographer," ABT, https://www.battlefields.org/learn/articles/sg-elliott-california-railroad-swindler-turned-civil-war-cartographer.

68. From the 34th NY Volunteer Infantry Regiment, monument inscription. According to the LCS record, the 34th NY, also known as the "Herkimer Guards," suffered 114 casualties at the Battle of Antietam. The monument was dedicated in 1902. LCS 392, 025. The 34th NY and the 15th MA regiments were both part of Maj. Gen. John Sedgwick's 2nd Division, Sumner's 2nd Corps. Sedwick's division suffered about 2,225 casualties in twenty minutes of fighting in the West Woods. Frye, 96.

69. Frye, 75.

70. Frye, 152–53. Reardon and Vossler, 292–94. John W. Schildt, "Lincoln at Antietam: In the Footsteps of Lincoln; A Self-Guided Tour" (unpublished booklet, n.d.), 7–12.

71. According to the NPS, the U.S. Civil War produced 1,125,453 casualties (642,427 Union and 483,026 Confederate), categorized as follows: 204,100 killed in action (110,100 and 94,000); 469,200 wounded (275,174 and 194,026); 388,580 diseased (224,580 and 164,000); and 61,192 captured (30,192 and 31,000). NPS, "Facts," https://www.nps.gov/civilwar/facts.htm. But different categories are required to estimate "total deaths" that would include mortal combat wounds and fatal battlefield illness. William F. Fox (who fought at Antietam) and Thomas L. Livermore used muster lists,

military reports, and pension records, in their landmark 1889 study to conclude that the U.S. Civil War produced 618,222 total deaths (360,222 Union and 258,000 Confederate). In 2012, J. David Hacker consulted 1850–80 census records and recalculated the death toll as being 750,000 (and perhaps up to 850,000). J. David Hacker, "A Census-Based Count of the Civil War Dead," *Civil War History* 57, no. 4 (December 2011): 307–48. The matter is by no means settled.

For context, the NPS estimates U.S. Civil War enlistment strength as follows: 2,672,341 (Union) and 750,000–1,227,890 (Confederate). On the Union side, 2,489,836 were "white;" 178,975 African American; and 3,530 Native American. Confederate records are incomplete or destroyed. NPS, https://www.nps.gov/civilwar/facts.htm.

72. Clara Barton to President Lincoln, February 1865, *Clara Barton Papers, 1861-1952*. Image 6, Library of Congress, https://www.loc.gov/resource/mss11973.064_0732_0808/?sp=6.

73. Stephen B. Oates, *Woman of Valor: Clara Barton and the Civil War* (New York: The Free Press, 1994), 368. For a more recent study, see Donald C. Pfanz, *Clara Barton's Civil War: Between Bullet and Hospital* (Yadley, PA: Westholme Publishing, 2018).

74. Quoted by Clara Barton Missing Soldiers Museum, "Opening Clara Barton's Missing Soldiers Office—1865," https://www.clarabartonmuseum.org/opening-missing-soldiers-office. Misspellings in Barton's letter are also reproduced by the NPS. See NPS, "Clara Barton, a Tireless Effort in the Face of Disaster," https://www.nps.gov/articles/clara-barton-a-tireless-effort-in-the-face-of-disaster.htm.

75. Thibodeau, "Gathering Your Gear," 49–53.

76. Maryland State law requires that all persons under sixteen years old shall wear an approved helmet while operating or riding on a bicycle or bicycle trailer on public property. See Maryland Department of Transportation, State Highway Administration, https://www.roads.maryland.gov/mdotsha/pages/Index.aspx?pageid=599, which summarizes Maryland Transportation Code Section 21-1207.1, "Helmet use required for bicycle riders."

77. Bike Washington, "C&O Canal Bicycling Guide," http://bikewashington.org/canal/plan-camping.php. This link contains a listing of campsites along the towpath from M11.5 to M184.5. For official NPS information and alerts on hiker-biker camping, see https://www.nps.gov/choh/planyourvisit/camping.htm and https://www.nps.gov/choh/planyourvisit/conditions.htm.

78. These excellent resources will get you started: BikeCandO, https://bikecando.com/default.aspx. C&O Canal Trust, https://www.canaltrust.org. NPS (C&O Canal), https://www.nps.gov/choh/planyourvisit/conditions.htm. NPS (Potomac Heritage), https://www.nps.gov

/pohe/planyourvisit/index.htm. PedalShift, https://pedalshift.net/bicycling-the-co-canal/. Thomas F. Hahn, *Towpath Guide to the C&O Canal* (Harpers Ferry, WV: Harpers Ferry Historical Association, 2015). *TrailGuide: Official Guide to the C&O Canal Towpath and the Great Allegheny Passage*, http://bikewashington.org/canal/.

79. On the surrender at Harpers Ferry, see Dennis E. Frye, "Stonewall Jackson's Triumph at Harpers Ferry," ABT, https://www.battlefields.org/learn/articles/stonewall-jacksons-triumph-harpers-ferry.

80. Capt. James S. Brown commanded a Virginia battery at Antietam. From 1:00–4:00 p.m., Brown's guns pointed east from this elevated ground above modern-day Branch Avenue. They exchanged fire with the Union 9th Corps, who by this point had taken the Rohrbach Bridge over Antietam Creek and were advancing to this location. Brown sustained a severe foot wound.

81. For a brief introduction to U.S. Civil War activity along the C&O Canal, see Gary M. Petrichick, "The War Moves North," C&O Canal Association Website, http://www.candocanal.org/articles/civwr15.html.

82. Frye, 171–73. Frye's book is a rich collection of chronologically ordered facts about the Battle of Antietam and the establishment of Antietam National Battlefield and Cemetery.

83. Soldiers from the following Union and Confederate states fought at the Battle of Antietam but do *not* have a state monument. In the following list, bracketed numbers identify the military units who fought at Antietam from each of these states. Ordinal markings are omitted for brevity. PA reserve numbers appear in parentheses before their infantry number.

Thirteen Union states: Connecticut [infantry: 8, 11, 14, 16]; Delaware [infantry: 1, 2, 3]; Illinois; Maine; Michigan; Minnesota; New Hampshire; Ohio [infantry: 5-7-66, 8, 11, 12, 23, 28, 30, 36], [artillery: 1st Battery Light]; Pennsylvania [infantry: (3) 32, (4) 33, (7) 36, (8) 37, 45, 48, 50, 51, 90, 100, 124, 125, 128, 130, 132, 137, Philadelphia Brigade (69-71-72-102)], [artillery: Durrell's Battery D], [cavalry: 12]; Rhode Island; Vermont [infantry: Vermont Brigade, Co. F 1st U.S. Sharpshooters, Cos. E and F 2nd U.S. Sharpshooters]; Wisconsin; and (West) Virginia.

Eight Confederate states: Arkansas; Alabama; Louisiana; Mississippi [infantry: 11]; North Carolina; South Carolina; Tennessee; and Virginia [infantry: 6, including the "ANV Monument"].

84. The NPS database has the monument's height as 12 feet. LCS 397, 029A. The Waymark database records the height as 18 feet. Waymarking, https://www.waymarking.com/waymarks/WMDDBN. Steve Hawks records the height as 15.5 feet. Hawks, "State of Georgia" https://antietam.stonesentinels.com/monuments/confederate/state-of-georgia.

85. The breakdown is as follows:

Infantry Brigades (Longstreet, 20):
Howell Cobb (3); Paul J. Semmes (2); Wright (3); Robert A. Toombs (4); Thomas F. Drayton (2); George T. Anderson (5); William T. Wofford (1).
Infantry Brigades (Jackson, 19):
Marcellus Douglass/Lawton (6); James A. Walker/Trimble (2); James J. Archer (1); Edward L. Thomas (4); Roswell S. Ripley (2); Alfred H. Colquitt (4).
Artillery Batteries (Longstreet/McLaws): Samuel P. Hamilton (2).
Artillery Batteries (Pendleton): Allen S. Cutts (4); William Nelson (1).
Cavalry Battalion (Stuart): Wade Hampton (1).

86. LCS 472, 098. The J.N. Forbes Granite Company is located in Chambersburg, PA.

87. Ibid. Also: Hawks, "Indiana Monuments at Antietam," https://antietam.stonesentinels.com/monuments/indiana/state-indiana-monument.

88. Initial strength: 443. Killed: 41. Wounded: 168. Loss (percentage of initial strength): 47.2%. *Antietam on the Web*, "27th Indiana Infantry," http://antietam.aotw.org/officers.php?unit_id=324.

89. *OR* 19:1, 328–29.

90. SIRIS lists all but the June 2006 rededication dates. AIC IAS MD000369. LCS lists June 2006. LCS 404, 035. Gindlesperger identifies June 3 as the last dedication (for repairs to the copper dome). Gindlesperger and Gindlesperger, 77.

91. The NPS lists the monument's height as forty feet. LCS 404, 035.

92. From a tablet installed near the bas-relief of the "Charge of Second Maryland on Burnside Bridge."

93. LCS 481, 107. John W. Schildt, *Monuments at Antietam* (Chewsville, MD: Antietam Publications, 1991), 65. The NPS website contradicts its own LCS database; it indicates that the MA State Monument was dedicated in 1920. Hawks also identifies 1920 as the dedication year. Hawks, "State of Massachusetts Monument," https://antietam.stonesentinels.com/monuments/massachusetts/state-massachusetts-monument.

94. Schildt, *Monuments at Antietam*, 65.

95. Gindlesperger and Gindlesperger, 24.

96. AIC MD000362.

97. Schildt, *Monuments at Antietam*, 75.

98. Excluding the 13th NJ regiment, the military units identified on the NJ State Monument all belong to the 1st NJ Brigade. The brigade has two additional monuments erected at Antietam National Battlefield and one at

Crampton's Gap (part of the Battle of South Mountain). The inscription for Capt. William Hexamer's Battery A, 1st NJ Artillery, has some interesting detail: "After engagement at Crampton's Pass Sept. 14, 1862, the battery was engaged on Sept. 17, at three different points on this field. From three to six o'clock the battery fired 280 shells, 200 shrapnel and 15 canisters, forcing out of position two Confederate batteries and repelling an infantry force."

99. LCS 382, 019. AIC MD000362.

100. AIC MD000363. Schildt, *Monuments at Antietam*, 88.

101. LCS 405, 036. Ulysses Ricci (1888–1960) and Angelo Zari (1873–1956) were partners in the New York City architecture firm, Ricci & Zari.

102. LCS 405, 036. AIC IAS MD000363.

103. Schildt, *Monuments at Antietam*, 88. Quoted without attribution by LCS 405, 036. The monument's height is noted by Schildt, 88, and Frye, 173. The NY State Monument is second only to the Philadelphia Brigade Monument in terms of its height.

104. The 27,000 number is from LCS 405, 036. The source for the land purchase and monument height is Frye, 173.

105. Schildt, *Monuments at Antietam*, 88.

106. From the monument inscription.

107. The A.N.V. marker is a simple, low to the ground marker near the entrance to the Piper farm (on private property). The marker has this inscription: "A.N.V. / Near this spot an abandoned Confederate gun manned by a Second Lieutenant of the 6th Virginia Infantry Mahone's Brigade and two Infantry Volunteers from Anderson's Georgia Brigade, was placed in action September 17, 1862."

Gen. Robert E. Lee's Headquarters Monument is a modest monument that has this inscription: "C.S.A. / On this site in an oak grove from Sept. 15 to Sept. 18, 1862 stood the Headquarters tent of General Robert E. Lee, Commanding the Confederate forces. / Purchased, restored and marked by the West Virginia Division United Daughters of the Confederacy. Unveiled Sept. 17, 1936."

The Gen. Robert E. Lee Equestrian Monument (dedicated June, 2003) was commissioned with private funds and erected on private property near the Middle Bridge over Antietam Creek, on Boonsboro Pike, which in 1862 would have been the middle of the Union line. (Lee's headquarters was not on the east side of town). In 2005, the NPS purchased forty-five acres of land around the Newcomer House, which includes the statue. For more information, see the commentary in Waymarking, https://www.waymarking.com/waymarks/WMC9K3_General_Robert_E_Lee_Keedysville_MD. The monument was vandalized in July, 2020.

108. Priest, *Antietam: The Soldiers' Battle*, 339. Priest counts six guns, citing Joseph Mills Hanson, "A Report on the Employment of the Artillery at

the Battle of Antietam, MD" (Washington, DC: NPS, 1940). However, Johnson and Antietam on the Web each count eight (not six) guns. Johnson and Anderson, 76. Antietam on the Web, "Federal Guns at Antietam 9/17," http://antietam.aotw.org/images/Artillery_in_Md.pdf. For an introduction to artillery at the Battle of Antietam, see NPS, "Artillery at Antietam," http://npshistory.com/brochures/anti/antietam-artillery.pdf.

109. From the monument inscription. Also, Priest, *Antietam: The Soldiers' Battle*, 339. For regimental losses, Priest cites the *OR* without details (but Capt. Upton's report is not in the *OR*). Johnson and Anderson list 14 battle casualties, which is one more than Priest and not further categorized into killed, wounded, and missing. Johnson and Anderson, 122.

110. Priest, *Antietam: The Soldiers' Battle*, 290–91.

111. Report of Capt. Emory Upton, Chief of Artillery, 1st Division (Slocum's), VI Corps, of the Battle of Antietam, September 26, 1862, Henry Jackson Hunt Papers, Library of Congress. Quoted by Johnson and Anderson, 116–18. The *OR* does not include Capt. Upton's report.

112. Capt. Alonzo Snow was absent due to illness.

113. Antietam on the Web, "Federal Guns at Antietam 9/17." Johnson lists six (not eight) guns. Johnson and Anderson, 76. A record for Vanneman's (Snow's) Battery B is not included in Priest, "Appendix," *Antietam: The Soldiers' Battle*, 317–45.

114. Carman, 305.

115. Priest, *Antietam: The Soldiers' Battle*, 196. For a map that marks Battery B's position from Noon to 1:00 p.m., see Priest, 197.

116. *OR* 19:1, 404–05.

117. Carman, 306.

118. *OR* 19:1, 404–05.

119. From the monument inscription. Also, Priest, *Antietam: The Soldiers' Battle*, 343.

120. Priest, *Antietam: The Soldiers' Battle*, 343.

121. Lt. Col. B.L. Simpson's official report, dated September 27, 1862. *OR* 19:1, 515. Other details are from Bradley M. Gottfried. Bradley M. Gottfried, *The Maps of Antietam* (El Dorado Hills, CA: Savas Beatie, 2012), 168–69, 182–83.

122. Reardon and Vossler include a map of the "Final Actions around the Dunker Church" that shows how the retreat of the 13th NJ and the attack of the 49th NC forced the Purnell Legion to withdraw from the area via Smoketown Road. The map includes the Union positions of the 3rd MD, 111th PA, and 28th PA regiments on the south and west sides of Dunker Church. It also shows the Confederate positions of the 3rd AK, 27th NC, 35th NC, and 49th NC regiments. Reardon and Vossler, 192.

123. Priest, *Antietam: The Soldiers' Battle*, 341. The monument inscription says: "Engaged, 187 men, loss 18 killed, 46 wounded, 3 missing." On September 20, Brig. Gen. James Nagle wrote in his official report to Brig. Gen. Samuel D. Sturgis: "The loss in my brigade on the 17th and 18th was 35 killed, 154 wounded, 15 missing; total, 204." *OR* 19:1, 445–47. Gindlesberger says: 18 Killed, 48 Wounded, 3 Missing. Gindlesperger and Gindlesperger, 162.

124. Wilmer, L. Allison, and J.H. Jarrett, George H. Vernon, State Commissioners, *History and Roster of Maryland Volunteers: War of 1861-65*, (Baltimore: Press of Guggenheimer, Weil & Co., 1898), 100–07. Cited by Antietam on the Web, Citation 13023, http://antietam.aotw.org/officers.php?officer_id=12287.

125. Priest, *Antietam: The Soldiers' Battle*, 341.

126. Hawks, "2nd Maryland Volunteer Infantry Regiment (U.S.A.)," https://antietam.stonesentinels.com/monuments/maryland/2nd-maryland. Also according to Hawks, Lt. Col. J. Eugene Duryea, 2nd MD commander, resigned his army commission five days after the Battle of Antietam, because he was angry that Maryland Governor Bradford had visited the battlefield but neglected to visit his regiment or its hospital. The 2nd MD's attempt to take the Rohrbach Bridge was supported by the 6th and 9th NH regiments. The Marylanders also fought in The Final Attack once they crossed the bridge.

127. The middle initial "M" matches the attribution in *OR* 19:1, 510–11.

128. Priest, *Antietam: The Soldiers' Battle*, 343. However, the monument marker counts three more killed: "Loss, 4 killed, 25 wounded." Hawks agrees with Priest, but with one more missing: 1 killed, 25 wounded, 4 missing. Hawks, "3rd Maryland Volunteer Infantry Regiment (U.S.A.)," https://antietam.stonesentinels.com/monuments/maryland/3rd-maryland. The NPS database counts 29 casualties. LCS 401, 039.

129. *OR* 19:1, 510–11.

130. Priest, *Antietam: The Soldiers' Battle*, 337. The 5th MD monument in the Bloody Lane says, "Loss, 43 killed, 123 wounded" (versus Priest's calculus of "25 Killed, 123 Wounded, 15 Missing"). The monument's higher "killed" number suggests the inclusion of "missing" men in Priest's tally. Gindlesberger's numbers might be from the monument inscription. Gindlesberger and Gindlesperger, 96.

131. Reardon and Vossler, 161. See also a helpful map of the Union attack through the Roulette farm and the Confederate defense on the Piper farm. Reardon and Vossler, 155.

132. *OR* 19:1, 324.

133. Although Capt. "Beau" Brockenbrough commanded the Baltimore Light Artillery, he was not a Maryland man. He was born in Lexington, VA; graduated from the University of Virginia and the Washington College of Law;

and would practice law in Lexington, where his father was Judge John W. Brockenbrough. However, a "Special Dispatch" from Baltimore to the *Richmond Times* indicates that John Bowyer Brockenbrough's wife was "of this city" (Baltimore). See "Major John Bowyer Brockenbrough Death," *The Richmond Times*, November 17, 1901, https://www.newspapers.com/clip/16321424/major-john-bowyer-brockenbrough-death.

134. Antietam on the Web, "Confederate Guns at Sharpsburg 9/17," http://antietam.aotw.org/images/Artillery_in_Md.pdf. Also, Johnson and Anderson, 95. Another source counts the Blakely as a "twelve-pounder" Blakely rifle. Gindlesberger and Gindlesberger, 59. Priest does not list a 12# Howitzer, but a cast iron tablet in West Woods describes a "12-pounder iron howitzer." Priest provides this listing: one 3" Ordnance rifle, one 12# Napoleon and two rifled Blakely's. Priest, *Antietam: The Soldiers' Battle*, 338. In terms of ordnance losses in Brockenbrough's Battery during the Maryland Campaign, Johnson lists one broken but recovered 12# Blakely and one disabled but recovered 10# Parrott. Johnson and Anderson, 107.

135. Priest, *Antietam: The Soldiers' Battle*, 328. Carman, 609.

136. *OR* 19:1, 1007-8.

137. The NPS database has the monument built in 1890. LCS 451, 076.

138. Johnson and Anderson, 104. Although Dement's Battery manned four cannons at Harpers Ferry, there is no record that the battery arrived in Sharpsburg in time to fire their artillery during The Final Attack.

139. Carman and Cope, Map 14.

140. At the Battle of South Mountain on September 14, 1862, two generals died at Fox's Gap, where monuments stand in their honor: Union Maj. Gen. Jesse L. Reno and Confederate Brig. Gen. Samuel Garland.

141. Reardon and Vossler, 156–57.

142. Calculated from the inscription on the north side of the monument: "The spot where Gen. Mansfield fell is a few yards Easterly from this monument / Born December 22, 1803 / Killed September 17, 1862."

143. The details of Mansfield's death are from Ezra J. Warner, *Generals in Blue: Lives of the Union Commanders* (Baton Rouge: Louisiana State University Press, 1964), 309. Mansfield died at the George Line farm on September 18. Reardon and Vossler, 37.

144. Warner, *Generals in Blue*, 403. Frye notes that "the mortal wounding of division commander Israel B. Richardson contributed to the federal failure to exploit the breach in the Confederate center." Frye, 112.

145. *OR* 19:1, 293–95.

146. *OR* 19:1, 1008.

147. NPS, "Facts," https://www.nps.gov/civilwar/facts.htm.

148. Frye, 71.

Index

CPSIA information can be obtained
at www.ICGtesting.com
Printed in the USA
LVHW071645271020
669965LV00018B/2454